THE PRACTICE
OF MULTINATIONAL
BANKING

Recent Titles from Quorum Books

THE PRACTICE OF MULTINATIONAL BANKING

MACRO-POLICY ISSUES AND KEY INTERNATIONAL CONCEPTS

Dara M. Khambata

106677

QUORUM BOOKS
New York • Westport, Connecticut • London

Library of Congress Cataloging-in-Publication Data

Khambata, Dara, 1948-
  The practice of multinational banking.

  Includes bibliographies and index.
  1. Banks and banking, International.   2.   International
finance.   I. Title.
HG3881.K265   1986   332.1'5   85–31253
ISBN 0–89930–139–8 (lib. bdg. : alk. paper)

Library of Congress Catalog Card Number: 85–31253
ISBN: 0–89930–139–8

First published in 1986 by Quorum Books

Greenwood Press, Inc.
88 Post Road West, Westport, Connecticut 06881

Printed in the United States of America

The paper used in this book complies with the
Permanent Paper Standard issued by the National
Information Standards Organization (Z39.48–1984).

10 9 8 7 6 5 4 3 2 1

To FK, TK, MK, and NK

CONTENTS

PREFACE

This book is designed to help the reader understand the environment and modus operandi of multinational banks, with the focus on policy- and concept-oriented issues in the arena of international banking. It fills what I feel is a pressing need in the field of international business. Each of the twelve chapters addresses the theory and practice of international banking. The contents are suitable for the practitioner as well as MBA and advanced undergraduate students. However, a basic knowledge of international finance and economics is presumed.

The subject's broad scope adds interest but creates problems. There is a long menu of possible topics that may be included in a book of this nature. The difficulty of selecting what to include is especially acute for professors who are structuring college-level courses in international banking. Other books specialize in related fields such as foreign exchange operations or international trade-related activities. This volume, instead, takes an approach that is both narrow and broad—the former in the sense of focusing only on important macro-policy issues and key international concepts, the latter in the sense of covering twelve major subject areas.

One final comment on content should also be mentioned. Most books dealing with contemporary issues are vulnerable to the possibility of events overtaking them. Today's issues become tomorrow's history. This book reduces the problem by including selections of issues that are relatively timeless.

Comments and reviews at various stages of the book's development have improved its coverage and organization. I am particularly grateful to Whitney Watriss for her painstaking review of my chapters and useful suggestions concerning content.

This book owes much to many people. Any deficiences in style or substance are the responsibility of the author.

Dara M. Khambata

THE PRACTICE
OF MULTINATIONAL
BANKING

1

DEVELOPMENT AND ROLE OF MULTINATIONAL BANKING

The modern system of multinational banking is the byproduct of hundreds of years of economic interaction among the nations of the world. But it is the present era that has shown us the extent to which the respective financial conditions of those nations can affect our everyday lives. Every day brings further news of banks on the verge of collapse and of imminent default on national debts. These crises seem to have a more dramatic and personal impact because the lenders are found throughout the world. Few nations have economies that are insulated from the rest of the world, and the failure of one nation's economy can easily affect the performance of another's.

Despite the universality of foreign banking today, the analysis in this book deals primarily with the United States. This emphasis is both because it is the home nation of the author and because it offers more ready sources of information. Also, the prominence currently enjoyed by the United States in multinational banking means that any analysis of its international financial dealings will of necessity touch quite extensively on the financial dealings of the rest of the world. Each year the international operations of many U.S. banks have accounted for a larger and increasingly important share of their total activities and profits, and each year their dealings have involved more and more nations, both as partners in operations and as borrowers. Parallel with that growth in business has been an increase in the scrutiny to which the U.S. banking world has been subjected, particularly in light of recent world problems on the political and economic fronts and with respect to debt servicing. Banks have come under sharp criticism for the haphazard way they have been lending, often neglecting to investigate thoroughly the political and country risks of their borrowers. In the United

States this scrutiny has been public to a large extent and has yielded much information on the foreign activities of American banks.

For purposes of conciseness, the focus here is on the international role of U.S. banks from 1920 to the present, their foreign financial activities before this time not being of such global importance as they are today. The remainder of this chapter, however, does examine some of the actions and regulations that occurred prior to the 1920s in order to show the evolution of the international economy and U.S. banking practice more accurately. In addition, it provides a general review of trends in the twentieth century by way of context for the more detailed topical chapters that follow.

The balance of the book is organized as follows. Chapter 2, "Regulation of International Banking," focuses on the U.S. regulatory environment and on foreign regulation as it affects the operations of U.S. banks overseas. As such, the chapter reviews the types of foreign representation a U.S. bank can have and the factors affecting the choice among them. It also reviews the principles and policies underlying U.S. international banking law and provides capsule descriptions of the most important legislation. Finally, the chapter describes the functions of U.S. regulatory agencies.

Chapter 3, "World Financial Markets and International Banking Centers," contains descriptions of the main capital markets and banking centers in which U.S. international banks carry out their transactions. The emergence of the markets and centers and their main features, such as the types of transactions in which they specialize, the foremost participants, and any limitations they pose to banks, are also covered.

Chapter 4, "Foreign Exchange Management," looks at a key area of international banking operations today, given the volatility of foreign exchange rates at present. The focus is primarily on how banks balance the currencies in which their thousands of transactions are denominated, for example, through options in the forward market and hedging techniques. Given the importance of reasonably accurate prediction of exchange rate trends, special attention is paid to the role of forecasting models.

Chapter 5, "Country Risk Assessment," deals with another primary concern of international banks today, in light of the recent and ongoing debt crisis. Many banks found themselves in the early 1980s with an overabundance of loans to countries that were unable to meet the terms of their lending. Their own management, spurred by the regulatory authorities, has led to far greater attention to the analysis of country risk. This chapter looks at the evolution of this management tool and how it is applied to bank operations, for example, how risk is defined, how the assessment is carried out, and generally what resources are required. An interesting trend now is the use of country risk assessment as an overall management tool, rather than just applying it to decisions about whether to make specific loans.

Chapter 6, "Multinational Banking Services," reviews some of the financing instruments that banks provide to their customers, such as letters of credit, drafts, bankers' acceptances, securities underwriting, shipping loans, and leasing facilities.

Chapter 7, "Asset and Liability Management," covers another vital area of bank operations today. Again, its importance is an outgrowth of the problem loans afflicting many banks, as well as of the changes in the nature of the banking industry, such as the greatly intensified competition and the rapidly rising costs of operations. The chapter opens with a quick review of the nature of the international banking environment that covers the risks and opportunities and the all-important interbank market. It then reviews what constitutes assets and liabilities management from two perspectives—internal bank policy and practices, and external tools that banks can use to balance their assets and liabilities.

Chapter 8, "Project Financing," addresses a relatively recent and quite complex form of lending. The discussion covers why project financing evolved—to address the constraints involved in financing very large, capital-intensive, and sometimes risky projects—and how it works, including the various financing options, organizational alternatives, and common procedures. As a guide to the key issues banks need to address, the chapter concludes with a look at why projects fail.

Chapter 9, "International Syndicated Loans," discusses another unique area of lending that once again involves large sums. The chapter opens with a short historical overview of syndicated lending, which has gone through a number of boom and bust cycles. It then describes the syndication process from the perspective of the lead bank. The chapter closes with a look at the future of this activity.

Chapter 10, "International Institutions in Multinational Banking," offers thumbnail descriptions of the main official international and national financial organizations that are involved with international banking. It is written from the perspective of the commercial bank; thus the focus is on how these organizations interact with the private sector in channeling funds to countries in need of financing. However, it also looks at what programs and resources the organizations offer to promote the development and stability of the world economy.

Chapter 11, "Sovereign Debt," addresses the now massive lending that has gone to governments, particularly third world ones, and the origin of the present debt crisis. It offers some possible approaches to dealing with the current debt crisis and some recommendations for avoiding future ones.

Finally, Chapter 12, "A Look at the Future," suggests what trends might be anticipated in the next five to ten years. Many of them are already underway, such as deregulation and the electronic telecommunications revolution. Others are likely to emerge as banks try to cope with the nature of today's international banking environment. They include, for example, greater specialization by smaller banks in terms of services and clientele, as well as new management standards and practices.

U.S. BANKING AND NATIONAL DEVELOPMENT: TO 1920

The banking system in the United States was designed, initially, to finance internal development. The backward conditions of America in the eighteenth and nineteenth centuries relative to the more advanced nations of Europe prevented banks from gaining a position of great importance in the world financial system. The United States was still trying to build a transcontinental railroad at a time when Europe had already completed railways not only at home but also in overseas colonies far from home. European nations were, by contrast with America, involved in sophisticated mercantile transactions around the world and were forging ahead in many new directions. Of course, even in 1900, the United States' presence was still large by any standard, just by virtue of its size and resources, but in relation to its potential, its participation was eclipsed by that of Great Britain and France.

While the United States traded internationally for capital goods and sought financing for its development projects, it did not do so on a major scale. One reason was its sporadic pursuit of an isolationist policy. Another was the National Bank Act of 1863, which authorized the federal government to charter banks for national purposes. Because foreign branches of U.S. banks were deemed contrary to national development, these new "national" banks, as they were called, could not set them up. Although state-chartered banks, the earliest ones to be established, could move abroad, as a rule they chose not to.

In addition to the prohibition on foreign branches, national banks could not accept drafts (such as trade acceptances). This ban, coupled with the lack of a developed secondary U.S. market for acceptances, prevented American banks from gaining a strong foothold relative to European competitors.

It should also be remembered that the foreign operations of European banks were drawn against their old colonial ties. The colonial system was itself primarily an economic and commercial one; while there were some political benefits and humanitarian justifications, financial rewards were the greatest motivator. Nations of limited resources such as Great Britain better served their interests by controlling territories offering commercial benefits (a policy clearly evidenced by Britain's retreat from Bechuanaland). As European businesses moved to the colonies, their home banks followed them. Even when the colonial system began to break apart, those economic ties still provided ready markets for European banks serving the overseas operations of their domestic customers, which continued to carry on their overseas business.

The United States was not involved in this sort of colonial process. The development of its own territory was challenging enough, and as a former colony, it could ill afford the hypocrisy of pursuing that which it had fought to be free of. For this reason, too, the United States lagged far behind its European counterparts in establishing foreign bank branches. In fact, the United States in the nineteenth century was in many ways still a large, developing economic colony that had never really broken its commercial ties with Great Britain.

Thus, by the early 1900s, most international financial dealings were based in Europe. Acceptances, bills of exchange, and insurance on international shipments of goods were still largely denominated in British pounds sterling, the accepted trade currency of the early 1900s. London was considered the financial capital of the world, while New York was seen as merely a large city that, because of unfavorable banking regulations, would never rival London.

THE INTERNATIONALIZATION OF U.S. BANKING

Clearly, if U.S. banks were to gain a foothold of any sort in the international financial community, national banks had to be able to establish a presence overseas. That condition was finally met in 1913.

The Federal Reserve Act of 1913

The passage of the Federal Reserve Act of 1913 dramatically changed the role that American banks could play in the international financial markets. The act gave national banks the right to set up branches overseas, and in 1914 the first one opened in Buenos Aires. There followed a general move to establish foreign branches. Initially, most American banks chose to open them in South and Central America, a not surprising pattern. Banks usually follow their domestic customers; in the absence of American colonies, U.S. businesses looked to nearby markets with abundant supplies of the natural resources in demand in the United States as well as Europe. South and Central America held out the most potential for American businesses, and therefore for American banks.

The Federal Reserve Act also allowed national banks to accept drafts and to have them discounted in the domestic markets. As the larger American banks began to perform this function, a secondary market in the acceptance-discounting trade developed, most prominently in California and in Chicago and New York. New York City eventually became the major financial center in the United States. Moreover, one result of increased participation by American banks abroad was a move toward having terms of trade denominated in U.S. dollars instead of the usual British pounds. As the discounting of time drafts was an accepted practice in international trade (drafts were often discounted for financing under the terms of letters of credit, the established trade fixture of the time), American banks were able quickly to make themselves felt in other markets throughout the world.

The Impact of World War I

The effects of World War I were far-flung, but most of the impact was felt in the industrialized nations of Europe. The sudden conversion of so much of their productive power (as well as labor and other resources) to war uses drained both their economies and their industrial capacities. And there was the unparalleled destruction of physical assets and infrastructure.

The United States, to the contrary, weathered the trauma of war with minimal damage relative to other industrialized nations and found itself at the beginning of the 1920s in the enviable position of having its finances and production power relatively intact. Thus, after the war, it had a clear advantage in international trade. As a result, during this time American financial centers grew in importance in the world economy. While London was still considered the financial capital of the world in 1920, it soon became apparent that the United States was moving forward very rapidly.

Immigration and Technology

Other factors were at play in this period. Through immigration, the population of the United States was growing continuously. Equally as important, many of the immigrants maintained personal (and later financial) contacts in their home countries. Not only did the United States have a much larger, international population, but along with the rest of the world, it was experiencing the benefits of improved transportation and communications technology. The world began to shrink, and financial transactions across national boundaries became much easier. Finally, as a nation in a growing phase, the United States held an advantage over countries that were already developed or that were stagnating under the burden of less developed economies, because it was able readily to adopt new advances in technology and new ideas.

Legislative Changes

The expansion of U.S. banks also received a boost from the Congress. In 1919, the Federal Reserve Act was amended in order to stimulate the financing of American businesses abroad. For purposes here, the most important of the amendments involved Section 25(a). The amendment, commonly known as the Edge Act, authorized "banking corporations"

to be organized for the purposes of engaging in international or foreign banking or other international or foreign financial operations, or in banking or other financial operations [abroad] . . . either directly or through the agency, ownership, or control of local institutions in foreign countries. . . . [1]

U.S. banks could also serve as fiscal agents of the federal government.

While giving banking corporations broad latitude to function overseas, the Edge Act limited their domestic operations: "No corporation organized under this section shall carry out any part of its business in the United States except as [it is] . . . incidental to its international or foreign business. . . ."[2]

Despite the government's hopes, the banking community saw the Edge Act as very limiting and did not take advantage of it until the early 1960s.

ENTERING THE WORLD ECONOMY: 1920–45

The international financial situation evolved rapidly after the war, with the United States moving quickly to exploit the opportunities it saw. This action was not the result of hasty opportunism, but reflected a recognition that much of Europe would require retooling after the war and that the United States was in the best position to aid that process.

American business abroad rose dramatically in this period: from 1914 to 1920, foreign commerce (the combined total of all exports and imports) increased from $4.3 billion to $13.5 billion. As American enterprises moved overseas, American banks followed them. Whereas prior to 1914, only 26 foreign branches of American banks were in operation (mostly state-chartered banks), by 1920 there were 181, of which 122 were in Latin America. Despite their growth, however, U.S. banks still lagged far behind Europe in branches, which counted roughly 2,000 by 1920.

The Perilous 1920s and 1930s

Despite the boom in business overseas and the growth in U.S. bank branches abroad, American banks proceeded quite cautiously in the first years of the 1920s, keeping their exposure to foreign risk at a minimum. That pattern changed explosively in 1927, when there was a major surge in short-term loans to foreign banks (the "due from" account). This surge, which lasted about three years until late 1929, left the major New York banks, according to some estimates, with a total exposure of about $1.8 billion. Given that these banks had been only marginally involved in the foreign markets a few years earlier, this exposure was significant.

It was also ill-timed: in 1929 the U.S. stock market crashed and the Great Depression was underway. The overextension of credit, declining prices for raw materials throughout the world, and a lack of public confidence in banks that was made manifest in massive withdrawals of funds brought a wave of financial failures and bank closures. In the first three years of the 1930s, the credit structure erected in the 1920s was swept away.

This period of wholesale liquidation underscored the inadequate lending techniques then in use and induced a period of caution. Moreover, during the remainder of the 1930s, exchange controls and the fermenting world political situation made new credit extension very hazardous. By the end of 1939, U.S. banks had reduced their outstanding short-term assets to only $600 million, while the United States itself had become a net debtor nation to the tune of $2.6 billion.

More Legislative Change

The Great Depression led to the passage of legislation that changed the role banks could play in American business. New restrictions concerning the branching of banks and the activities banks could engage in seriously curtailed their operations. It was assumed these changes would remove the riskiness of some of the financial operations that banks had gotten into in the past; they would make them secure and avert any further large-scale failures.

Perhaps the most visible of the new regulations was that imposed by the Glass-Steagall Act of 1933; banks were barred from entering the investment banking field. Instead, it was reserved for those firms that did not take deposits from customers who expected their funds to remain safe and liquid over long periods. Critics of the measure claimed that it would weaken the competitiveness of American banking relative to its European counterparts, which faced no such restrictions.

The outcome of Glass-Steagall was not to be known immediately. World War II exploded in Europe, creating massive dislocations that precluded observation of a normal response to new legislation. By the time the war ended and business returned to usual, the regulations had been in force for ten years, and American banks and companies had grown used to them.

The recovery of the U.S. economy from the Depression was on the whole aided by World War II, albeit a brutal and costly solution. However, whereas many Americans may have found their financial situations to have improved, the international position of U.S. banks continued to retrench. When the war ended in 1945, they had only 72 foreign branches, less than half the number in 1920.

AN ERA OF RECONSTRUCTION: 1945-60

The economic effects of World War II were similar to those of World War I, although greatly intensified because of the extensive, heavy bombing and broader geographic range of the war. All the major industrialized nations except the United States suffered enormous physical damage, and for the most part the world's financial system had practically collapsed. France,

Germany (now divided into two), and the other industrialized nations on the continent suffered from the wholesale destruction of most of their capital production capacity. The United Kingdom fared little better, having had to bear the strain of heavy enemy aerial attacks and to convert most of its industrial assets to the manufacture of war material. The European economies, having shifted so completely to support a war on a scale never before experienced, were incapable of effecting an instant turnaround to peacetime production. Nor were the resources immediately available to do so.

Structuring a New Financial System

In one regard, World War II had a paradoxical effect. Certainly it devastated the economies of the major European industrialized countries. At the same time, in an economic sense, it introduced an international financial system that might prove more stable in the long run. Certainly the old one had revealed fatal flaws.

Confident that they would triumph, the United States and its allies began to plan that system even before the war ended, drawing on their experiences before the war as lessons in what not to do. The major industrialized nations met at Bretton Woods, New Hampshire, to produce their new system. The Bretton Woods agreement provided for the development of a new economic order that would help rebuild Europe into a viable economic power as fast as possible.

Two key instruments were to be the International Monetary Fund (IMF) and the World Bank. Set up early in 1946 by the major industrialized nations, the IMF was to administer what was then believed to be an acceptable system for stabilizing currency prices in the European nations. Although the gold standard had collapsed in the depressed economy that preceded the war, it was now reinstituted. The U.S. dollar was to be valued at $35.00 per ounce of gold, with the remainder of the currencies placed at some par value with respect to the dollar. This system thus gave them a direct relationship to the gold standard, with the dollar the currency for trading purposes. Each nation was allowed to set the par value of its own currency against the dollar. The Fund permitted a transitional period for implementation, given the reality of payment restrictions and the inconvertibility of some currencies. This step, although flawed, worked in the short term to stabilize the currency situation.

The World Bank was set up as a mechanism to channel funds from the wealthier nations to those most in need. Its immediate purpose was to facilitate the reconstruction after the world war. Eventually, it would serve as a means of helping less developed nations attain sustained economic growth and a standard of living equal to that of the industrial countries.

The Marshall Plan

The World Bank may have been designed to rebuild Europe, but in that endeavor it was outshone by the Marshall Plan. The intent of the plan was similarly to pour tremendous amounts of money into Europe so as to rebuild it in record time, with the Bank picking up the slack in forgotten sectors of the economy. The Marshall Plan was also politically motivated, in that it was a response to the perceived Soviet threat. The Soviet Union, invited to join the plan, declined on its own behalf and that of the nations it had enveloped during the war. To this day, there is a severe disparity between economic conditions in East and West—the Soviet bloc countries have never caught up with their West European counterparts in terms of production capacity and economic viability.

The Marshall Plan was an overall success. It provided for the rebuilding of Europe at a reasonable cost, and without destroying the delicate currency situation that existed after the war. However, it attacked only the problem of the long-term reconstruction of Europe and Asia. It did nothing about the short-term effects of the postwar currency crunch. As the demand of European consumers for goods returned to normal after the war, the United States had the only economy capable of meeting those needs. America was also perhaps the only source of the industrial goods European nations required. The catch was the shortage of U.S. dollars with which to buy the goods. After the war, as noted, the U.S. dollar had become the accepted trading currency, bypassing the British pound. Many national governments had imposed strict controls on the import of American goods to minimize the strain on their own currencies and to allow them to save their dollars for reconstruction.

The Eurodollar Market Emerges

During the 1950s, when the dollar became entrenched as the leading currency, many expected that the result would be large deficits in the U.S. balance of payments and a redistribution of gold and assets throughout the rebuilt nations. Both predictions came true. During this period, American banks did not venture into foreign markets readily, content to stay home and let the national banks of other nations worry about the financing of reconstruction. They were leery because of numerous exchange crises in Europe. The United Kingdom alone went through four between 1955 and 1957. Moreover, the 1950s were characterized by flights from one country's currency to another's, and under the terms of the IMF agreement, each nation was required to maintain parity of rates with the U.S. dollar.

It was in this period that Eurodollars first emerged, although they were not treated as they would be in the 1960s. The International Monetary Fund and the governments of industrialized nations had, as noted, been holding dollars in their reserves to finance the reconstruction of their economies. As a result, in the early years after the war, businesses in the rebuilt nations rarely had an opportunity to buy American dollars for their own purposes. In the later 1950s, however, European enterprises began to buy U.S. dollars in the open markets. At this time, they found a ready supply—through branches of American banks located in such tax havens as Panama, the Bahamas, Cayman Islands, and the U.S. Virgin Islands.

What had happened was that at the close of the 1950s, U.S. banks were ready to reenter the overseas banking market. By 1958, the currency situation had finally stabilized to the point where U.S. dollar accounts and foreign currency accounts could be maintained within the parity boundaries and there was convertibility of currencies for most trade transactions. The pressure on most European currencies to be maintained within the prescribed limit of the IMF agreement disappeared, as the currencies found a comfortable position within the economic structure.

Once convertibility was reached, the structure of the IMF held the prices of currencies within tolerable limits. There was no "free-floating exchange rate" at the time, and a lack of concern over this risk factor helped bring international banking back to prewar levels. As long as nations were required to respond to market influences upon their currencies, a bank could suffer great losses from currency fluctuations. But the political stability that had emerged since the war years created confidence; trade flourished and with it, international banking.

THE INTERNATIONAL BANKING BOOM: 1960–73

The period 1960–73 saw a tremendous increase in international banking operations both by U.S. banks in foreign countries and by foreign banks in the United States.

International Operations of U.S. Banks

American banks expanded their foreign banking operations at a rate almost three times that of domestic operations. Prior to 1960, there had been only about 100 U.S. branches overseas, and they were controlled by only 8 commercial banks. By contrast, from 1960 to the early 1970s, U.S. banks were opening branches abroad at a rate of 42 a year. Branches were set up in London, Hong Kong, the Bahamas, and many other locations. By the end of 1972, 34 American banks operated 45 branches in London alone, which, it turned out, had more American banks represented than New York City did. While most domestic operations by U.S. banks showed a decline in foreign lending, there was a significant increase in the amount and number of loans being offered by these overseas offices. Within the United States,

Edge Act corporations, largely ignored since their inception in 1919, became fashionable.

The increase in business by U.S. corporations overseas was an important factor in the growth of U.S. banks' international activities, but it was by no means the only one. Some underlying, indirect reasons were the emergence of the United States as the principal economic and financial power after World War II, the growth of the world economy since 1950, the need of the American economy for additional capital from abroad, and the demand of U.S. consumers for a wider variety of goods. These factors helped create an environment conducive to international trade.

Other conditions contributed more directly. A very key one was restrictive U.S. regulations. U.S. controls over capital limited the level of funds that banks could loan or invest abroad from bases in the United States. The result was a rapid build-up of foreign branches of U.S. banks as the only way for them to continue to serve the offshore needs of their clients, especially the multinational corporations. U.S. banks also faced ceilings on the interest rates applicable to domestic business, a constraint imposed by Regulation Q. It did not apply, however, to overseas transactions. Thus American banks moved to finance domestic loan demand through the Eurodollar market. The domestic credit crunch of 1969 led many banks that had never before considered opening a foreign branch to do so in order to get into the Eurodollar market. Many of these branches, particularly those in the Bahamas, Cayman Islands, and similar tax havens, were merely shells, or addresses where U.S. banks could book their transactions, which were actually handled at corporate headquarters. Their function was to allow U.S. banks to escape the restrictive domestic regulations. These shell branches, along with the Edge Act corporations, allowed smaller banks to enter the international financial scene without large investments.

Foreign Bank Operations in the United States

Foreign banks also entered the United States in droves, where they faced very favorable operating conditions in relation to domestic banks. Foreign banks were not subject to the restrictions on capital that American banks found so onerous. Federal reserve requirements did not always pertain, nor did foreign banks necessarily have to obtain Federal Deposit Insurance Corporation (FDIC) insurance, with its costly premiums. In some instances, however, these exemptions did not work to the favor of foreign banks. Some customers wanted to do business only with banks that carried that insurance. Moreover, banks that chose to hold reserves with the Federal Reserve were eligible to use the central bank's discount window.

On the down side, foreign banks were required to register in a particular state, which did not necessarily have the same requirements as another state. New York, for example, allowed foreign branches to accept deposits without

FDIC insurance, whereas California required all banks to have it. That California condition created an unusual situation. While the state had no law against opening foreign branches, as noted, all foreign branches had to have FDIC insurance, but federal law prohibited them from having that insurance. The end result was an absence of foreign branches in California. It did have foreign subsidiaries, however, as these institutions were recognized by the Federal Reserve and therefore were eligible for federal insurance.

Traditionally, European banks sought to establish their offices on the East Coast, while Japanese banking concerns were more prominent on the West Coast.

The Legislative Environment

Domestic banks complained bitterly about the more favorable conditions for foreign banks. They claimed that they were being held back by regulations far more stringent than their competitors faced. As a result, during this period, the U.S. government amended the banking regulations somewhat to let American banks compete on a more equal footing. For the most part, however, the changes were geared toward making American banks more competitive overseas, so as to sustain a strong U.S. influence in the international financial arena. Thus Section 25 of the Federal Reserve Act was amended in 1962 and 1965 to allow foreign branches of American banks to participate in activities on foreign soil that were closed to them within the United States. National banks could even hold stock in foreign banks if they met certain criteria. In contrast, little was done at this time to deregulate domestic banking.

Parallel with this trend, international banking began to change. The competition became very intense, and increasingly banks found they had to play with very large numbers and very small spreads and ever higher volumes in order to make their branches even marginally profitable.

RECENT DEVELOPMENTS IN INTERNATIONAL BANKING

World prosperity drew to a close in 1973. The financial bubble burst. The oil embargo, the deteriorating balance of payments deficit being experienced by the United States, and other economic factors suddenly made it more difficult to prop up the U.S. dollar as the supreme trading currency. The private price of gold had skyrocketed way over the $35.00 an ounce standard set in 1946 to which the dollar and other currencies were pegged. Other major currencies also underwent staggering fluctuations.

The oil crisis of 1973 had the single most important effect on the international capital markets. In late 1973 and early 1974, oil prices tripled. As a result, the oil-producing countries found themselves with massive increases in revenues and little capacity to absorb them. An enormous pool of capital assets—$335 billion—appeared in the financial markets of the world.

Buffeted by these various forces, in 1974 the United States lifted most of its currency regulations, and the U.S. dollar was allowed to float freely on the foreign exchange markets. This step by the United States marked the end of the managed float system set up under the IMF.

Since the financial crisis of 1973, the U.S. government has sought to stabilize the international operations of both its own banks and those foreign ones operating within its borders. Its policies in the last decade or so have had three purposes: to help domestic banks compete with foreign banks, to insure fair competition within the United States, and to protect the financial assets of Americans doing business with banks. In keeping with these goals, there were a number of major legislative and regulatory changes in this period. Unlike the earlier period of reform, the focus this time was on domestic issues, with stated U.S. policy to treat all banks, domestic and foreign, equally.

The major change was the passage of the International Bank Holding Act of 1978. To deal with the inability of U.S. banks to compete effectively with many foreign counterparts, the act provided for the creation of yet another type of banking entity. Domestic bank holding companies could set up international banking facilities (IBFs) that could provide domestic banking services to foreign nationals, subject, however, to a number of restrictions, such as the size, nature, and duration of deposits and the nature of the business the transactions could support. Because the IBFs were treated as offshore banks owned by bank holding companies, they were immune from certain federal regulations, even though they operated within the United States. They could also cross state lines.

In keeping with the domestic policy of equal treatment for all banks, foreign banks were also allowed partial ownership of Edge Act and Agreement corporations. They could also set up IBFs. Their involvement with these latter facilities has been quite extensive. According to *Business Week* (July 23, 1984), 75 percent of the IBF assets in New York were held by foreign banks, with half that amount in the hands of Japanese bankers.

To address the confusing array of ways foreign banks could enter the U.S. market, with each one subject to different state and federal requirements, all foreign branches could qualify for FDIC insurance. Additionally, the 1978 act removed some of the restrictions on foreign banks' acquisition of domestic banks.

A later act allowed national banks to own, at least in part, certain overseas investment and export trading companies whose business was nonfinancial, an option that had been closed to them under the Glass-Steagall Act. And there is an ongoing effort to loosen the Glass-Steagall provisions even further. Although the act has not yet officially been revoked, banks have begun to acquire firms previously denied them, and the regulatory agencies have looked the other way. An example is the purchase of Charles Schwabb & Co. by Bank America Corp. In general, the feeling is that bank holding companies will be permitted to enter other financial industries.

INTERNATIONAL BANKING TODAY

The extent to which the United States has come to play a major role in international banking is clear from some figures that appeared in the July 23, 1984, issue of *Business Week*. In 1976, international lending by banking facilities in the United States and by offshore branches constituted 22.5 percent of the global total. By 1983, the figure was 34.1 percent. By contrast, the levels for Great Britain were 25.7 percent in 1976 and 27.5 percent in 1983. The volume of foreign exchange trading in New York went from $23.4 billion in 1978 to $33.5 billion in 1983. Much of this business is attributed to foreign banks, whose presence in New York alone went from 149 in 1980 to 207 in 1983.

There is little question but that U.S. banks will continue to play a major role and that the international operations of many will continue to expand. But just as the international banking environment has changed dramatically since the early twentieth century, and even more dramatically just since the early 1970s, so, too, will it change in the next few years. The worldwide trend in deregulation will open up new opportunities and new markets at the same time that it will increase the competitiveness of the industry. The interlinkage of banks will become even closer thanks to the rapid advances in telecommunications. The ongoing debt crisis and the more stringent supervision of regulatory authorities, particularly in the United States, have led banks to tighten up their management and operations. The need for greater loan loss reserves in the face of the continuing debt crisis and for a higher capital gearing ratio have led to shifts in the nature of banking business. The shrinking profit margins on many transactions have reinforced that shift. Instead of a heavy concentration on lending, many banks are now looking to activities that generate fees and commissions and that do not affect the balance sheet, as well as to less risky ventures. Lending will tend to concentrate on sounder borrowers or areas that promise higher spreads, such as credit cards. There could be still further changes, depending on unpredictable global conditions such as worldwide economic growth, natural disasters, and political upheaval. The one point that does stand out throughout the history of banking, however, is that the banking community is extremely resilient and dynamic, with a capacity to adapt readily to and to exploit whatever new conditions arise.

SUMMARY AND CONCLUSIONS

While American banks are not newcomers to the field of foreign banking, they only became extensively involved after World War II. During the nineteenth century, to the contrary, international banking was for the most part the domain of British and continental financial houses that had already set up branches of their banks in areas where important colonial or commercial interests existed. At that time, only state-chartered U.S. banks could venture overseas, and almost none chose to. Among the foreign financial centers, London was preeminent, and most trade financing, the dominant early international banking activity, was carried out there.

The Federal Reserve Act of 1913 authorized national banks to establish foreign branches and accept foreign drafts. This act, coupled with the outbreak of World War I and the extensive damage it occasioned in Europe, gave rise to an expansion in American banking overseas after the war. To boost the U.S. presence and its foreign trade, in 1919 the Congress passed the Edge Act, although U.S. banks did not take immediate advantage of the wider powers it afforded them. Still, U.S. banking grew by other means until brought up very short by the Great Depression. The advent of World War II sustained the deep contraction in international banking operations.

Even after World War II, the growth of American foreign banking remained slow. One reason was that U.S. exports proved essential for postwar reconstruction, and the dollar quickly emerged as the key currency. Consequently, it was in short supply around the globe. Foreign countries responded by placing stringent restrictions on their foreign exchange reserves that inhibited their banking systems from taking overseas deposits and lending abroad. Instead, the dollars that financed trade and provided for the capital requirements were supplied largely through the Marshall Plan and other programs of the U.S. government, and not through the private banking system. Finally, the still shaky international scene caused bankers to hold back.

Several factors came into play in the late 1950s that aroused new interest in international banking. One was the success of the Marshall Plan and with it the restoration of the economies of Europe and the freedom of exchange of the major European currencies. Another was the trend toward economic integration and interdependence, as well as the spectacular economic recoveries of West Germany and Japan and the less dramatic but still steady growth in many other countries. The dismemberment of the colonial empires favored the expansion of American trade, investment, and banking; it was yet another factor. And in the early 1960s, the governments of many of the newly independent former colonies began to borrow on a massive scale. They looked to the banks to be a steady and secure source of business for years to come. Concomitant with these trends, although not necessarily directly linked to them, the U.S. government began to introduce legislative and regulatory changes in the 1960s that would make U.S. banks' international operations more competitive with those of foreign counterparts.

Parallel with these international factors were some domestic stimuli for U.S. banks. They included the tendency of American industry and banks not only to internationalize, but also to decentralize within the United States. Although there was competition from foreign banks entering the U.S. market, often on more favorable conditions, the domestic banking industry weathered the situation well.

Most U.S. banks began to undertake international lending only in the 1960s, a period of dramatic growth. That pattern continued on into the early 1970s. In fact, during this period, the foreign activities of commercial banks rose at a rate almost three times that of their domestic business. In their endeavors U.S. banks were again assisted by some important legislative changes that equalized the treatment received by domestic and foreign banks operating in the United States.

Despite the good performance of U.S. banks, there is no escaping the extensive internationalization and competitiveness in the international banking world today. Of the top fifty banks in terms of assets, only eight are U.S., while eighteen are Japanese. Other top competitors are France with five, Canada and Great Britain with four each, West Germany with three, Switzerland and Italy with two each, and the Netherlands, Brazil, and Hong Kong with one each. Still more countries feature farther down the list.

This competitiveness and its intensity are not likely to let up, and international banking business will continue to grow, sometimes rapidly, sometimes more slowly, depending on world economic conditions and the internal situation of banks themselves. Many have had to take stock in the last few years because poor lending practices left them with excessively risky portfolios and lessened earnings as a result of the various debt servicing problems of many borrowers. To their credit, many of the banks have put their houses in order, bolstering their loan loss reserves, writing off problem loans, and expanding their capital. Earnings have been rising as a result of these measures and higher net interest margins and greater income from fees for services. Many banks, spurred in part by regulatory agencies, have also instituted procedures to avoid a recurrence of current problems. U.S. banks are also likely to be abetted by further changes in domestic regulations. There has been, for example, a strong push to allow interstate branching. Thus the future for international banking looks promising for those banks that choose their opportunities wisely and manage their assets well.

NOTES

1. U.S.C., title 12, sec. 611, as amended December 14, 1919 (41 Stat. 378).
2. Ibid.

REFERENCES

Aliber, R. Z., "Towards a Theory of International Banking," Federal Reserve Bank of San Francisco *Economic Review*, Spring 1976, pp. 5–8.

Bank for International Settlements, *The Maturity Distribution of International Bank Lending*, Basel: BIS, 1984.

Dufey, G., and I. Giddy, *The International Money Market*, Englewood Cliffs, N.J.: Prentice-Hall, 1978.

Giddy, Ian H., "The Theory and Industrial Organization of International Banking," in Robert G. Hawkins et al., eds., *The Internationalization of Financial Markets and National Economic Policy*, Research in International Business and Finance, vol. 3, Greenwich, Conn.: JAI Press, 1983, pp. 195–243.

Gisselquist, David, *The Political Economics of International Bank Lending*, New York: Praeger, 1981, Chapters 1, 2, and 3.

International Monetary Fund, *World Economic Outlook*, Washington, D.C.: IMF, 1985.

Korth, Christopher M., "The Evolving Role of U.S. Banks in International Finance," *The Bankers Magazine*, July–August 1980, pp. 68–73.

Lever, Lord Harold, "The International Debt Threat," *The Economist*, April 30, 1983.

Mathis, F. John, ed., *Offshore Lending by U.S. Commercial Banks*, 2nd ed., Philadelphia: Robert Morris Associates, 1981, Chapter 9.

Quinn, Brian Scott, *The New Euromarkets*, New York: John Wiley & Sons, 1975.

Salomon Brothers, *United States Multinational Banking*, New York: Salomon Brothers & Co., 1976.

Terrell, Henry S., and John Leimone, "The U.S. Activities of Foreign-Owned Banking Organizations," *Columbia Journal of World Business*, Winter 1975, pp. 87–97.

Vernon, Raymond, *Sovereignty at Bay: The Multinational Spread of U.S. Enterprises*, New York: Basic Books, 1971.

Williamson, John, *The Open Economy and the World Economy*, New York: Basic Books, 1983.

World Bank, *World Development Report*, Washington, D.C.: World Bank, 1985.

2

REGULATION OF INTERNATIONAL BANKING

As international financial activities grew over the twentieth century, so, too, did the range of forms banking institutions took and the activities they engaged in. In many cases, the major determinant was the banking laws and regulations of the countries in which they were active. For example, the major expansion of U.S. banks overseas in the 1960s came about in response to regulations at home that both limited their business options and imposed additional costs that made it difficult for them to compete with foreign banks. As U.S. banks entered foreign markets, the nature of their representation and activities was often determined by local laws and regulations. Similarly, when foreign banks entered the United States, they were able to carry out activities and to locate their operations in ways not permitted domestic banks, and they were exempt from some regulations that allowed them to offer customers more favorable terms. Much of the U.S. legislative activity in the 1970s and 1980s has been directed at equalizing the treatment of domestic and foreign banks.

This chapter looks at the factors involved in choosing the type of foreign presence to establish and at the pros and cons of various options. It also reviews the key U.S. laws affecting international banking by American banks abroad and foreign banks in the United States, as well as the main regulatory authorities overseeing banking in this country. A final section looks at some of the trends now underway in the regulatory area that will influence the nature and structure of banking in the next five to ten years.

CHOOSING A FOREIGN BANKING PRESENCE

The reason a bank wants to be overseas determines in part what type of presence it establishes. If it wants simply to explore the market, a small specialized office might suffice. If it has a major loan exposure in a moderately risky country, it might want a more sophisticated unit able to monitor the project and country risk. Other key factors are:

Host country legislation. Many foreign countries prohibit entry of full-service foreign banks or limit involvement in domestic banking to certain areas. For example, they may prohibit branches, in the belief that they compete too effectively with local banks. On the other hand, they may allow minority interests in local banks and permit local lending. Some countries preclude any presence, in which case foreign banks must resort to correspondent banking or perhaps representative offices or agencies.

A bank's size, resources, international experience, and volume of business. Setting up an overseas office of any size can be very costly both financially and in terms of manpower. Smaller banks may not have sufficient resources for a full-scale overseas presence or may not have sufficient overseas business to justify the expenditure. Moreover, a bank may want to develop contacts and build up business before entering the country. It may be constrained by a lack of sufficient manpower for a full-scale foreign office, as the host country may restrict alien work permits. It is widely agreed that the success of a foreign office, whatever form it takes, is closely tied to the qualifications and abilities of staff, and this issue cannot be ignored. Finally, a bank lacking in foreign experience may be unwilling to rush into a costly and complex move overseas.

Bank strategy. Most banks have formulated, or should have done so, medium- and long-term plans that specify where and how they intend to proceed in the future. For some, international banking may be assigned a key role in terms of affording new markets and higher profits than domestic business offers. In some cases, banks may choose to emphasize the somewhat riskier but more profitable world of financing for developing countries. Other banks may choose to specialize in certain areas, such as energy or heavy industry, while still others may focus on leasing, foreign exchange dealings, or investment banking. Thus a bank's strategy and geographic interests will influence the nature and location of its overseas presence.

Tax considerations. Basically, there are two tax-related issues. One is the desire to avoid taxes: they increase the cost of doing business and hence a bank's ability to offer competitive financing and services relative to banks affected by lower taxes. The other is to take advantage of certain tax breaks that accrue from international business.

Avoidance of domestic regulations. Domestic operations of U.S. banks are subject to certain requirements regarding reserves, interest rates, and areas of activity. Sometimes these requirements can be avoided by establishing a banking entity overseas.

Entry into the Eurocurrency markets. Until recently, there was no vehicle through which U.S. banks could participate in the Eurocurrency markets from their home office. Moreover, federal reserve and other requirements made the cost of U.S. banking business higher than that of its competitors. This situation resulted in a large-scale establishment of branches in other countries, especially the tax-free havens of the Bahamas and the major financial centers such as London.

Clearly, the nature of a bank's presence is also mutable. Many banks that have started out with nothing more than a specialist at the home office who travels extensively have ended up with extensive in-country facilities of different types, from branches to merchant bank subsidiaries. Nor is this pattern likely to stop in the near future. Banks will continue to look for better organizational forms tailored to specific needs, circumstances, and markets.

The U.S. government, as have most other national governments, has sought to control the banking system and its impact on national economic health. Thus a large body of law, typically complex, has emerged that addresses most aspects of international banking. Local governments have also passed their own laws. Inevitably, there has been inconsistency in the various bodies of law and their application, as well as many gray areas that complicate international transactions. For example, how are the terms of loans across borders to be enforced? In the event of disputes, what country has jurisdiction and what laws apply? To what activities and organizations do tax laws and regulations apply? How can national interests such as economic stability and growth be reconciled with the desire to attract foreign capital and business?

In the United States, legislation has followed two tracks: one involves the regulation of domestic banks and their overseas activities, the other the operations of foreign banking institutions in the United States. Particularly since the 1970s, there have been major changes in the laws, and the two tracks have moved closer together as the government has sought to equalize the treatment of both categories of banks.

It is unlikely that supervision will diminish anywhere in the world in the near future, as the competitiveness of international banking is growing more intense, the field more complicated, and the risks and interconnectedness of countries' banking systems more extensive. Moreover, the bank crises of the 1980s revealed the pitfalls and weaknesses of the present international banking system.

International Banking Options

Banks have devised a range of alternative organizational structures for their overseas activities in response to legislation, regulation, tax and accounting requirements, and business opportunities. This chapter looks primarily, however, at U.S. regulation and at the forms U.S. banks operating overseas and foreign banks operating in America have taken. At one extreme is the international department at the bank's home office, at the other the global financial supermarket with local networks offering a range of services. In between are correspondent banks, representative offices, agencies, foreign branches of different types, subsidiaries, affiliates, specialized facilities such as leasing or factoring companies, Edge Act and Agreement corporations, international banking facilities, and joint ventures.

International Department in a Home Office

Generally, a first step in developing international banking business is for a bank to establish an international department at its home office. Such a setup is necessary whatever the subsequent nature of a bank's foreign activities and presence. The department will in the long run be the center of the bank's international activities in terms of planning, coordination, administration, and supervision and is often the point of contact with the regulatory agencies. An international department can be very similar to a bank itself, handling deposits and collections, paying debts, transferring funds, serving as correspondent banker, and taking care of customers' international business needs, such as letters of credit and bankers' acceptances. While this option is less expensive than most overseas offices, it still entails a considerable outlay, and the operating expenses, particularly if there is extensive travel abroad, can be substantial. Perhaps the most serious drawback, however, is that it does not permit the in-depth, ongoing collection of country information and development of foreign contacts that is so important to international banking today.

Correspondent Banks

Correspondent banks provide a range of services to banks located in other countries that do not have local offices or whose local office is not permitted to conduct certain transactions. Common activities are accepting deposits, extending credit, handling bankers' acceptances and letters of credit, processing securities, and dealing in foreign exchange. Correspondent banks may also be an important source of referrals for business to be carried out in the home country of the bank requesting the services. Credit-related activities, which are the dominant activity, involve normal international transactions, such as confirming letters of credit, creating U.S. dollar acceptances, making advances and covering overdrafts, and running credit checks on potential customers. U.S. banks traditionally have provided dollar lines of credit and have offered short-term credit facilities through the money markets, by which means foreign correspondent banks can use local liquidity more profitably. Foreign banks also help foreign bank customers with local transactions. A special type of correspondent bank is the reimbursement bank, a third bank used to settle certain transactions that cannot be handled by the correspondent bank, such as high-volume business.

What a bank looks for in a correspondent institution is timely, high-quality services; error-free transactions, or at least a reliable means of detecting and correcting mistakes quickly; accurate and current account balances and information on transactions; and fast decisions in the case of such activities as foreign exchange dealing.

For many banks, correspondent banking is the best alternative for today's banking environment, with its lower spreads and reduced profitability. They see it as a relatively cheap, easy, and flexible way to enter and operate in foreign markets. Moreover, it has become more important recently because of the problems with required asset growth and capital ratios, inadequate yields, and the credit risk involved in international banking. Another important point is that correspondent banking is not threatening to local banks or the host country government, but rather is viewed as a source of opportunities. Indeed, it may be the only type of involvement a foreign government will permit.

As demand has grown, the quality of correspondent banking has improved. The international correspondent market now offers relatively large clearing balances, excellent credit profiles, and a range of timely services. Clearly, the revolution in communications has made it far easier to provide the kinds of services at the speed that bankers want. Some banks, realizing that the popularity of correspondent banking is growing, are now aggressively marketing that service for foreign financial institutions. Both credit and noncredit services offer potentially large earnings and a ready source of funds. Correspondent sight deposits, for example, offer high yields, low capital requirements, and ready cash.

Representative Offices

Representative offices may perhaps best be defined by what they cannot do. They cannot engage in certain direct financial and commercial activities, such as deposit-taking, financing, and collections. Instead, their services tend to be more personal and developmental—establishing good relations with contacts important to the parent bank, seeking out and setting up investment and business opportunities, negotiating mergers and acquisitions, setting up business deals, advising on business opportunities in the home country, and similar activities.

Representative offices may also play a key role in internal bank operations. They may serve as conduits for up-to-date information on such topics as country risk, economic and political trends, business opportunities, and regulatory changes. They may also be asked to make recommendations on the approval of loans or on the level of country exposure and to monitor outstanding loans. They can be used to run credit analyses on potential borrowers or business associates. Often they are used as a training ground for promising staff. Some offices are assigned responsibility for administering customer accounts and services.

Generally, banks choose this option for three reasons. One, the host country may prohibit any other type of physical presence. Second, a representative office usually does not take much investment to set up and does not pose a major loss if assets are seized by the government. If a capital base is required, the amount is usually small. Third, the representative office is a good interim step for a bank exploring the option of a more intensive involvement in-country. Should the decision be made to establish some other type of presence, such as a branch, the representative office will have already laid the groundwork in terms of developing contacts and business, as well as firsthand knowledge of the host country. Representative offices are also a good idea in locations where there is a strong local demand for foreign currency loans but where the banking market is characterized by an under-developed local currency market that cannot sustain funding of local branches and where local savings are insufficient. It is also viable where the risks call for a low profile. On the other side of the coin, representative offices do have restricted scopes, the decision-making takes place elsewhere, the post is not always desirable to qualified personnel, and the resources may not be available for the desired in-depth research.

The decision to set up a representative office should be an outgrowth of and consonant with the overall strategic plan of the bank, including its credit policy objectives. And the final decision should be based in part on a feasibility study. That study will probably cover such points as the "full measurement" cost of the office (will it earn enough profits to cover the direct expenses and contribute to the parent's loan loss reserve and return on capital and asset ratios, and what will be the incremental or opportunity costs of this option versus others?). Before actually opening the office, it is a good idea to do some advance business development. A prime marketing area is the host country government, as well as correspondent banking services offered through the home office. Then the move can be made into private sector marketing.

The key to a successful representative office is the representative. Usually it is someone who has been with the bank several years and has had lending experience. Rarely do banks use local hires.

It is likely that banks will continue to use representative offices, partic-ularly in connection with country risk analysis and because of the restrictions on other types of presence.

Edge Act and Agreement Corporations

Originally U.S. national banks were prohibited by law from engaging in international operations. State-chartered banks, on the other hand, could do so. In 1916, to rectify this situation and to encourage national banks to further U.S. commerce abroad, the Congress authorized national banks to invest in state-chartered banks and corporations that would conduct inter-national banking and financial business. These state-chartered institutions in turn had to agree to abide by federal reserve requirements and regulations, hence the name "Agreement corporations." Because this law did not produce the desired results, in 1919 the Congress authorized the Federal Reserve to charter corporations to engage in international financing and banking in furtherance of U.S. trade and commerce. These corporations are called Edge

Act corporations after the name of the act establishing them. In 1978 this right was extended to foreign banks as well.

Edge Act and Agreement corporations can accept deposits from foreign governments and agencies, individuals residing abroad, and people whose business is primarily conducted abroad; make loans; and provide other banking and financial services. Note that domestic retail deposit-taking is excluded unless the depositor is engaged primarily in international business. Thus the Edge corporations have to support, directly or indirectly, international U.S. trade and commerce.

A very important provision of the act is that Edge corporations, unlike other domestic banks, can cross state lines by establishing branches wherever state law permits it. This provision is important in two respects. One, it puts U.S. domestic banks on a more equal footing with foreign ones, which until 1978 were able to cross state lines freely. It is also critical to foreign banks, for it allows them to continue having a presence in more than one state despite the fact that they were excluded in 1978 from having branches and agencies in more than one state.

Yet another part of the 1919 act allows Edge Act corporations, when calculating the maximum loan permissible to a single borrower (10 percent of the capital and surplus of the corporation) to use as a basis the consolidated capital and surplus of all related branches in all states. Thus far larger loans are possible. On the other hand, Edge corporations have to maintain capital and surplus equal to 7 percent of their risk assets. Moreover, in general Edge Act corporations are subject to the same reserve requirements and interest limitations as Federal Reserve member banks are.

A second key provision is that Edge Act corporations, again unlike national banks, can hold stock in nonbanking enterprises and are allowed to conduct business in foreign countries, including long-term financing. Moreover, Edges can underwrite, distribute, and deal in debt and equity securities outside the United States.

One area that is somewhat unclear at present is how the nonbanking investment provision will be applied to foreign banks. Normally, foreign banks with branches and agencies in the United States are subject to stringent constraints on their nonbanking activities. However, foreign banks whose U.S. operations involve only Edge corporations are exempt from these restrictions. The Federal Reserve Board, which charters Edge entities, may not be willing to adhere to the exemption.

International Banking Facilities

International banking facilities, or IBFs, are recently authorized financial vehicles designed to allow U.S. banks to become involved, subject to certain restrictions, in the Eurocurrency markets from domestic bases. It was hoped that this authorization would attract back to the United States the business that banks had taken overseas, such as in the Bahamas, in order to participate in the Eurocurrency markets. IBFs and the activities permitted them were also seen as a way of increasing the international competitiveness of U.S. banks relative to foreign ones that can deal in these markets freely. Since part of U.S. noncompetitiveness relates to the extra cost embodied in federal requirements as to reserves, interest rates, FDIC insurance, and the like, IBFs are exempt from those provisions. Because state and local taxes have also imposed a disadvantageous cost, in an effort to attract the facilities many local governments have exempted IBFs from that taxation as well. Finally, the Federal Reserve Board favors IBFs, as they enhance its ability to conduct monetary policy.

The restrictions are that IBFs can offer their services only to foreign customers, who may be individuals, corporations, or governments. They are only permitted to accept time (not demand) deposits, and those are subject to a minimum deposit period of two business days. All deposits and withdrawals must be at least $100,000. The instruments for time deposits are not negotiable. However, in the case of time deposits of foreign offices of U.S. depository institutions, other IBFs, or parent institutions of IBFs, the deposit period is overnight. Finally, IBFs can extend credit to foreign residents (including banks), other IBFs, or parent institutions of IBFs. Loans and deposits may be in U.S. dollars or foreign currencies. As with the Edge corporations, IBF transactions cannot be used for domestic business, except to the extent that it relates to foreign commerce. IBFs must inform customers of these restrictions on the use of funds and obtain from the customers acknowledgment that the services are not being used to avoid the interest rate restrictions and reserve requirements.

In many ways, IBFs are similar to the shell branches set up by many U.S. banks overseas in that they are mainly record-keeping entities. They are also similar to Edge corporations in that the IBF corporation can operate multiple IBFs within the same corporate structure and can cross state lines.

Virtually any U.S. depository and foreign banking institution, including branches, agencies, and Edge corporations, can establish IBFs in any state that permits them. They must get permission from their primary federal or state supervisory agency, but this has never been refused. They must, however, have a legal domicile in the United States. Moreover, they must maintain separate records and accounts. The main operators of IBFs now are U.S. commercial banks and nonbank depository financial corporations, Edge Act and Agreement corporations, and U.S. branches and agencies of foreign banks. In 1985 they held approximately $250 billion in assets.

All these organizations belong to CHIPS—The Clearing House for Inter-Bank Payments Systems—an international electronic check-transfer system that moves money between major U.S. banks, branches of foreign banks, and Edge Act subsidiaries of out-of-state banks. CHIPS has enabled transactions to be settled close to the end of each business day.

Foreign Subsidiaries and Affiliates

Subsidiaries are legally incorporated companies in which the investor owns a majority of the voting stock, directly or indirectly, or exercises effective control. The advantage of this option is that incorporation protects the parent corporation or head office from legal liability. Moreover, subsidiaries are sometimes permissible alternatives in some countries that prohibit branches. Similarly, subsidiaries can carry out certain services or activities that branches, which are direct extensions of banks, are not allowed to. For example, the subsidiary may be a merchant bank and as such can underwrite securities, whereas a branch would be precluded from doing so. One disadvantage of the subsidiary involves the method for computing the maximum loan size for a single borrower—here the 10 percent is based only on the subsidiary's capital and surplus, and not on the parent corporation's assets as well.

Initially subsidiaries were set up to attract retail business, such as deposits and loans. Now, however, they are often specialized entities that conduct activities that the parent corporation cannot. They have been a favorite vehicle of small banks (for example, midwestern banks) and have also been used by foreign banks operating in the United States. The latter see them as a good investment in terms of access to modern, high-technology banking and because the United States is a stable and profitable economic environment in which to invest. There was a spurt of acquisitions or establishment of subsidiaries by foreign banks beginning in the late 1970s.

Subsidiaries of foreign banks can be either state-chartered or federally chartered and can engage in the full range of banking services. They are subject to the same restrictions as U.S. banks are and are subject to the supervision of the regulatory agencies of jurisdiction and to the same restrictions and requirements that domestic banks are.

An affiliate bank, by contrast, is a local bank in which the investing bank has only a minority interest. It offers the advantage of immediate, albeit indirect, access to full-range banking. In such an arrangement, most foreign business typically goes to the affiliate, which reciprocates in terms of any domestic business in the investor bank's home country. The disadvantage is the lack of control over decisions and operations. However, once again, affiliation may be the only option.

Agencies

Agencies, also known as investment companies or commercial lending companies, are low-overhead entities that engage only in wholesale international commercial banking. Their sphere of interest is mainly commercial and industrial lending and the financing of international transactions. One advantage of the agency is that it is not subject to the limit on the size of a loan to a single borrower that foreign branches and subsidiaries are. Therefore, they can extend credit to U.S. customers at reasonable rates. In general, the relations of agencies with the regulatory bodies in the United States are easier than is the case with other types of banking alternatives. On the other hand, agencies cannot sell certificates of deposits, accept deposits from host country residents, or handle trust functions. They may, however, accept "credit balances"—accounts to which the proceeds of loans or collection can be credited. These balances may not be obtained from the general public. Moreover, the balances must be designated for specific purposes, and an amount that is reasonable relative to the size and nature of the account must be withdrawn within a reasonable time and be used for the stated purpose. The sources of agency funds are interbank borrowing in the host country money market or the Eurocurrency markets, and resources of parent and affiliate banks.

Many agencies of foreign banks in the United States serve as the fiscal agent for their home country government and as financier of trade for home country customers. The Canadians and Japanese, for example, have set up quite a few agencies in the United States. The former use them as a source of funding for parent banks or affiliates, and also to hold trade balances and dollar proceeds from securities issued by the Canadian government and corporations. The Japanese use agencies to finance Japanese companies setting up shop in the United States, for which large amounts of financing are necessary. These foreign agencies are active in the U.S. money market, particularly in terms of portfolio management. They also deal heavily in foreign exchange markets or place dollar loans in the Eurodollar market at attractive interest rates. They are often engaged in fairly risky activities.

Foreign Branches

Foreign branches of U.S. banks account for the largest share of overseas operations. There are now around 800 U.S. foreign branches in over 100 countries, with more than $400 billion in assets. U.S. foreign branching exploded in the 1970s, followed closely by European countries, Canada, and Japan (the latter also experienced a rash of branching in the late 1950s).

Initially, branches were set up to serve the multinational customers of the head office. Now, however, that share of the market is relatively small. As to the activities into which branches have shifted, that depends in part of where they are. Those located in the major financial centers such as London may focus on the Eurocurrency market, often the reason for their having been set up. This market is important for two reasons. One, it affords a good opportunity to lay off surplus domestic funds and to do so more profitably, as the transactions are not subject to U.S. reserve requirements and interest rate limits. Second, the Eurocurrency market is frequently necessary for funding large international transactions. Even smaller banks have been resorting to this market as a way to increase profits.

Retail banking, especially deposit-taking, has not been a dominant area for branch activity, largely because of the restrictions that host countries impose. In addition, foreign branches often cannot compete effectively with the network of a well-developed local bank. On the other hand, wholesale dealings with local businesses have grown. That latter piece of the market is what provides the bulk of profits and justifies the cost of a branch, which is considerable.

The predominant activity of branches has been extension of credit. The bulk of the credit has gone across borders, usually denominated in U.S. dollars. Most of this lending has been term, with a floating interest rate at a fixed spread over the cost to the bank of financing the loan through the purchase of one-, three- or six-month time deposits. Typical borrowers have been multinational corporations of industrial countries, banks, and governments of developing countries. Given this type of clientele, it is not surprising that foreign branches in the major financial centers have increasingly been engaged in loan syndications, loan management, leasing, project financing, and other activities geared to the large, complex, often risky lending required for major industrial projects, general economic development, balance of payments deficits, and the like. How long this focus will continue is uncertain, however, because international lending is now extremely competitive, a situation that has brought profit margins down to the bare bone.

Perhaps because of the lending picture, but also in response to the increasing complexity of the international market, many branches are now engaging in or looking for other activities. Many large banks are setting up branches solely to handle and manage loan syndications. A new service of branches is international money management for multinational corporations. Banks may provide advice and assistance on setting up acquisitions and mergers or on investments in U.S. companies, for which services the branch charges a fee. Branches also advise trust departments on investments in foreign stock. Many foreign branches now offer specialists for these various transactions and areas. Companies engaged in or considering conducting business in foreign countries may turn to branches for advice, a service that may be provided free as a sort of loss leader.

An activity that has been growing recently and that is providing good profits is interbank placements, or "redeposits." Here one bank places funds in time deposits at another bank. Usually this activity is combined with another business that offers low profit margins but high-volume returns—foreign exchange trading. This activity is often handled by specialized traders, frequently out of the head office. While some banks avoid this activity, many others seek to take advantage of the potential for good earnings, of which it is an important source. The interbank placements are also used to finance short-term international trade, along with credit extensions to exporters on behalf of foreign customers and to importers. In fact, import financing is a big business, particularly for developing countries that are short of hard currency. The need for that short-term financing may be an inducement for foreign governments to allow foreign branches.

A specialized foreign branch is the shell, frequently no more than a post office box. A number have been set up in tax havens such as the Bahamas. Often they have specialized in a particular area—many in the Bahamas handle largely Eurodollar deposits and loans, a not surprising specialization, given that they were set up to avoid the domestic restrictions on participation in those markets. Banks book loans and make interbank placements with the shell, but do the actual trading and dealings with the Eurocurrency and other money markets from the head office.

Many banks prefer foreign branches because they have direct control over the operations, and branches can offer full services. In addition, this structure affords some benefits in terms of federal regulation. For example, the loan maximum is based on the combined assets of the parent and branch, not just on the assets of the branch. Thus, branches can offer larger loans than, say, subsidiaries. Moreover, foreign branches are exempt from the reserve requirements and ceilings on interest rates to which the parent is subject, especially in cases in which deposits are payable outside the United States. Depositors at foreign branches are now liable for nonpayment hindrances (external factors that prevent the bank from repaying the deposit). Should the parent bank guarantee to pay depositors of foreign branches, the branch would lose its exemptions.

Foreign banks have chosen to set up branches rather than subsidiaries in the United States for one additional reason: under U.S. law, subsidiaries must have a separate board of directors, the majority of whom must be U.S. citizens. With a branch, the foreign bank can use its existing board. In addition, branches require less capitalization because of the parent company's capital base.

While foreign branches offer many advantages, they also entail some disadvantages and risks. For one, they are a physical asset, often a costly one, and in unstable or otherwise risky countries there is potential for loss. Parent banks may have more of a loss in the event of bankruptcy than a subsidiary would.

Because of their heavy international, particularly short-term, lending and the less stringent regulations they are subject to, many foreign branches have liquidity and capital ratios that would be unacceptable domestically. As a result, increasingly they ask for guarantees by local banks or other parties as a condition for the loan.

The most common restriction on branch activities is a prohibition on local deposit-taking and limited access to stable sources of local currency in tight money markets. For example, branches may not have as much access to a central bank's rediscounting facilities, while local corporate customers always withdraw their money from foreign branches first. So branches depend to a greater extent on money market sources, which are costlier and drier. One solution is for a branch to arrange a standby commitment with a local bank for local currency for a set time. This agreement is made reciprocally: the home office extends the same facility to local foreign branches of host country banks. Governments may also limit such transactions, which are tantamount to currency swapping.

Other problems that U.S. foreign branches face relate to staffing. For one, expatriate staff are expensive relative to local hires, although that differential is disappearing now. Some governments limit the number of foreign staff who can be hired by restricting the issuance of work permits. This restriction is a major problem, because good staff, especially the manager, are vital to successful operations of a branch. Sometimes the establishment of a branch can jeopardize important correspondent bank relations, although the restrictions on local retail banking lessen this possibility.

Under U.S. law, a U.S. foreign branch is considered to be a legal and functional extension of the parent bank. The branch has no separate assets or liabilities. As such, it is subject to the same regulations and regulatory agency as the parent bank. The parent in turn is subject to suit under local law for grievances against the branch. U.S. foreign branches must be approved by the Board of Governors of the Federal Reserve system, which generally does so, although it can attach certain conditions to ensure sound operations and financial health. Branches are supposed to have a certain level of capitalization as called for by federal or local law, although in reality they have all of the capital of the parent behind them. Branches are supposed to operate within the governing charter of the parent, that is, to undertake only what the parent can legally do. However, if other banks in a host country can carry out certain activities prohibited to the parent bank at home, and hence to its foreign branches, and that prohibition renders the branches uncompetitive, the Board has the right to authorize those activities.

Despite the institutional and legal ties to parent banks, foreign branches can be very independent. They keep their capital separate, do their own hiring, hold their own reserves at the central bank in the host country, and put their surplus funds in the local money market. Often they have quite extensive decision-making authority, and their recommendations as to loan approvals or country exposure limits can carry a lot of weight. Other banks in the key international financial centers may deal directly with the branches, which can accept Eurocurrency deposits and issue Eurocurrency certificates of deposits in their own names.

The future of branches is uncertain, at least with respect to new ones. The trend in foreign countries is not toward liberalization of foreign banking opportunities. Smaller countries are concerned that an excessive number of foreign branches will shut out local banks and are therefore restricting new entries. Moreover, local banks may receive more favorable treatment. In some cases, however, the restrictions are reciprocal ones imposed because of the home country's treatment of the host country's banks. In addition, as operating costs go up, many banks are taking a close look at whether branches are really necessary, given the nature and volume of business and the alternatives possible through modern, high-speed telecommunications.

It seems that American banks are undertaking less branching (particularly in Latin America), except for the larger ones. Smaller banks have more alternatives now than before—money brokers, other correspondent banks, Edge Act corporations, and IBFs—and better telecommunications systems through which to carry out their international business themselves.

Joint Ventures

Joint ventures, which involve two or more partners who have shares in the entity, are generally set up for specific purposes. The reason for this choice of organization may be to gain local contacts and expertise, share the risks, develop greater political leverage against the possibility of a take-over, or meet local legal requirements. It may also be that other preferred institutional forms are closed to foreign banks.

With joint ventures, a key issue is obviously the choice of partners. Others are the role of the major participants in management and the role and composition of the board of directors. In some cases the shareholders may serve as officers and managers in the joint venture, in other cases officers and managers may be hired. It is important to be clear what each partner is to provide in the way of capital, management, resources, planning, decision-making, staffing, and other needs and tasks.

Export Trading Companies

The Export Trading Company Act of 1982 authorizes bank holding companies to organize and operate, or to invest in and operate, companies whose primary purpose is to facilitate or engage in the export of U.S. goods and services. Typical activities for export trading companies are trade financing, advice on markets, shipping and transport services, information dissemination, insurance, warehousing, and the like. To accomplish the goal of promoting U.S. commerce, export trading companies are exempt from many of the restrictions that banks normally face with respect to international business, for example, in terms of activities in which they can engage. However, the trading companies are still subject to some restrictions. Bank holding companies cannot invest more than 5 percent of their capital and surplus in one trading company and cannot extend credit in excess of 10 percent of their consolidated capital and surplus to one company. Export trading companies cannot engage in any domestic business, such as agriculture or manufacturing, unless it relates to exporting.

Consortium Banks

Consortium banks are separately incorporated entities owned by two or more banks, usually of different nationalities, which are direct shareholders.

The rationale for setting up a consortium bank is to pool capital and management resources, to obtain business referrals from other members, and to engage in activities otherwise prohibited to the individual partners.

Consortium banks have tended to focus on certain activities. One category specializes, for example, in medium-term lending in the Eurocurrency market; this group includes some of the oldest and largest consortium banks. Often they manage medium-term syndicated loans. Another category is the multipurpose consortium—it undertakes medium-term lending and international investment and merchant bank activities, specialist financial services, mergers and acquisitions, project financing, and syndications, the latter a nonbanking service that has become a lucrative source of nonasset, fee-based earnings. Participation in a consortium bank is one way U.S. banks have been able to enter these types of markets. A third category is based on geographic coverage of wholesale and retail banking—the intent is to exploit certain markets that a single bank would be hard pressed to cover or enter. Consortium banks may also be a vehicle for avoiding the prohibition on foreign branches.

The consortium bank has had a checkered history. They first appeared in the early 1900s and grew rapidly, but friction among partners and mistrust led many to disband. Around 1964 there was a resurgence of these institutions, with the added feature that they were multinational. Most were comprised of medium-sized banks that could not afford their own branches. The failure of one consortium in 1974 revealed a number of problems, however, and the concept again fell into disfavor. Moreover, the medium-sized banks were becoming more adept at meeting their needs in other ways. As a result, the number of consortium banks fell. Another problem is that consortiums often compete in areas in which a member also has a subsidiary, such as merchant banking—a situation that poses a conflict of interest. Today there are only a limited number of both specialized and general consortium banks, most based in London.

Merchant Bank Subsidiaries

As noted above, one way U.S. banks have gotten around the restriction on Euromarket participation and investment financing is through consortium banks. More recently, however, they have begun to resort to merchant bank subsidiaries, perhaps because they realize that the syndication lending and investment banking business is a permanent source of income.

U.S. banks set up merchant bank subsidiaries to specialize in Eurocredit syndication; generally they represent the parent bank's entire network in this area of business. As a rule, merchant banks are headquartered in London but may have their own subsidiaries elsewhere. These banks also carry out Eurobond underwriting and private and project financing, and offer advice on mergers and acquisitions and other activities. The rise of merchant banks has been one cause of the gradual demise of consortium banks.

Domestic and Foreign Holding Corporations

While not strictly an alternative form of international banking in and of itself, this organizational structure must be mentioned because it is often a prerequisite for use of some of the options discussed above, e.g., subsidiaries, Edge Act corporations, etc. Banks have often resorted to holding companies as a means of avoiding certain restrictions and regulations, and many of the largest and oldest banks are themselves now parts of bank holding companies.

The bank holding company has evolved because of the fundamental principle in U.S. economic policy that banking and commerce be conducted separately. This principle, which applies to both domestic banks and to foreign banks in the United States, does not pertain in most other countries. In an effort to compete more effectively and broaden their base of earnings, domestic banks have set up bank holding companies as an indirect means of acquiring companies involved in nonbanking business.

Bank holding corporations must have at least a 25 percent equity interest, or controlling interest, in the commercial bank subsidiary, which must be registered with the Federal Reserve Board. Bank holding companies in turn can invest up to 5 percent of their consolidated capital and surplus in export trading companies and can extend to them credit up to 10 percent of their capital and surplus. The same is true for investment in Edge Act and Agreement corporations. Holding corporations may also invest in foreign companies that do not do business in the United States.

Deciding on a Foreign Banking Structure

A number of factors were mentioned earlier as determinants of the structure a bank will choose for its international operations. Generally, the direction in which a bank moves is determined by its medium-term plan, which sets goals and priorities, defines a marketing strategy, indicates what resources are available, and outlines procedures for management, staffing, and the like. If an equity investment is contemplated, the bank will usually call for a feasibility study, whose content and format will be predetermined. The study will look at all key variables and provide projections. They include such factors as the host country's economy and overall business environment, the banking market and opportunities, the foreign exchange situation, the legal and regulatory environment, the risks (including political, economic, and social conditions), and the likelihood of achieving certain specified targets. The study will also provide an analysis of the potential costs and benefits to the parent corporation, both direct (profits) and collateral. It should also indicate the most appropriate management style, structure, operating strategy, and approach. The content of the feasibility study will vary depending on the type of equity presence being contemplated. It is likely to be less extensive if only a representative office is being considered, while it will be quite inclusive if a foreign branch is at issue. Affiliates or joint ventures also necessitate analyses of the creditworthiness and status of foreign participants.

As a rule, a bank prefers wholly owned branches or subsidiaries, as they afford unilateral control. However, they may have to weigh that desire against other factors, some internal, some external. They include:

Foreign legal and regulatory restrictions. Perhaps the foremost external factor in influencing the choice of presence is foreign laws. Some countries prohibit certain types of structures, for example, branches or subsidiaries, and permit only correspondent banking or representative offices, and perhaps limit equity in a local bank to a noncontrolling interest.

Tax considerations. These include avoidance of state and local taxes on foreign transactions that raise the cost of U.S. financing and services in relation to foreign competitors. Favorable tax treatment along with confidentiality is what led so many U.S. banks to set up shell or other offices in the Bahamas. Banks may also want to take advantage of certain tax credits available for international activities. Moreover, certain structures offer better tax benefits than others. Earnings and losses incurred by foreign branches of U.S. banks affect a parent's tax liabilities directly, whereas those for subsidiaries are taken into account only in the case of divestiture or liquidation. Moreover, the income of subsidies is calculated after dividends are issued, not before.

Tax and regulatory considerations have become increasingly important as more foreign banks have entered the international arena, because frequently they have been able to offer lower-cost financing and services because of more favorable treatment. Ironically, this difference has been particularly true of foreign banks operating in the United States, as the laws until recently afforded them important cost and other operational advantages. As to taxes, they were one of the moving forces behind the authorization of IBFs and other changes with respect to international banking.

REGULATORY LEGISLATION IN THE UNITED STATES

As noted, the alternative forms of U.S. foreign banking have evolved in large measure as a result of banks' trying to get around regulations and restrictions on their activity or have been created by legislation aimed at righting some problem in the domestic or foreign banking system that renders U.S. banks uncompetitive. In turn, the legislation has been formulated to a large extent on the basis of some fundamental principles underlying banking policy in this country. It is useful to look at those principles as a backdrop to the discussion of the laws themselves.

Underlying Principles

One of the unique features of the regulation of the U.S. banking system is its dual nature. That is, licensing, regulation, and supervision of banks is the responsibility of both state and federal governments. A bank has the option of choosing whether to be chartered federally or by a state and may change that decision at any time. Banks may also choose whether or not to join the Federal Reserve system; member banks are called national banks and have access to the system's rediscount, clearing, and borrowing facilities. This duality, which has been in existence for 100 years, is an outgrowth of the principle that states have the right to manage and control activities within their political jurisdiction. This is a right the states have guarded carefully. On the whole, the dual system operates quite smoothly, with a fair degree of comparable regulation by both levels of regulators. At the same time, it creates an underlying tension.

Given the emphasis on states' rights, it might be asked why the federal government is involved at all. One reason is the relationship of banking activities to national monetary policy and the overall stability of the economy. In addition, the federal government has the role, through the vehicle of the central bank, of lender of last resort: in times of crisis, the Federal Reserve will act to maintain the stability and health of the banking system by advancing credit to solvent but temporarily illiquid financial institutions. From these roles comes the second principle—that the federal government has the duty to impose prudential measures designed to ensure the soundness of the system and to monitor and examine banks to ensure compliance and to identify problems before they become severe. This function is considered even more important today, given the ever-growing and complex links among banks, both nationally and internationally. The domino theory is seen to be potentially at play here—if one of the pieces falls, so will the rest.

A third principle is that the Federal Reserve system should be responsible for monetary policy, as it is a key tool in maintaining the stability of the economy overall. Because that policy hinges on management of bank reserves, the federal government claims the right to intervene and to supervise this aspect of banking.

A fourth principle, referred to earlier, is that banking should be kept separate from commercial, industrial, and certain financial activities. Thus banks traditionally have been excluded from direct involvement in non-banking activities, although they now are permitted carefully delineated indirect participation. They have been excluded from underwriting securities issues. With the increasing competitiveness of international banking, this principle has been a thorny issue, as many foreign banks are not so limited as to fields of endeavor. Much of the recent legislative change has been directed at correcting this inequity, a task that is still in process.

A fifth point is that to prevent the possibility of monopolies and an overconcentration of power in a few institutions, banks have not been permitted to branch out outside the borders of their home state, although they may establish branches within it. To some degree, that restriction has been circumvented by the practice of setting up bank holding companies that can acquire part or total interest in banks and other companies in other states, and by other newer banking entities such as the IBFs. Moreover, a number of states now permit regional interstate banking, with provision for national interstate banking after a certain period.

Sixth, the federal and state governments have felt it necessary to protect the retail consumer, a responsibility that resulted from the plight of the many people who lost all their savings in the bank failures of the nineteenth century and during the Great Depression. Banking authorities protect the consumer through regulation and insurance, obtained primarily from the FDIC, as well as some state insurance institutions. Again, with the advent of foreign banks to the United States and increasing U.S. banking overseas, this social benefit has run up against the question of relative competitiveness in the marketplace. FDIC and other insurance raises the cost of business for U.S. banks relative to foreign ones not subject to FDIC premiums.

The seventh principle relates to policy toward foreign banks in this country. Here the federal government has been guided by two objectives. One is to further U.S. business and commercial interests for the benefit of the economy. The second, which is related to the first but also independent of it, is that U.S. policy on international banking should be guided to the extent possible by a combination of reciprocity and respect for existing foreign practice. That is, foreign banks in the United States should not be prevented from doing what they would be permitted to do in their own countries. One reason for that belief is that U.S. banks abroad want to receive comparably favorable treatment in order to be competitive. However, this principle has often put U.S. banks at a disadvantage domestically, as they have been subject to more restrictive legislation than is found in the home countries of many foreign banks. Righting this disparity has likewise occasioned many of the legislative changes over the years, and more changes are still being debated.

As noted, banking law with respect to international activities has changed, sometimes dramatically, in response to changes in international banking and national objectives. One major change is the increasing role of the federal government over the years. Initially, the states had primary control and responsibility over banking. Then, as problems such as bank failures arose, and given the federal government's role as lender of last resort and implementor of monetary policy, the federal government moved in. The need to balance state versus federal rights has, however, always been an element in the debate relating to any change.

Key Legislation

The following reviews briefly the key pieces of legislation that bear on international banking.

The Federal Reserve Act of 1913

The Federal Reserve Act of 1913 was the federal government's first attempt to deal with the knotty issues of international banking. U.S. banks were prohibited from international banking, and the 1913 act loosened that ban somewhat.

According to the act, U.S. national banks with capital and surplus of $1 million or more could set up branches for the purpose of furthering U.S. commerce and to serve as fiscal agents of the U.S. government, with the approval of the Federal Reserve Board. (State member banks and privately incorporated banks already could do so.) Each branch was to maintain separate records and would be subject itself to federal supervision by the Federal Reserve, the FDIC, and the Office of the Comptroller of the Currency. These branch institutions were authorized to accept bankers' acceptances. At the same time, national banks still could not own foreign banks. Finally, the act established the Federal Reserve as the central bank of the United States.

The conflicts that would emerge later in terms of inequitable treatment of foreign and domestic banks operating in the United States were not apparent at this time, as there was little foreign banking here.

The Edge Act of 1919

The way had been paved for the Edge Act of 1919 by the Agreement Corporation Act of 1916. Both were designed to promote international banking and financing operations by U.S. banks in the furtherance of U.S. trade. The 1916 law gave national banks with capital and surplus in excess of $1 million the right, individually or together, to invest up to 10 percent of their capital and surplus in state-chartered banks and corporations that would conduct international banking business. In return, the state-chartered banks had to enter into an agreement with the Federal Reserve Board to be bound by its rules and regulations, for example, its reserve requirements and interest rate ceilings. This stipulation occasioned the name "Agreement corporations."

Despite expectations, the 1916 act produced little activity. Therefore in 1919 the Congress passed the Edge Act, which authorized the Federal Reserve Board to charter corporations that would engage in international banking and financing. Edge Act corporations had to have a minimum capitalization of $2 million, a majority of the shareholders had to be U.S. citizens, and the board of directors had to be composed of U.S. citizens. The corporations could engage in long-term financing and investment in nonbanking firms that carry on foreign business. They were allowed to receive deposits outside the United States and within it if the funds were to be used for foreign commerce. On the other hand, they could not issue bonds or debentures. The corporations were required to maintain a reserve requirement of 10 percent on all deposits. These provisions still apply today, with minor revisions.

The McFadden Act of 1927

The McFadden Act authorized national banks to establish branches, provided the states permitted it, in the municipality of the head office. It specifically prohibited them from crossing state lines. Later amendments allowed national banks to branch elsewhere in their home state, but still not across state lines. This law has been considerably diluted recently, and it is now widely believed that national interstate banking is a certainty in the fairly near future.

The Glass-Steagall Banking Act of 1933

The next important piece of legislation addressing international banking, Glass-Steagall, came in response to the bank failures and financial panic of the Depression. Its purpose was to control abusive, risky bank practices, the sorts of practices that had led to the partial failure of the banking system. Its main provision was to prohibit banks from engaging in commercial and investment—or nonbanking—activities. Its intent was to prevent a concentration of economic power and to protect deposits. A particular concern was bank involvement in securities transactions, and the Glass-Steagall Act prohibited banks from engaging in that business and member banks from being involved in certain ways with companies engaged in that business. The main exceptions were public issues of securities and securities transactions made in connection with foreign customers. This restriction on nonbanking activities applied to both state member and national banks and to bank holding companies. Moreover, banks could not purchase securities worth more than 15 percent of their capital and 25 percent of their reserves, or 10 percent of the securities outstanding. Banks or bank holding companies holding equity business securities had to divest them. The reason for the inclusion of holding companies was that banks had been growing in part by setting up holding companies as a way to acquire other banks or to acquire state-chartered banks beyond federal control.

Several banks have found loopholes in the law and have purchased discount brokerage businesses. Because of the competition banks now face from nonbanking institutions such as insurance companies and major retail chains, as well the banks' proven ability to exploit loopholes, the consensus is that the restrictions of Glass-Steagall will be modified in the years ahead, though how much is unclear. The prohibition against underwriting securities issues may be maintained, for example. In the interim, the regulatory authorities have taken a lenient stance on nonbanking activities by banks.

The Bank Holding Company Act of 1956

Holding companies were again addressed in the Bank Holding Company Act of 1956. It too was passed in order to regulate the process by which banks were using holding companies to expand and acquire additional banks and to engage in nonbanking business. The act also sought to reinforce the separation of banking and commercial activities. Henceforth bank holding companies had to obtain approval to acquire a voting share in excess of 5 percent of a bank or company, and state law had to permit the investment. Bank holding corporations were prohibited from acquiring a bank outside the bank's principal state of operations unless the state permitted it.

There was a major loophole in the law, however—holding companies with only one bank were excluded. Moreover, the act did not define the factors and weights to be applied by the Federal Reserve Board in deciding on acquisitions or mergers. These oversights were corrected somewhat by the 1966 Douglas Amendment to the act and by a 1970 amendment. The former spelled out in greater detail the factors to be used in deciding whether to authorize an acquisition or merger. The latter brought the single bank holding company under the provisions of the Bank Holding Company Act. As a result of the 1970 amendment, holding companies and banks are now treated equivalently.

The International Bank Act of 1978

The amendments did not address foreign banks, which remained outside the 1956 act as amended unless they were members of the Federal Reserve or in control of a subsidiary U.S. bank. This exclusion was a major issue with domestic banks. As noted, foreign banking in the United States was expanding rapidly in the 1970s, for the most part under the laws and supervision of the states rather than the federal government. As such, foreign banks had a number of important competitive advantages over domestic ones. Even federal law, however, offered foreign banks certain advantages not available to domestic ones. Many U.S. bankers claimed that the favorable treatment bestowed on foreign banks was responsible for the tremendous inroads they had made in the U.S. banking industry. Specifically, foreign banks could cross state lines, engage in nonbanking activities, hold equity in U.S. securities firms, benefit from lower capitalization requirements, ignore federal reserve requirements and interest rate ceilings, and decline FDIC insurance and related assessments. Thus, not only did the foreign banks have more business latitude, but they could offer their banking services more cheaply because they did not have to comply with Federal Reserve regulations. For its part, the Federal Reserve Board was concerned about the status of foreign banks not only because of the disparate treatment, but because its inability to control their reserves made it very difficult to implement federal monetary policy, which relies on management of reserves. To the Board, there was a clear gap in federal control.

Although there seemed to be unanimity on the need for change, there was no agreement on what forms it should take. The larger international U.S. banks feared further restrictions on foreign banks, as they felt foreign countries would in turn retaliate against them. Smaller and regional banks, on the other hand, were concerned over the competition posed by foreign banks and wanted the federal government to clamp down. For its part, the Board wanted to strengthen its hand with respect to both domestic and foreign banks.

The International Bank Act sought to achieve more equal treatment of domestic and foreign banks in the United States and abroad by striking a balance among the various interests. It called on the U.S. Treasury to conduct a study of banking and then for the Federal Reserve Board, Comptroller of the Currency, and FDIC to promulgate regulations on international banking. The act itself, however, specifically retained the dual state and federal chartering and licensing system so dear to the states. At the same time, it required all foreign banks to register with the Federal Reserve Board. Existing foreign bank agencies and branches could choose either a state or federal charter, but new ones had to join the Federal Reserve if the parent bank did not already have a charter or if the state permitted it. Foreign banks were not allowed to locate agencies and branches in the same state.

In another area, the act specified that foreign branches and agencies were to be supervised by the Comptroller of the Currency, federally insured state branches by the FDIC and state agencies, and non-federally insured state branches and agencies, as well as commercial lending companies, by state examining bodies. However, the Federal Reserve was given residual authority for special examinations of all foreign branches and agencies. The Federal Reserve, in keeping with the authority given it by the act, imposed the same federal reserve requirements and interest rate ceilings on all foreign banks with consolidated assets of more than $1 billion as applied to national banks. In return, foreign banks gained access to the central bank's rediscount, borrowing, and clearing facilities.

As to interstate banking, foreign banks were now allowed to establish or acquire Edge Act corporations. One important aspect of that authority was that Edge Act corporations were not covered by state restrictions on entry. Thus the act gave foreign banks an opportunity to enter states prohibiting subsidiaries or branches. On the other hand, interstate expansion of deposit-taking facilities by foreign banks was frozen. Foreign banks that already had deposit-taking facilities in more than one state had to designate a home state and could not have subsidiaries in other states. They could, however, establish non-deposit-taking agencies and branches, e.g., Edge corporations, where the state permitted it, and then they had to follow the Edge Act deposit rules. Again, this act contained a loophole—a grandfather clause— that exempted existing foreign banks from the requirements. This clause left some banks with their substantial advantages intact. For example, if a bank already had a deposit-taking unit in one state and an agency in another, it could choose as its home state the one in which the agency was located and legally convert it into a deposit-taking entity. Thus, it could end up with deposit-taking facilities in two states. Since enactment of the law, expansion by foreign banks has largely involved agencies and limited branches—ones that follow the Edge corporation rules on deposit-taking.

Edge Act corporations were permitted to merge the capital of all like organizations under the holding company when calculating the loan limit of 10 percent. The intent was to make Edge Act entities more competitive with foreign banks. In general, those banks were able to make larger loans because the parent banks were larger and had more capital than U.S. ones. Thus foreign branches were often at an advantage in terms of the permissible maximum loan size. Further, the old minimum reserve requirement was eliminated and replaced with one equal to 7 percent of the corporation's risk assets. Finally, Edge corporations could finance domestic production of goods and services for export, in addition to providing other export-related services such as insurance and storage.

As to domestic nonbanking activities, the quite stringent restrictions of the Bank Holding Act were made applicable to foreign banks with branches and agencies and to foreign commercial lending companies. The restrictions did not apply, however, to foreign banks whose U.S. presence consisted solely of Edge corporations.

FDIC insurance was made mandatory for all retail deposits of less than $100,000, except for the domestic-based deposits of foreign bank branches, which could choose whether to comply. Parent companies were required to make a surety bond or to pledge assets because of the additional risk to the FDIC of dealing with a foreign company. However, because of certain other regulations of the FDIC and the Comptroller, most foreign banks have been able to avoid deposit insurance when they wanted to. In addition, foreign bank branches and agencies with $1 billion or more in assets now have to comply with the reserve requirements (the requirements are somewhat different for Eurodollar liabilities). In return, foreign entities are able to use the Federal Reserve's rediscount, clearing, and borrowing facilities.

Finally, according to the act, federal branches and agencies, foreign and domestic, must maintain eligible assets (dollar deposits and permissible investment securities) on deposit with a member bank in the same state up to certain amounts.

Other provisions of the act were directed toward the operations of Edge Act corporations. The intent was to eliminate or modify the provisions that discriminated against foreign-owned banking institutions and that constrained Edge Act corporations from competing effectively with foreign banks in the United States and abroad. Edge corporations were allowed to acquire equity in foreign countries.

The provisions of this act still apply, with only minor modifications.

The Depository Institutions Deregulation and Monetary Control Act of 1980

A major issue that had not yet been resolved was the prohibition of domestic U.S. bank involvement in the Eurocurrency markets. It was that very situation that had led to the rapid growth of shell and other foreign branches in the 1960s and 1970s. On the other hand, foreign banks in the United States were free to deal in these markets. The issue had emerged as particularly important, since the Eurocurrency market was a necessity for financing the large-scale loans common in the 1970s.

The solution, enacted in this 1980 law, was to permit U.S. and foreign banks, any U.S. depository institution, and Edge or Agreement corporations to set up IBFs in any state allowing them. These facilities could accept Eurocurrency deposits of $100,000 or more. The act precluded the IBFs from taking deposits from U.S. offices of foreign firms and banks, nor could funds be used to support domestic economic activities. IBFs were required to have separate asset and liability accounts. While IBF transactions have been subject to federal taxes, many states and localities have chosen to waive their taxes in order to attract the business. The act also eliminated the reserve requirements on Eurodollar holdings of foreign branches in the United States and of U.S. foreign branches aboard. However, deposits were subject to insurance premiums.

Aside from the obvious advantages that large international banks gained, smaller banks also benefited, as participation in international banking became more possible.

Export Trading Company Act of 1982

The Export Trading Company Act of 1982 was designed primarily to promote exports of U.S. goods and services. This landmark legislation removed the threat of antitrust violations for American businesses, including banks interested in setting up joint ventures to explore export markets. It also permitted commercial banks to own an interest in export ventures.

The act authorized the U.S. Commerce Department to promote export trading companies (ETCs) and to facilitate interaction between the producers of exportable goods and services and firms offering export services. The antitrust issues were to be resolved by Commerce in consonance with the Justice Department. Finally, the law instructed the Export-Import Bank to set up a loan guarantee program for ETCs and to liberalize the rules to increase the negotiability of commercial paper used in international financial transactions.

According to the act, an ETC must be engaged in business in the United States primarily for the purpose of exporting goods and services produced in the United States and of assisting unrelated companies in the export of their products overseas. Thus, ETCs could only export goods and services or provide facilitating services for unrelated exporters. As such, they could also engage in importing and trade between third countries.

ETCs could be owned by either U.S. or foreign companies. The act authorized bank holding companies and bankers' banks to invest up to 5 percent in and to loan up to 10 percent of their capital and surplus to an ETC. With respect to loans to ETCs, a bank was exempt from the collateral requirements called for in the Federal Reserve Act. Moreover, they could own up to 100 percent of an ETC's stock. However, the Federal Reserve Board had to approve any proposed investment, although the procedure was quite simple, involving only notification of intent. If the Federal Reserve Board did not respond in 60 days, the investor could go ahead. The Federal Reserve Board was also assigned a monitoring role. By granting antitrust preclearance to traders, the Board would substantially limit antitrust lawsuits that could be brought by private parties.

In other words, the new law gave American business the chance to use government-sanctioned export trading institutions. In addition, the act did not specify what an ETC was, only what it could and could not do. Thus businesses were free to use their ingenuity and imagination to structure whatever type of ETC best met their needs.

The Future

While the legislative changes to date have addressed many of the issues that have beset international banking, there is continued agitation for further change. It is highly likely that still more modifications will be made that will intensify the scope of financial activities and the competitive environment. It is also likely that there will be increasing equity investment by foreign banks in U.S. ones.

REGULATORY AGENCIES

As noted, the U.S. banking system is a dual state and federal one. Thus supervision and oversight of U.S. banks rest with both federal agencies and state examining bodies.

The Federal Regulators and Their Responsibilities

Three federal agencies share responsibility for international banking: the Federal Reserve system, the Comptroller of the Currency, and the Federal Deposit Insurance Corporation. Interestingly, the respective roles of the agencies are not clearly spelled out in legislation, but have evolved on their own over time. The same is somewhat true with respect to the areas of jurisdiction of federal and state agencies. On the whole, there has been a substantial degree of accord among the regulatory groups.

The Federal Reserve regulates all member, or national, banks, and supervises bank holding companies, Edge Act corporations, overseas affiliates of U.S. banks and foreign branches of U.S. banks, and all foreign banks with consolidated assets greater than $1 billion operating in the United States. It also has residual authority to conduct special studies of all foreign banks under state supervision. Its regulatory and supervisory role with respect to bank holding companies actually gives the Federal Reserve considerable influence over banks themselves, as the holding companies are now the chief mechanism by which banks expand.

In addition to these monitoring and supervisory functions, the Federal Reserve of New York undertakes periodically to rank foreign countries on the basis of their ability to service their external obligations. This ranking is based on five ratios (e.g., current account deficit/exports). The information is used in evaluating a bank's risk exposure.

The Office of the Comptroller of the Currency (OCC) supervises all national banks with assets of $10 billion or more, all national banks with overseas branches, and federally chartered foreign branches and agencies in the United States. It shares with the states the regulation and oversight of non-federally insured state-chartered foreign branches. In addition, the OCC is responsible for centralizing national policy and for the operation of international regulations. To facilitate this role, in 1978 the OCC established the Multinational Banking Division, which now handles examination, analysis, and supervision of multinational banks and policy coordination. Also under the OCC is the Interagency Country Exposure Review Committee (ICERC), which measures the exposure of U.S. banks to "sovereign risk" loans.

The Federal Deposit Insurance Corporation supervises all banks that it insures, although it shares that responsibility with the states in the case of state-chartered banks that are not members of the Federal Reserve. It also advises other agencies.

Because of the increasing riskiness of the banking business, the FDIC is seeking to obtain the right to set the charge for premiums so as to reflect that risk. It has proposed two schemes to that end. First, it does not want to provide full coverage for deposits placed in banks by brokers, who find the funds in regions with excess deposits and sell them where money is in short supply. Second, it has asked the Congress to permit it to charge higher premiums for deposits at risky banks.

Given the division of supervisory responsibility, coordination has obviously been a concern. In 1979 the Federal Financial Institution Examining Council was set up to coordinate the agencies' international activities.

Nevertheless, the regulators differ in their philosophies about bank regulation, a situation that has caused some confusion with respect to activities such as state banking, loans to other countries, limited service banks, capital requirements, brokered deposits, disclosure, and bank examination.

It is also important to note that concern for coordination and more uniform supervision has emerged at the international level as well, a not surprising fact given the nature of the banking industry today. While it has proven difficult to get countries to agree to common standards, procedures, and thoroughness, some general accords and international coordinating organizations have emerged. The Bank for International Settlements, for example, has set up a Committee on Banking Regulations and Supervisory Practices to which mostly industrial nations belong. An understanding (Basle Concordat) prepared under the auspices of the committee establishes principles of cooperation and mutual obligations. The Organization for Economic Coordination and Development (OECD) has an Export Banking Group, and there are also regional bodies, such as the Center for Monetary Studies in Latin America. One area in which work is ongoing is the development of global consolidated accounting systems. Finally, participants in certain transactions, e.g., syndicated loans, often specify in the contracts such points as the governing law and jurisdiction.

There are in addition private bank-rating companies, such as Keefe Bruyette and Woods, which publishes "Bank Watch" and rates 300 U.S. and 100 foreign banks. Other private companies include Moody's Investor Services, Duff & Phelps, and McCarthy, Crisanti and Maffei Co.

Monitoring and Supervision

The various regulatory bodies monitor and supervise their charges fairly closely and routinely. The purpose is to prevent problems from arising by insisting on sound banking practices and management. Further, by conducting regular reviews and inspections, it is assumed that the agencies will detect problems and propose solutions before they become serious. In fact, the Comptroller of the Currency maintains a list of banks that it considers to have excessive exposure and that it monitors even more closely until the problem is resolved.

The regulatory bodies carry out a combination of routine examinations, both on-site and from their headquarters. In the case of the latter, the review involves the reports and documentation that all banks and banking institutions are required to submit periodically. Discussions are also held with bank officers and staff. Examiners look at a number of variables, such as country risk, foreign commercial credit, foreign exchange, interbank dealings, international operations systems and controls, the bank's operating environment, its range of activities, its system of external and internal controls, the quality of its assets, its portfolio management, its capacity to analyze risks, its funding and dealing operations, compliance with domestic and host country laws and regulations, and the bank's performance relative to its strategic plan and objectives. These variables are examined in the context of the effect of international operations on the bank's consolidated safety and soundness. In sum, the examiners look at both the external factors affecting a bank's operations and the internal systems and procedures that ensure good control and management and ready identification of problems, as well as the ability to respond to them.

Perhaps the greatest attention is paid to the quality of management. Elements that characterize a good management system include ongoing evaluation of economic, social, and political trends; country exposure limits; current, adequate, and accurate reporting systems (management information systems) for country and loan risk assessment; good portfolio structure in terms of the diversity of investments and loans by geography, customer, use, maturities, and interest and exchange rates; and an emphasis on forward planning. Good financial management is characterized by the provision of prudent sources of liquidity, to be available for anticipated needs, and sensitive management of the interest rate between assets and liabilities to provide adequate net interest earnings. Banks should also have clear goals and policies. Recently the examiners have also been emphasizing banks' foreign exchange and interbank deposit dealings. Increasingly they themselves are applying country risk assessment techniques to their analysis of the soundness of banks' portfolios.

To facilitate the monitoring, each bank or banking institution is required to maintain separate records and must periodically file reports with specific information, such as its country exposure, to the regulatory bodies, where it is analyzed by computer.

Depending on the nature of any problems found, examiners may choose to talk informally with a bank's upper-level management and board. In addition, examiners must provide reports on their studies to the Federal Reserve Board of Governors. Deficiencies include such things as an over-concentration of loans to one customer, geographic region, or repayment factor (e.g., a mineral resource), poor internal controls, and an inadequate management information system.

Supervision of Foreign Banking Institutions in the United States

As noted, it is only in the last ten to twenty years that regulation of foreign banking institutions operating in the United States has been an issue. However, the disparities in treatment of domestic and foreign banks and the rapid growth of foreign banks in the United States, particularly in terms of acquisition of U.S. banks, led to calls for reform of the legislation. A third critical factor in bringing about recent reforms was the Federal Reserve's feeling that it was being hampered in its efforts to carry out monetary policy by the number of institutions, especially foreign ones, exempt from its reserve requirements.

As mentioned earlier, several conflicting objectives have come into play in determining U.S. policy toward foreign banks in this country. One has been the belief that foreign banks should not be precluded from activities permissible in their home countries, largely because it was felt that doing so would result in reciprocal restrictions being placed on U.S. banks abroad. On the other hand, the principle of reciprocity would seem to suggest that restrictions be placed on the banking institutions of those nations imposing the most constraints on U.S. banking facilities. Nevertheless, U.S. policy has been to treat all foreign banks equally.

A third factor has been the need, in setting policy, to balance the objectives of the large multinational banks and the smaller state and regional banks with respect to the position of foreign banks. The former want less restrictions across the board, the latter more restrictions. The Congress has also sought to balance state rights versus federal economic policy and management needs.

The main areas at issue relate to entry of foreign banking institutions into the U.S. market, the scope of activities permitted those entities, the application of regulations, and the extent of supervision and examination. As to entry, because of the dual banking system, foreign banks can still choose between state and federal chartering. However, the International Banking Act of 1978 did close some doors by making entry of certain types of banking institutions a federal responsibility. For example, foreign banks cannot acquire banks in more than one state, although they can have branches and agencies. The following are now subject to federal approval: acquisition of national or state banks, establishment of federal or state branches and agencies, formation of an investment company (or commercial lending company), establishment of an Edge corporation, and formation of a representative office. For the most part, the Federal Reserve has approved all applications, although it may attach prudential conditions as it sees fit. Generally, the decision is based on the Comptroller's assessment of the effect the entity will have on competition in both U.S. domestic and foreign commerce, the financial and managerial resources of the parent bank and its prospects, and the convenience and needs of the community to be served.

With respect to scope of activities, in the end the government chose not to restrict foreign banking institutions unduly, a decision that meant affording more equal opportunities to domestic banks. On the other hand, to a large extent foreign banking institutions were brought under the regulatory umbrella. Subject to certain exemptions, foreign banking institutions must meet capitalization and federal reserve requirements and adhere to ceilings on interest rates. Again with certain exceptions, foreign banking institutions must have FDIC insurance for retail deposits.

As to monitoring and oversight, foreign banking institutions are required to provide certain information and reports to the regulatory agencies, probably more than is required at home in many cases. Examiners also review these records and the institutions' activities and operations to ensure compliance with regulations. Because the reporting requirements are often greater than would be required in their home countries, the examining agencies afford confidentiality.

POSTSCRIPT

A final point needs to be made about the regulation of banking. The trend today is toward greater deregulation, not only in the United States, but also in other countries. In terms of international banking, deregulation is likely to open up more countries to foreign banks and to afford them freer and more equal operating conditions. It will also mean that more banks will be able to enter a wider range of activities.

Many have feared that deregulation will bring with it greater problems. In particular, they note that the current crises have all arisen since banks entered the unregulated Euromarkets in a big way.

While only time will tell if deregulation proves problematic, it is important to note a parallel and counteractive trend—an increase in supervision and an insistence on sounder banking practices and management by regulatory authorities. At the same time, banks themselves were scared by the crisis of the early 1980s, a fear that persists as the difficulties prove to be more intractable than anyone thought. Thus, of their own accord, banks have tightened their operating procedures. In addition, the increased competition spurred in part by deregulation has forced banks to become more efficient and to cut back on risky operations that might jeopardize already slim profit margins. (See also the final chapter of this book for a closer look at the likely impact of deregulation in the coming years.)

REFERENCES

Adam, Nigel, "How America Rediscovered Correspondent Banking," *Euromoney*, February 1982, pp. 79–91.

Aliber, Robert Z., "International Banking: A Survey," *Journal of Money, Credit and Banking*, November 1984.

Atcheson, Al K., *Bretton Woods Revisited*, Toronto: University of Toronto Press, 1972.

Bee, Robert N., "The Consortium Bank Is Alive and Well," *Euromoney*, November 1979, pp. 139–41.

Brewer, Elijah, et al., "The Depository Institutions Deregulation and Monetary Control Act of 1980," Federal Reserve Bank of Chicago *Economic Perspectives*, 4, September–October 1980, p. 5.

Burr, Rosemary, "Consortium Banks at the Crossroads," *The Banker*, November 1977, pp. 115–19.

Cambitsis, Andres, *The Eurobond Market*, Geneva: Institut Universitaire de Hautes Etudes Internationales, 1974.

Carson, Teresa, "Big Bank Problem Loans Exceed Equity," *American Banker*, March 17, 1983.

———, "Second-Tier Latin Loans Equal Equity," *American Banker*, April 6, 1983.

Darity, William A., "Loan Pushing: Doctrine and Theory," Board of Governors of the Federal Reserve System, Washington, D.C., 1985.

Edwards, Franklin R., "The New International Banking Facility: A Study in Regulatory Frustration," *Columbia Journal of World Business*, Winter 1981, pp. 6–18.

Eitman, D. K., and A. I. Stonehill, *Multinational Business Finance*, Menlo Park, Calif.: Addison-Wesley, 1973.

Enzig, Paul, *The Euro-bond Market*, London: Redwood Burn, 1975.

———, *Foreign Dollar Loans in Europe*, London: Macmillan, 1965.

Federal Financial Institutions Examination Council, "Country Exposure Lending Survey," Statistical Release E.16, Washington, D.C., April 1985.

Federal Reserve Board, *Federal Reserve Bulletins*, Washington D.C., 1979–84.

Fisher, Frederick G., III, *The Eurodollar Bond Market*, London: Euromoney Publications, 1979.

Folkerts-Landau, Eleona, "The Regulatory Origins of the International Debt Crisis," *Bankers Magazine*, September 1984.

Geisst, Charles R., *Raising International Capital*, Farnborough, Eng.: Saxon House, 1980.

Golembe, Carter H., and David S. Holland, *Federal Regulation of Banking*, Washington, D.C.: Golembe Associates, 1983.

Guttentag, Jack, and Richard Herring, *The Lender-of-Last Resort Function in an International Context*, Essays in International Finance, no. 151, Princeton, N.J.: Princeton University Press, 1983.

Hall, William, "Consortium Banks Adapt to a New Environment," *The Banker*, November 1981, pp. 135–39.

Handbook for National Bank Examiners, Washington, D.C.: U.S. Comptroller of the Currency, 1982.

Hogan, W. P., and I. F. Pierce, *The Incredible Eurodollar*, London: George Allen & Associates, 1982.

Holland, David, "Making Use of Export Trading Companies," *Banking Expansion Reporter*, November 15, 1982, pp. 1–15.

Ireland, Jenny, "International Banking Facilities: The Bahamas Eyes Its Future," *The Banker*, July 1981, pp. 51–56.

———, "International Banking Facilities: Miami–Benefactor or Competitor?" *The Banker*, July 1981, pp. 57–60.

Johnson, G. G., *Aspects of the International Banking Safety Net*, Washington, D.C.: IMF, 1983.

Khoury, S., *Dynamics of International Banking*, New York: Praeger, 1980.

Mendelsohn, Stefan, *Money on the Move*, New York: McGraw-Hill, 1980.

Officer, Lawrence H., et al., eds., *The International Monetary System*, Englewood Cliffs, N.J.: Prentice-Hall, 1969.

Park, Yoon S., *The Eurobond Market: Function and Structure*, New York: Praeger, 1974.

Quinn, Brian Scott, *The New Euromarkets*, New York: John Wiley & Sons, 1975.

Reed, Edward W., Edward K. Gill, and Richard K. Smith, *Commercial Banking*, 2nd ed., Englewood Cliffs, N.J.: Prentice-Hall, 1980, p. 427.

Rose, Peter S., *Money and Capital Markets*, Plano, Tex.: Business Publications, 1983.

Roussakis, Emmanuel N., ed., *International Banking Principles and Practices*, New York: Praeger, 1983.

Rudy, John P., "International Correspondent Banking," *The Banker*, February 1982, pp. 49–54.

Short, Genie D., and Betsy B. White, "International Bank Lending: A Guided Tour Through the Data," Federal Reserve Bank of New York *Quarterly Review*, Autumn 1978, pp. 39–46.

———, "A New Supervisory Approach to Foreign Lending," Federal Reserve Bank of New York *Quarterly Review*, Spring 1978.

Tschoegl, Adrian E., *The Regulation of Foreign Banks: Policy Formation in Countries Outside the United States*, New York: Salomon Brothers Center for the Study of Financial Institutions, New York University, 1981.

U.S. Congress, House of Representatives, *An Act to Amend Certain Sections of the Act Entitled "Federal Reserve Act,"* Approved December 23, 1913, P.L. 270, 64th Cong., 1916, H.R. 13391, pp. 43–48; U.S. Congress, Senate, *An Act to Amend the Act Approved December 23, 1913, known as the Federal Reserve Act*, P.L. 106, 66th Cong., 2d sess., 1919, S. 2472, pp. 378–84.

———, *Banking Act of 1933*, P.L. 66, 73d Cong., 1st sess., 1933, H.R. 5661, pp. 184–85, 188–90; and *Banking Holding Company Act Amendments of 1970*, P.L. 91–607, 91st Cong., 2d sess., 1970, H.R. 6778, pp. 1760–68.

———, *Depository Institutions Deregulation and Monetary Control Act of 1980*, P.L. 96–221, 96th Cong., 2d sess., 1980, H.R. 4986, pp. 132–93.

———, *International Banking Act of 1978*, P.L. 95–369, 95th Cong., 1978, H.R. 10899.

Weston, Rae, *Domestic and Multinational Banking*, New York: Columbia University Press, 1980, Part 4.

White, Betsy B., "Foreign Banking in the United States: A Regulatory and Supervisory Perspective," Federal Reserve Bank of New York *Quarterly Review*, Summer 1982, pp. 48–58.

Woolridge, J. R., and K. D. Wiegel, "Foreign Banking Growth in the United States," *The Bankers Magazine*, January–February 1981, pp. 30–38.

Yassukovich, S. M., "Consortium Banks on Course," *The Banker*, February 1976, pp. 165–71.

3

WORLD FINANCIAL MARKETS AND INTERNATIONAL BANKING CENTERS

Lending and borrowing of dollars and other currencies outside a country of origin takes place largely through a number of international money markets, which are centered around certain key banking sites. While originally these money markets focused primarily on trade-related transactions, their scope has grown tremendously in the last twenty years or so, along with the volume of international business and complexity of operations. The huge amount and mobility of capital funds are predominant features of today's world financial markets and are likely to remain so and to intensify in the years ahead.

This chapter reviews the main capital markets (Eurodollar, Eurobond, Asian dollar Special Drawing Right [SDR], and European Currency Unit [ECU]) and the major banking centers (Asia, Europe, and the Caribbean).

WORLD FINANCIAL MARKETS

Eurodollar Market

The substantial increase in the volume of capital flows in the 1970s can be traced largely to the emergence of the Eurocurrency market in Europe. Today's extensive international financial integration is now closely associated with the high level of capital turnovers in and expansion of this market, which is the largest of the financial trading centers. Eurodollars are in turn the largest component of the Eurocurrency market. For this reason, the Eurocurrency market is sometimes referred to as the Eurodollar market.

The Eurodollar market is now the primary means of transferring short-term funds across national boundaries; it provides a mechanism for shifting funds from banks, corporations, and other institutions with temporary surpluses to those with temporary deficits. For example, from 1973 to 1977 it provided one-half the capital needed to finance the current external payments deficits of all the world's oil-importing countries by recycling the petrodollars placed in short-term Euromarket bank deposits. At present, the volume of business is probably between $1.5 trillion and $2 trillion a year.

The Origins of the Eurodollar Market

The Eurodollar market can be traced back to a number of factors. One was the huge quantities of resources the United States transferred overseas to Europe and Asia under the Marshall Plan. Another was the move by the Soviet Union and other centrally planned economies, because of the perceived risk of holding dollar balances in New York in light of the Cold War, to transfer their assets to banks in London (Moscow Narodny Bank) and Paris (Banque Commerciale pour l'Europe du Nord). Yet another factor was that western central banks, commercial banks, and businesses also shifted their funds to the Eurodollar market, in this case to take advantage of the higher yields.

A fourth reason for the emergence of the Eurodollar market was the response of the British government to the sterling crisis of 1957. When the pound weakened in that year, the British authorities imposed tight controls on U.K. bank lending in order to retain their leading position in world finance. As a result, London soon emerged as the center for international trading in the U.S. dollar.

Events in the United States itself were a further cause. For one thing, the U.S. balance of payments deficits in the 1960s led to an accumulation of dollars in the hands of nonresidents. That same problem led to the passage of legislation in the 1960s designed to control the outflow of capital from the United States. The U.S. Interest Equalization Tax of 1963 imposed a tax on foreign borrowers in the U.S. capital markets. In response, U.S. banks transferred massive amounts of funds to European branches so as to be able to lend without incurring the tax. In 1965 the U.S. government called for American corporations to impose voluntary restrictions on their foreign direct investment; with the response less than hoped for, in 1968 the government made the restrictions mandatory. Finally, there was Regulation Q. Up until 1983, it imposed interest rate ceilings on all savings and time deposits in the United States, whereas there was no such limit in the Eurodollar market. Predictably, Regulation Q also led to a transfer of funds overseas.

There was also the glut of petrodollars deposited by Arab nations in European banks following the oil price increases. For political reasons, they had chosen not to place these in U.S. banks. These Euromarket funds constituted a major source of short-term financing.

Although a number of these conditions no longer pertain, once the Eurodollar market got going, it gained a momentum and life of its own. And it has had a lasting impact on the nature of international banking. It has shifted to London and Europe a major part of the dollar borrowing formerly transacted in New York. It has raised the importance of the dollar as a key international currency. It has increased the competition between commercial banks for deposits and loans. Certainly it has moved the major money markets closer together, particularly those within Europe itself. Many European central banks, such as the Bundesbank, now use the Eurodollar market to control the liquidity of their domestic banks, although they also recognize that the capital inflows into the markets make it hard for them to tighten credit when that policy seems necessary.

The Operations of the Eurodollar Market

A Eurodollar is created when a U.S. dollar is transferred from a bank in the United States for deposit in another country, either in a foreign bank or in a branch of an American one. Eurodollars are also created when someone outside the United States acquires dollars and deposits them in a bank outside the United States.

Types of Deposits. Eurodollar deposits, which usually take the form of certificates of deposit (CDs), range from "call" or overnight deposits to ones with three-year maturities. Typically, however, the maturities run from one to six months. (Longer-term transactions of one year or more generally take place in the allied but separate Eurobond market, discussed later.) The CDs can be marketable or nonmarketable. Deposits are usually made in blocks of $1 million, with the minimum being $500,000, and no collateral is required. Thus, a Eurodollar deposit is not a demand deposit that can be used to settle a debt, but is a type of money market instrument.

Nonmarketable or straight-term deposits are placed in a bank for a specific maturity at a specific interest rate and require the approval of the bank for early withdrawal. They account for 85 to 90 percent of all Eurodollar deposits.

Marketable or negotiable deposits, which have varying maturities, are highly liquid and may be sold at any time on the secondary market. That market is maintained by twenty broker/dealer firms that are members of the International CD Market Association. Banks find that negotiable CDs are cheaper, while investors like them for their liquidity and anonymity. First introduced in 1966 in London, they now account for the remaining 10 to 15 percent of Eurodollar deposits.

A common type of CD issued by Eurobanks is the tap CD, which has different yields for different maturities. Usually the maturity is one to twelve months, with three to six months very typical. However, maturities up to a few years are possible. A second common type of CD is the tranche, which is made up of a series of identical parts—or tranches—with the same yields, interest payments, and maturities. Each tranche can be liquidated according to prearranged installments. In cases where the tranches are to be liquidated, the interest rates differ, i.e., interest rates may be lower on the remaining balances. A third type of CD, first offered in 1980, is denominated in Special Drawing Rights. These CDs are based on the five currencies used to calculate the value of the SDR. The amount of the deposit is hypothetically converted into SDRs on the date of deposit at the rate prevailing then. On maturity, the depositor gets back the amount of the SDRs plus interest converted back to dollars at the then prevailing rate. Thus this CD may serve as a hedge against depreciation in the currency of deposit. Credit Suisse–First Boston maintains the secondary market for SDR CDs.

The basic rate for borrowers in the Eurodollar market is tied to the London Interbank Offered Rate (LIBOR), the deposit rate applicable to interbank transactions. Customer rates on loans are calculated as a premium on top of the LIBOR, with the level of the premium tied to the borrower's creditworthiness and the terms of the credit. The loan itself is rolled over every six months at a new rate that reflects changes in the LIBOR. This practice allows banks to decrease the risk posed by long-term lending using short-term funds. Customers pay the interest on their loans every six months, depending on the premium over the LIBOR. Some Eurocredit maturities run ten or fifteen years.

Participants. The Eurodollar market is supplied with dollars by U.S. and foreign commercial banks. Swiss banks rank first among the suppliers, central banks second. Institutional investors such as insurance companies, mutual funds, and multinational corporations constitute a third group of depositors. Finally, there are wealthy individuals. Bank funds come from the liquidity reserves of commercial banks that are located in countries without organized money markets. Despite this diversity of depositors, the Eurobank market is basically an interbank one, with 75 percent of the Eurodollar liabilities owed among banks.

The major users of Eurodollars include governments, companies involved in international trade, foreign as well as U.S. banks, and speculators. Many times a Eurobank places Eurodollars deposited with it in another European bank, including U.S. branches. These interbank transactions clearly inflate the statistical value of deposits in the market. Banks may also lend the money to another bank user, such as an importer or exporter. A further option is to transfer the funds to a U.S. branch bank in Europe, which in turn loans them out to its head office in the United States. These Eurodollar deposits at branches can be an additional source of funds for parent banks in the United States, especially when monetary policy there is tight.

The Pros and Cons of the Eurodollar Market

The Eurodollar market has grown fast and is continuing to expand because it offers a number of advantages to depositors and investors. A key one is the narrower interest rate spread. The difference between deposit and loan rates in the Eurodollar market is often less than 1 percent, whereas in the United States it is 2 percent. The narrower spread means that depositers can earn more in the Eurodollar market than in the United States. Financing is also cheaper for borrowers, as the Eurodollar market is interbank. The wholesale nature of the market—involving unsecured CDs of $500,000 or more—also keeps rates low. Moreover, the borrowers are mainly international banks, multinational corporations, or governments that qualify for low rates because of their credit standing and the size of their transactions. As to deposit rates, they are higher in the Eurodollar market because of the absence of U.S. reserve requirements and Regulation Q, which limits the interest payable on time deposits. Moreover, the Eurodollar market has no watchdog agency such as the Securities and Exchange Commission.

The efficiency and convenience of the Euromarket as an instrument for holding excess corporate liquidity are other attractions. So is the efficiency of the market as a source of short-term bank loans to finance corporate working capital needs, including the financing of imports and exports. Further, Eurodollar deposit maturities are flexible and thus can be fitted to the needs of investors. The market also offers investors a way to improve their liquidity by buying dollars in the market and lending them in the form of Eurodollar deposits. In addition, the market can be used for covered or uncovered interest arbitrage, in which the differentials between interest rates and forward foreign exchange contracts guarantee profits.

There are also some disadvantages to the Eurodollar market. First, it has no lender of last resort similar to the Federal Reserve in the United States to help banks out in case of liquidity problems. Nor is there any type of insurance such as that provided by the U.S. Federal Deposit Insurance Corporation. Third, on a broader scale, the Eurodollar market has made it far harder for countries to appraise and manage domestic monetary conditions. A fourth problem that emerged during the glut of petrodollars was the excessive risks that banks incurred when they recycled those funds into loans to unstable countries. That overexposure eventually provoked the current banking crisis. Finally, the extensive speculation being carried out in foreign exchange markets has produced a destabilizing and volatile effect on many currencies.

Many of the traditional risks that accompany international financing also apply to the Eurodollar market. One is credit risk, associated with a borrower's inability to repay and a lender's failure to require collateral as a basis for lending. When the transactions take place across boundaries, there is also sovereign and country risk. Lending institutions that do not manage their assets and liabilities well may run into liquidity problems. Finally, there is risk associated with the extreme mobility of interest rates and relative foreign exchange rates. To some degree, these risks can be reduced by using the spot and forward markets and by periodically adjusting interest rate charges on loans in keeping with changes in the LIBOR.

Conclusions

The Eurodollar market has evolved into a highly efficient form of financial intermediation that has drawn depositors and borrowers alike away from purely domestic transactions. It offers investors high yields and safe, liquid investments, while satisfying the needs of businesses and governments for low-cost funds with some assurance of availability. Because of these features, the Eurodollar will remain a permanent feature of the international financial world. Only a return to nonconvertability or extensive restrictions on capital flows, or a loss of confidence by investors in the worldwide usability of the U.S. dollar, will disrupt it.

The Eurobond Market

Eurobonds are securities that exist almost entirely outside the United States. They may be denominated in U.S. dollars, deutschemarks, yen, or Swiss francs. Generally, the Eurobond market is defined as a market for dollar securities offered by a syndicate of international banks to investors in two or more nations where their distribution is legal. The reason for this system is that U.S. law requires that publicly offered securities be registered with the Securities and Exchange Commission and conform to its disclosure requirements. Eurobonds are not registered with the commission and hence cannot be placed in the United States or with U.S. citizens as new issues.

Emergence of the Eurobond Market

International bond issues first appeared in the early nineteenth century. At that time, and up to World War I, saving was considered virtuous and relatively easy, at least for the well-to-do, who were not taxed as heavily as today. Moreover, political stability and the absence of major wars increased people's willingness to save. The fact that capital movements were not subject to international restrictions and that exchange controls were rare were other favorable factors. Nor did countries suffer from balance of payments deficits.

The leading European international capital markets in the nineteenth and early twentieth centuries were London, Paris, and Berlin. After World War I, New York, spared the ravages of battle, became the leading international capital market. But its reign was brief—the stock market crash of 1929 and the ensuing Depression brought about a temporary demise. There was a resurgence after World War II, again brought on by the United States' favored position in the world and its continued balance of payments surpluses; New York regained its role as a leading international bond market. However, it should be noted that most of the U.S. surpluses were attributable to *public* capital transactions such as the Marshall Plan, the Anglo-American Financial Agreement, and foreign bond issues in New York, as opposed to private transactions, which were virtually nonexistent.

As Europe rebuilt itself and gained economic strength, the shortage of dollars gradually receded, and the U.S. balance of payments surplus shrank in direct proportion. By the mid–1950s, the United States was experiencing constant deficits. Then in 1958, the major European countries reestablished the convertibility of their currencies for nonresidents and even reduced the foreign exchange restrictions on residents.

U.S. gold reserves declined along with the continuing deficits. These problems, combined with the lack of response to U.S. pleas that Europe raise its capital in its own markets, eventually led the U.S. government to restrict the massive outflows of capital in the form of Yankee bonds. It did so by implementing the Interest Equalization Tax in 1963. The tax was based on the purchase price of the foreign investment made by a U.S. citizen and varied with its maturity, ranging from 2.75 percent for bonds of at least three years of remaining maturity (but less than three and a half) to 15 percent for bonds of more than twenty-eight and a half years of remaining maturity. In theory, this tax was to raise the attractively low U.S. interest rates on Yankee bonds to the same high levels as European rates. It was anticipated that as a result the foreign markets would expand to accommodate the European borrowers now shut out of the New York market. In February 1965 the government also instituted the Voluntary Foreign Credit Restraint Program, which called for U.S. corporations voluntarily to restrict overseas investments in subsidiaries and affiliates. In 1968 the program was, as noted, made mandatory.

Except for certain public issues, such as those sponsored by the World Bank, the Yankee bond market indeed came to a halt. In turn, Europe was flooded with dollars. This flow was reinforced by the continuing U.S. balance of payments deficits and the substantial government spending on Vietnam.

While other countries could have revalued their domestic currencies, most chose instead to increase their dollar reserve holdings. However, in 1964 the West Germans opened the first important nondollar currency sector by imposing a 25 percent withholding tax on domestic investment in deutschemark bonds by nonresidents. The success of the deutschemark bond brought other new currency sectors into the market—the first Euro-French franc and Euro-Dutch guilder ones were floated in 1965. The opening of these nondollar sectors was important to the expansion of the Eurobond market in that they provided new capital resources and allowed borrowers a greater choice of currencies.

Another factor that led to the rapid growth of the Eurobond market was the quick adoption by the European banking system of New York's issuing techniques, modified by those techniques used by the merchant banks of London. Eurobanks soon found that they were able to mobilize vast sums in short periods.

Bond transfers were risky because they required no proof of ownership. Thus, during the formative period, Europe set about improving the security of its Eurobond market. The first clearinghouse, Euroclear, was established in Brussels in 1968, followed by Cedel of Luxembourg in January 1971. In April 1979 the self-regulatory Association of International Bond Dealers (AIBD) was set up to regulate the Eurobond market. It has been relatively successful in harmonizing Euroclear and Cedel and is responsible for the standardization of secondary market practices in the Eurobond market.

After extensions in 1965, 1967, 1969, and 1971, the Interest Equalization Tax was finally terminated in June 1974. While many have argued that it failed to solve the balance of payments deficit problem, it certainly did reduce the number of U.S. investors seeking to buy foreign securities. But in doing so, that and the other restrictive regulations forced the capital markets of Europe to reopen, in part by eliminating the direct competition from New York.

The Operations of the Eurobond Market

The Eurobond market's medium is the Eurodollar, usually in the form of a bank deposit and typically placed with a U.S. bank or foreign branch. Because Eurobonds can be bought and sold freely in the secondary market, they are quite liquid.

Types of Eurobonds. There are four main types of Eurobonds: (1) straight-debt, (2) convertible notes, (3) currency option, and (4) floating rate notes. Up to the end of 1977, nearly 85 percent of all Eurobonds were conventional *straight-debt*, with fixed rates of interest, as distinct from equities, which fluctuate with the borrower's profits. Interest is paid at regular intervals, usually annually, until the bonds are redeemed for their face value on the date of maturity.

Convertible bonds carry a fixed rate of interest, but investors have the option of converting them into the common stock of the borrowing company at a stipulated price during a stipulated period, with the stock issued in the investor's name. The conversion price is usually fixed at a premium above the market price of the common stock on the date of the bond issue. The investor is likely to convert only when the market price rises above the stipulated conversion price. The main advantage of the convertible bond is that it allows the borrower to buy fixed-interest capital at lower costs than are otherwise available, with the prospect of obtaining a wider spread of share ownership. The risk to the investor is limited by the fixed rate of interest, even though it is lower than that on a straight-debt bond. Ten percent of all Eurobonds prior to 1978 consisted of convertibles, of which one-half were sold in 1968–69 and 1972.

Some convertible Eurobonds are sold with "warrants," which are detachable parts of the bonds that investors can trade for common stock or sell to other investors. At the same time, the investor retains the balance of the fixed-interest security, as well as the option of converting it to common stock.

Currency option bonds allow investors the option of buying in one currency and making the payments of interest and principal in another. Most currency option bonds to date have been issued in sterling and one other currency, usually the dollar or deutschemark. In the past these bonds were referred to as sterling bonds.

As to *floating rate notes* (FRNs), here the lender adjusts the rate of return at regular intervals, usually every six months, to reflect changes in the short-term money market rates. This note is the only type of Eurobond without fixed interest. Prior to 1977, it accounted for only about 3 percent of all Eurobonds; it was most attractive to non-U.S. banks, as it allowed them to obtain dollars without having to cut into their credit lines with other banks, as happens when a bank obtains dollars in the interbank market or by issuing CDs for sale to other banks. Moreover, funds obtained from the interbank market and CDs do not count as capital, whereas government authorities in some countries are willing to consider the proceeds of FRNs as bank capital. Finally, inasmuch as banks usually lend FRNs, it is logical for them to obtain funds on the same basis.

Bond maturities tend to fluctuate according to a set pattern. They were quite long in the early years of the market—often up to fifteen years—when investor confidence in the future was high. During periods of uncertainty, such as in 1969 when the deutschemark was freed from its Bretton Woods parity, investors have, however, been hesitant to make long-term commitments, and the average maturity has fallen.

Participants. Eurobond investors are largely invisible: securities are in "bearer form," that is, no record is kept of their ownership. Most experts believe that about 60 percent of Eurobond investors today are individuals, a drop from the estimated 80 percent of the early 1970s. It is also believed that 50 to 60 percent of all Eurobonds ultimately end up in portfolios managed by Swiss banks on behalf of their clients.

The Secondary Market. The very important secondary market for Eurobonds assures investors of their liquidity. The secondary market is unofficial, or over-the-counter, and is free of government restrictions. As such, trading for the most part does not take place on the floor of a stock exchange. Instead, it is conducted by telephones and telexes around the world.

Even though trading does not involve a formal exchange, Eurobonds are still listed on the established stock exchanges. This practice gives Eurobonds several advantages in terms of marketability. The listing requires that certain information be available to investors, as a result of which the securities are better understood than might otherwise be the case. Moreover, the listing allows Eurobonds to escape the prohibition that some governments have placed on the purchase of unlisted securities by institutions such as pension funds and insurance companies.

Pros and Cons of the Eurobond Market

The Eurobond market offers borrowers several advantages. One is an alternative source of international capital that is easily sold because of the liquidity of and extensive secondary markets for Eurobonds. Moreover, numerous currencies are available, a situation that enables borrowers to match foreign exchange assets and liabilities in order to eliminate exchange rate risk. Borrowers can also improve their standing in any international market and obtain a wider diversification of international investment for their companies.

As for investors, the overriding advantage is that returns on Eurobonds and redemptions are exempt from withholding taxes, a provision that allows corporations to evade this tax. In a climate of inflation and depressed economic growth, securities that have fixed interest rates and are denominated in strong currencies offer very profitable investment opportunities. A last point is flexibility—investors can choose between fixed and floating rate securities.

However, there are also drawbacks. For borrowers, there can be a foreign exchange risk when a borrower obtains currencies for which it does not have or is unlikely to earn matching assets. Moreover, the relatively short maturities complicate longer-term planning. Access to the nondollar sectors of the market is limited. Finally, issuing a Eurobond is costly, while the distribution of new issues and trading in the secondary market are inefficient. The latter two conditions have kept some potential participants out of the market. In addition, some fraudulent business has been conducted on the secondary market.

Conclusions

Eurobonds have come a long way since they were first introduced in the early 1960s. They evolved out of the need for financing that preceded and followed World War II and were fueled by the Interest Equalization Tax of 1963 and other restrictive U.S. legislation. From that point on, the market has gathered its own momentum, until today it is a very significant component of the international financing scene.

Asian Dollar Market

The Asian Dollar Market (ADM), which got underway in October 1968, involves mostly trading in Eurodollars in Asia. It consists of a pool of offshore bank deposits comprising all offshore currencies in Asia. By the end of 1984, the ADM had grown to $128 billion, a huge leap from its paltry base of $20,000 in 1968. It is headquartered in Singapore and Hong Kong, but there are also centers in Tokyo, Manila, and other cities. In many ways the ADM is similar to the Eurodollar market; in fact, the main difference between the two is their location.

The Origin of the ADM

Several factors led to the creation of the ADM. By the 1960s, a number of Asian countries had experienced rapid economic growth. There was much new industry, while direct investment, particularly from the United States and Japan, had increased substantially. Multinational corporations were becoming more and more active in the Far East, leaving foreign currencies in private Asian hands. Many freely convertible currencies were held in substantial quantity by both residents and nonresidents of Asia. When the Sterling Area was abolished, international financiers found themselves in need of additional sources of finance. Concurrent with these trends, the United States was spending dollars freely in Asia as part of the Vietnam war effort.

Demand for these various funds grew in 1967–68, when the tightening of credit in the United States forced its corporations to look elsewhere for funds for their overseas activities. This demand forced interest rates in the Eurodollar market up. By comparison, the Asian supplies looked attractive to international banks.

The Operations of the Market

The ADM is a regional offshore market within the worldwide Eurodollar network. It is primarily a short-term money market, designed to help banks with their liquidity problems, as well as to mobilize surplus capital for development investment in Asia. The ADM permits small transactions, in contrast to the Eurodollar markets, in order to channel smaller bundles of resources into productive economic uses in Asia. Banks take in deposits as small as $5,000. The ADM also serves as a sort of intermediary between the major Asian countries and the Eurocurrency market and provides an arbitrage function among the markets of Asia, the Middle East, and Europe. It should be noted that the ADM (like the Eurodollar market) does not include checking accounts, i.e., demand deposits.

The ADM is characterized by very considerable interbank activity. In fact, its growth in 1984 was largely attributable to this category of transactions, which accounted for two-thirds of the gross size of the market. These interbank activities have been facilitated by the establishment of six international money brokers in Singapore and the development of the Singapore foreign exchange market. U.S. banks are the dominant institutions in the ADM.

The ADM offers a number of attractions. Foremost among them from the perspective of international bankers is the absence of reserve requirements and ceilings on interest rates.

Deposit and Loan Facilities. Banks offer a range of deposits, including sight, two- to seven-day notice (often limited to $100,000 or above), and fixed term with maturities of up to five years. The two- to seven-day notice deposits are designed for banks and large commercial firms that have excess funds for very short periods. The minimum maturity for smaller nonbank firms and individuals is generally seven days, with maturities commonly ranging from one to three months. As a rule, maturities are shorter than in the Eurocurrency market. The minimum amounts of deposits and interest intervals also vary from bank to bank and borrower to borrower.

The rate of interest on interbank loans is the Singapore Interbank Offer Rate (SIBOR). Corporate borrowers pay a premium over the SIBOR that is commensurate with the lender's assessment of risk.

Sources and Uses of Funds. Four groups supply funds to the ADM: commercial banks located outside Singapore, including the head offices and branches of foreign banks located there; central banks; nonbank companies; and individuals residing outside Singapore. The central banks in Asia hold sizable foreign reserves in U.S. dollars, and they constitute a major source of funds. They hold these reserves in the ADM in order to earn interest while still maintaining liquidity and safety. Among the nonbank companies, the major source is the large multinational and regional corporations in the Pacific area. They often invest substantial amounts of excess liquid currencies in the ADM for short periods in order to earn income. Many wealthy individuals put funds in the market for the same reason.

The major source of interbank ADM funds is the Eurocurrency market, especially the London market, the single largest net supplier. Other significant sources include New York, Zurich, and other offshore financial centers such as Hong Kong, Bahrain, Panama, and the Bahamas. The amount of funds from Asia itself has been increasing steadily, as is true of the Middle East.

The main borrowers on the ADM are large multinational firms, local power-generating companies, petroleum and petroleum-related corporations, and finance companies. Nonbank institutions have moved recently from being net depositors to net borrowers, and there was an 11 percent increase in lending to these customers in 1984. This shift reflects the opening up of business opportunities in the region. Nonbank financial institutions have been receiving direct loans, as have manufacturing industries. Some of these financial institutions have in turn acted as intermediaries in lending to local borrowers.

Conclusions

Although the ADM is still small in comparison with the Eurocurrency market, its growth and impact have been impressive. It has provided regional liquidity and has increased the flow of external capital into the area. The added funds have spurred economic growth, for example, in trade and foreign investment, as well as increased domestic savings. The dominant interbank activity of the ADM has been largely responsible for the funds going into nonbank loans used for economic growth. Perhaps one of the biggest benefits of the ADM, however, has been the inclusion of Asia in the international financial network, a trend that has in turn produced more sources of financing.

It is clear that the ADM is viable and here to stay. To maximize its growth, however, it will have to contend with some problems and weaknesses. Its capital market is still relatively undeveloped, as is the foreign exchange market. In addition, Singapore seems to be overflowing with banks now, and many experts believe it is overbanked. The growing worldwide trend toward protectionism and any slowdown in world economic growth will also affect the ADM adversely. However, as its customers are mainly in developing countries, a reasonably steady demand for funds can be expected. Nor has overborrowing been a problem to date, as in Latin America and Africa. The ADM also needs to develop longer-term sources of funds, a direction in which it has been moving, as well as to expand the bond market and to pull in a wider variety of currencies.

Commercial/Private Use of SDRs

The Special Drawing Right (SDR) is the unit of account for all transactions and operations of the International Monetary Fund (IMF). Since January 1981, the value of the SDR has been determined on the basis of a basket of currencies. At present, the basket is composed of the five most important currencies in world trade and international finance, with the following weights and values per SDR: the U.S. dollar, 42 percent, U.S. $0.54; the deutschemark, 19 percent, DM 0.46; the French franc, 13 percent, FF 0.74; the pound sterling, 13 percent, £0.071; and the yen, 13 percent, ¥34. The weighting basket is due to be modified in 1986. Some fifteen countries have pegged their currencies to the SDR, and it is also used by about fifteen international and regional institutions as the unit of account. Finally, the SDR is used in a number of international conventions to express monetary magnitudes, such as the limits of liability in the transport of goods and services across borders.

Emergence of Commercial/Private SDRs

Over the past ten years, there has been a move within the private international community to develop and gain acceptance for a "commercial," or "private," SDR, defined as SDR-denominated deposits in commercial banks. This move is the result of the search of international organizations, borrowers, and investors for a stable hedge against the volatility and uncertainty of interest and exchange rates.

Although the value of the commercial SDR is determined on the same basket of currencies as the official one, it is set by the marketplace, beyond the regulations of the IMF. This SDR is used to denominate many private financial transactions, such as deposits and syndicated loans. For the smaller or more conservative organization, the private SDR is a cheap and practical way to protect against the risk of exposure, particularly since they have neither the capacity nor the resources that larger corporations have to structure their own protective baskets of currencies. Use of the SDR cuts down on expensive monitoring, as well as on frequent, costly changes in currency positions. Returns are based on two items—exchange rate changes and interest income—and both are considerably more stable with SDRs. Nonetheless, the SDR loses its attractiveness when the dollar rises in value. Interest rates tend to move in the same direction across countries, hence interest income from SDRs will follow the same trends as with other currencies. Finally, the SDR is desirable because it affords inherent currency diversification across three major regions in the world.

The Slow Growth of Private SDRs

Given these advantages, it has been surprising to some that use of the private SDR has not grown more rapidly. For example, from 1973 to 1981, total bond issues in all units of account (European Currency Unit [ECU], European Monetary Unit [EMU], European Composite Unit [EURCO], European Unit of Account [EUA], and Special Drawing Rights [SDR]) came to just $2.6 billion. That figure represented a mere 1 percent of the total issues of international and foreign bonds. Of that, SDR bond issues specifically accounted for only 25 percent. At its peak in 1981, the SDR was used for only $386 million worth of issues, and no issues have been placed since. SDR deposits have similarly shrunk—by 50 percent since 1981. Despite some quotations of forward rates in specialized papers, the private SDR forward market is essentially dead.

There seem to be several reasons for the doldrums in the private SDR market. One is that investors, who are generally cautious, are not really familiar with this unit of account. Aside from engendering caution, that lack of familiarity necessitates certain "start-up" costs, for example, in terms of information gathering. Those costs would have to be included in the price of SDR transactions, with the inevitable effect on competitiveness. Other problems are that the spot and forward foreign exchange markets are too small and hence illiquid, transfers are more difficult, and there is a question of how to proceed should it prove impossible to determine the value of one of the five basket currencies or should the basket itself be changed. Other existing legal issues pose problems. For example, some countries prohibit banks from accepting SDR-denominated deposits. Another issue is whether the SDR really offers currency diversification. Some people have argued that it does so across the three most important currency zones; others argue that only a few firms have a foreign exchange exposure that matches the SDR basket. A particular concern is that the weight assigned the U.S. dollar in the basket is inappropriate for non-dollar-based investors. It is undoubtedly very difficult to balance SDR-denominated liabilities with equivalent SDR-denominated assets, a situation that forces an institution to hedge against foreign exchange risk in each currency in the basket. A final issue is that in general there has been no political backing for the SDR among official institutions, let alone private ones.

All of these problems would seem less significant if the rate of return on the SDR were excellent. Unfortunately, the return on investment is not at all attractive, especially when compared with that of dollars.

Are these concerns valid? While there is still no effective two-way inter-bank exchange market, many banks do quote both spot and forward exchange rates, precisely because the SDR currencies are few in number and widely traded. And as more contracts employ SDRs, the costs of writing them have gone down and become less constraining. On the other hand, it is extremely difficult to settle direct payments. There are no international clearing arrangements, and transactions have to be made in another currency or one of the five basket ones. Banks that handle SDRs for their customers are few in number and generally maintain accounts in that unit with one another so as to facilitate interbank transfers.

Based on the experience with the European Currency Unit, discussed in the next section, it would seem that one reason for the failure of the private SDR to take better hold is the absence of official institutional support for it. Another is that it does not encompass one homogeneous region with strong political and economic links.

It is also believed, as noted, that the SDR does not offer some organizations sufficient protection from exchange rate risk because of the weights assigned the currencies in the basket, particularly the relatively volatile U.S. dollar. This attitude is held mainly by European and non-dollar-based investors. The fluctuation in the weight of the dollar in the SDR from 42 percent in 1979–80 to over 50 percent in 1983 lends some credence to this argument. Other analysts counter by claiming that the weight of the dollar is probably temporary, as its excessive appreciation in the early 1980s is not likely to last. Moreover, the importance of the dollar in international trade and finance necessitates a heavy weight. In general, they maintain, the SDR is an attractive global hedge that is, however, inappropriate for certain classes of organizations with predominantly regional currency exposures.

Unquestionably, the small size of the private SDR market now leaves it vulnerable to changes in participation by heavily involved organizations, and it does not have extensive participation by or support from official institutions to shore it up, as has been true of the ECU.

Future Prospects

As to the future of the private SDR, it seems unclear. Some forecast its demise, especially considering that its main purpose is to provide an ordinary investor with a good hedge against foreign exchange risk, which it may not do. By the same token, it should receive a boost if the volatility and uncertainty of the exchange and interest rates persist and call for further hedging.

Certain changes in the private SDR system itself could strengthen it. One would be the establishment of a formal clearing mechanism so that balances could be settled easily. Another would be for the key international institutions such as the IMF to provide greater support and increase the private sector's familiarity with the SDR. Many economists believe the private SDR should be associated with the official one. One specific recommendation is for a clearing system that links the two SDRs and gives them the scale and liquidity that an international reserve asset requires. In addition, the IMF might take steps to provide full support for the private use of SDRs by borrowing SDRs itself from private sources, by encouraging other member countries to peg their currencies to the SDR, and by helping establish the clearinghouse and a system for settling payments in SDRs. The IMF could issue debt certificates denominated in SDRs in the private market and require that they be purchased with private SDRs, with the IMF paying interest by transferring some of its private SDRs. Moreover, the Fund could deposit SDRs with various banks as the liquid assets.

There is also a role for central banks. They could begin to use SDRs more widely in their own transactions, could denominate some of their foreign borrowing in SDRs, and could permit commercial banks in their jurisdictions to open SDR-denominated accounts with them.

Such measures could have a snowball effect. If more countries responded to these types of initiatives by pegging their currencies to SDRs, the greater foreign exchange risk in terms of payments in national currencies might increase the demand for SDRs. More SDR-syndicated loans and bond issues would produce a viable secondary market. As more private organizations were attracted to invest in SDRs, they would begin to issue debt in SDRs. Private bank use of SDRs in many areas would increase and interbank transactions with SDRs pick up. That shift would in turn provoke more transactions involving SDRs. The snowball would continue to grow.

Commercial/Private Use of ECUs

The European Currency Unit (ECU), created in 1979, functions as a unit of reference for the establishment of parities between European currencies and as a unit of account within the European Monetary System (EMS) in the operation of intervention and credit mechanisms, and more generally within European Economic Community (EEC) institutions. The ECU was in fact the first phase of the EMS. The ECU is backed by deposits of EEC member states to the European Funds of Monetary Cooperation (FECOM); these deposits are equal to 20 percent of members' dollar and gold reserves.

The value of the ECU is based on a basket of the currencies of member states. Their shares, in percentages, were as follows in 1984:

Deutschemark	37.38	Belgian franc	8.57
Pound sterling	14.05	Luxembourg franc	0.3
French franc	16.93	Danish krone	2.7
Italian lira	7.86	Irish punt	1.06
Dutch guilder	10.1	Greek drachma	0.4

Spain and Portugal were added in January 1986. Each country's share is fixed, having been calculated on the basis of a percentage established according to the economic importance of each member state.

At first the ECU market was centered in Belgium and Luxembourg, but it has since expanded to other European countries.

The Nature of the Private ECU Market

A private market in ECUs has been developing rapidly, based around ECU deposits made in certain banks by the European institutions, the European Investment Bank (EIB), the European Council, and Euratom. The EEC institutions have been entering into and paying for ECU-denominated contracts with private companies for several years now. Moreover, some countries have been extremely supportive. Italy, for example, allows Italians to hold ECU accounts and conducts over 20 percent of its exporting in ECUs. One result is that dollar usage has fallen from 90 percent to 50 percent. In addition, the ECU is officially quoted on the Rome and Milan exchanges, and assets and liabilities denominated in ECUs are recorded with the assets and liabilities in EEC currencies. This type of official support is a main reason for the rapid expansion of the ECU market. Nevertheless, the market as a whole is in the early stages of development, with most transactions still being carried out in dollars. At the same time, more and more companies are using ECUs.

In keeping with this growing interest, financial organizations and companies are using the ECU for an increasing variety of commercial and financial purposes, including borrowing, lending, paying, and charging. Over 350 European banks now provide a full range of ECU-denominated services. The Banque Internationale a Luxembourg, Lloyds Bank, and Banca Nazionale del Lavoro are all using negotiable ECU CDs, while the Bank of Luxembourg has introduced retail credit in ECUs and a Visa credit card billed in this unit. The newest service is to be ECU traveler's checks, in the belief that they will promote a unified currency structure in Europe. This market is expected to take off slowly but to have long-term potential because of its practical financial advantages.

The ECU also appeals to corporate treasurers. Besides serving as a shelter against exchange rate risks, it is a source of new funding and of diversification of debt. Moreover, since it is not subject to national currency regulations, treasurers gain exposure in currencies that otherwise might have been unavailable to them because of foreign exchange restrictions.

The largest part of the ECU business now involves bond issues. The average maturity of the ECU bond is eight years. Interest rates have held relatively stable, starting at 13 percent in 1981, rising to 14.25 percent at the end of that year, and then moving down to 12.5 percent in 1982.

The bond piece of the market has grown sensationally. The first bond issue of ECUs—35 million—was floated by the Kredit Bank on behalf of the SOFTE, an Italian communications company, in April 1981. Total bond issues in that year totalled $200 million. By the end of 1983, bond issues came to 2.8 billion ECUs ($2.5 billion) and made up between 4 percent and 5 percent of the volume of all Eurobond issues. By the end of 1984, Eurobonds denominated in ECUs accounted for more than 3 billion ECUs ($7.4 billion). In 1985 the ECU was the third most commonly used Eurobond denomination, after the U.S. dollar and the deutschemark, and ahead of the pound sterling and Swiss francs. Governments account for 42 percent of ECU bonds; international organizations, 30 percent; banks and corporations, 21 percent; and localities, 5.3 percent. In similar fashion, syndicated ECU bank loans went from 580 million ECUs at the end of 1983. Over 200 European banks accept deposits in this unit of account and are participating in the interbank market, which is estimated to be 10 billion ECUs ($12–15 billion a year).

An interbank market in ECUs emerged shortly after the ECU itself, in April 1981. Participants in the system can buy and sell ECUs directly. Organizations such as Euroclear and Cedel are also proposing to enter that business through their banking agents in terms of maintaining current accounts and overdraft facilities and providing transfer facilities. The interbank market is now estimated at around 20 billion ECUs a year.

The banks participating in the ECU interbank market have themselves become simplified clearinghouses in ECUs to facilitate their transfer, although this activity has focused informally around two banks: Lloyds, the largest force in the ECU money market, and Kredit Bank, the leader in overall use of the currency. Various banks have also opened mutual accounts in ECUs.

As a rule, the ECU system as a whole is not yet institutionalized, nor is the clearing capacity large enough. The leading banks are now seeking a central bank, or its like, to carry out the clearing operations and to act as lender of last resort. They want to be assured of an adequate supply of

ECUs to meet any liability in that unit. Several large banks, including Lloyds, Credit Lyonnais, and Morgan Guaranty, have asked the Bank for International Settlements (BIS) to take on those roles. However, the governors of the Bundesbank and the Netherlands Bank both sit on the BIS board, and both are unenthusiastic about the ECU. Thus it is unlikely the BIS will accept the task. Instead, it seems that Cedel, based in Luxembourg, will end up, as it is planning to do, handling the technical and operational aspects of a clearinghouse.

The rapid expansion of the ECU market clearly has not come about without controversy and problems. For example, while it is recognized that the market is now unsupervised, it is unclear who should control and supervise it. Nor is there an official clearinghouse or lender of last resort. While some European countries have been very supportive of the ECU, such as Italy, Belgium, and France, others have not. The West German Bundesbank not only does not recognize the ECU as a currency, it prohibits its use. One reason is the belief that the ECU prevents central banks like the Bundesbank from effectively implementing monetary policy. Since the ECU has the *de jure* or *de facto* status of a currency, it can be used by nonresidents in each member state for all banking operations. Residents, however, can make use of these facilities if the exchange control regulations in their countries permit identical operations in foreign currencies.

The Future of the ECU Market

Most experts agree that the use of ECUs will continue to grow. Some optimists say that they could eventually replace the dollar in financing European trade, particularly with respect to countries with weak currencies where the dollar is used most frequently. A real and major weakness of the ECU is the realignment of EMS parities that is carried out twice a year, an event that is always preceded by a period of uncertainty.

There is also speculation that just as an ECU market grew, so will U.S. dollar, yen, and other markets. The implications are twofold. One is the likely increase in competition between markets. Another is that the European governments will have to give up monetary control. The pound sterling will have to be included in the EMS, foreign exchange controls will have to be dismantled, and the ECUs will have to be made domestic assets, i.e., monitored and controlled by a European central bank.

The speculation raises another real problem with which adherents of the ECU will have to contend—the hostility of the Bundesbank and other central banks, born of a fear that the ECU will compete with domestic currencies and that its use will result in a loss of control over domestic monetary policy.

West Germany's attitude contrasts sharply with Italy's, as described earlier. Most countries lie somewhere between these two extremes. In France, for example, operations in ECUs are treated like foreign currency operations. Whether Europe will accept the ECU to the degree that it eventually replaces

Common Market currencies or the dollar in its business transactions remains to be seen. It is doubtful at this point, because of the vast differences in EEC economies.

INTERNATIONAL BANKING CENTERS

European Banking Centers

The key European banking centers are the United Kingdom, Luxembourg, and Switzerland.

United Kingdom

The United Kingdom has a 600-year-old tradition as an international banking center because of the time-honored position of London as a financial capital. Although the pound sterling is no longer the dominant currency it was up until World War I, and while many other cities have become active and important international centers of trade and finance, London has remained a foremost money center that is still growing and evolving.

The Advantages of the London Market. Why has London flourished as a center for so many decades, indeed centuries? For one, its political and regulatory environment has been stable and friendly to banking. Even though the British government has become more restrictive in the last couple of years, particularly in terms of taxes on bank business, the consensus is that London is still a good place to operate, with ample opportunities for taking advantage of new and old financial activities.

London's long history as a merchant, industrial, business, and financial center has meant the evolution of large, internationally oriented financial institutions of all types that engage in all aspects of international banking and finance. The city's strong domestic banking network provides clearing banks, accepting houses, issuing houses, discount houses, finance houses, and the like. Through its clearing banks, London has come to dominate sterling retail deposit banking, cash distribution, and money transmission in England, and by extension plays a major role elsewhere. These banks also handle international and wholesale banking. The accepting houses engage in the financing of international trade through acceptance of bills of exchange and also in wholesale banking, corporate lending, investment management, issuance of Eurobonds and securities, and many other services. As to the discount houses, their forte is making the markets in short-term financing, for example, through CDs, activities that produce liquid assets for the rest of the banking system. Leasing transactions and installment credit are typically handled by the financial houses, some of which are associated with other banks.

Most of the business in London is handled by the "big four" U.K. banks, Barclays, National Westminster, Lloyds, and Midland. All of them have excellent international reputations, as is true of England's banking network in general. As happened in other countries, particularly the United States, many found themselves saddled with risky overexposures in Latin America and Africa and have had to make provisions to cope with borrowers' debt-servicing problems. But even in a year—1984—when they were hit with major new taxes and the debt-servicing problems, the big clearinghouses were still able to raise their earnings by 20 percent on average, according to the *Financial Times* (May 13, 1985). While the London banking community was shaken by the unseemly demise of Johnson Matthey Bankers (JMB), a small banking subsidiary of Johnson Matthey, that event had little overall effect on the system's reputation or activities.

One reason for the staying power of London banks is their dynamism. They have always been at the leading edge of the banking business, willing, despite a generally conservative nature, to get into new activities. Thus London took the initiative in the Eurobond market and in syndicated lending. As the sterling declined in importance, rather than sitting back, the banks saw the potential of the emerging Eurocurrency market and moved quickly to establish themselves as its hub. Access to Eurocurrencies and the growth and importance of syndicated lending were primary reasons so many foreign banks, particularly U.S. ones, flocked to London. Many U.K. banks are now entering the securities market in a big way. And they are embarking on some major technological improvements that augur well for the future.

London's importance can be traced to still other reasons. As a result of its long history in international banking, London offers comprehensive expertise, much of it highly specialized, in all types of financial transactions. In addition, it offers markets and services of every type that complement its money and banking transactions directly and indirectly—interbank deposit networks, primary and secondary markets in certificates of deposit, diversity of currencies, insurance, shipping, legal and accounting services, and a global communications network. That latter asset is a logical outgrowth of England's traditional external orientation and extensive trade, which have over the years resulted in the development of strong links with every corner of the world. London is also helped by its central geographic location and favorable time zone, which in the course of the average business day permits contact with all regions of the world during their business day.

The Involvement of Foreign Banks. Much of London's growth as a financial center in the past three decades can also be traced to the explosion in the representation of foreign banks there. Whereas in 1970 London hosted some 161 foreign banks, fifteen years later the number was 400, of which 340 were branches or subsidiaries. U.S. and, to a lesser extent, Japanese banks handle the bulk of the business by foreign banks. Initially, foreign banks set up shop in London to serve their domestic customers in their international business. In addition, in the 1960s and 1970s, U.S. banks were motivated by a need for a supply of funds as a result of the tighter monetary policy imposed at home and by the desire to escape certain regulations that constrained international business conducted out of the United States.

It did not take long for the foreign banks in London to seize the many additional opportunities for profit-taking, and foreign banks became active in every area of international financing. Recently they have begun to expand into the one activity from which they had stayed away: most had chosen not to venture into the U.K. domestic retail banking market, in competition with the London clearing banks, largely because the latter were so dominant in the local market. That, too, has begun to change.

It is important to note some of the other conditions that have attracted foreign banks to London. England imposes no restrictions on foreign ownership of any company, and foreign banks can now buy local brokers. Beginning in 1986, there will be no fixed brokerage commissions. Further, there are no foreign exchange controls.

The Bank of England. The heart of the English banking system is, of course, the Bank of England, the central bank, which is under the Exchequer. The Bank of England is the government's banker, lender of last resort, supervisor of the banking sector, doyen of the national money supply, and manager of the national debt and foreign exchange, among other functions. It is also a primary economic advisor to the government on financial, monetary, and economic policy. More directly relevant to the international banking community, the Bank of England provides various services, such as the settlement of interbank balances for London clearing banks and, as part of its role as lender of last resort, a discount window.

The Future. Clearly time has not diminished London's importance in international finance and banking, nor is it likely to do so. In large measure that happy prospect can be traced to the strength of the network that has emerged over the last 600 years. It can also be attributed to the willingness of English banks to be forward-looking and active. It is likely that, given the collapse of JMB and the overexposure of many banks in risky loans, the Bank of England will keep a tighter supervisory rein in the future. Moreover, the government is unlikely to back away from the increased taxes it has imposed in its efforts to raise revenue, particularly since the banks seem to have coped well. In the long run, however, neither of these points should affect business.

Luxembourg

Another of Europe's key banking centers, Luxembourg, is noteworthy in part for being the headquarters of the Central de Livraison de Valeurs Mobilieres, or Cedel, the clearing system that provides a computerized administrative service for settling Eurobond trading. This organization was a logical outgrowth of Luxembourg's extensive involvement with the Eurocurrency market, particularly the Eurobond market. Cedel is also a safe repository for securities, which are held in fungible or nonfungible accounts.

Moreover, it serves as a clearinghouse for new issues, administers bearer depository receipts and organizes collateral credit lines from banks to its members. Most recently, it has undertaken to provide clearing services for dealings in gold on the Luxembourg Stock Exchange. Cedel's role in the Eurobond market is likely to grow further, given the difficulty European banks are having in getting official support for an ECU clearinghouse. Cedel has indicated a willingness to provide that service.

Luxembourg offers, in addition, a full range of traditional and banking services. As noted, the Euromarket has been a focal point, and Luxembourg banks have been dealing extensively in medium- and long-term international Eurocurrency lending, including syndications, and in short-term interbank currency operations. Luxembourg banks held an estimated 12 percent of the total volume of Eurocurrencies at the end of 1980.

Luxembourg banks may now have to look for new borrowers. Traditionally, they have lent to major companies and institutions in the industrialized world, particularly in Scandinavia and the Federal Republic of Germany. Those customers are now far more liquid and able to raise funds on their own in the securities markets.

The heyday of growth of Luxembourg as a center came mainly in the 1970s. At this time, the number of banks grew commensurately, and they now number around 117. West Germany has the strongest foreign presence, followed by Scandinavia. It has been suggested that further expansion is unlikely, given that Luxembourg now requires a reserve equal to 3 percent of a bank's liabilities. Government spokesmen note, however, that most banks have adapted well to that regulation and that that gearing is still below the level in many other countries. Perhaps of more concern is the new single-debtor rule that limits a bank's exposure to a single borrower. Even here, exceptions can be made for international banks, and the limits are not necessarily that onerous—50 percent of a bank's own funds for the first five years, 30 percent thereafter.

Finally, it should be noted that Luxembourg has an active international stock exchange that has become a trading center for equities and bonds, the latter denominated in a wide range of currencies and units of account, as well as SDRs.

Switzerland

Following London and New York, Switzerland is the third most important international money center, and it is now experiencing strong growth. According to the *Financial Times*, 1984 was its best year ever, with the balance sheet totals of banks up 10 percent.

There are many reasons for Switzerland's success. The country has a history of political stability and neutrality, as well as a strong economy, and a tradition of three key languages—French, German, and Italian. Because of its external orientation and neutrality, it has developed strong ties with most regions of the world. An important catalyst in its growth as an international financial center is that Switzerland has been a nation of savers and for a long time has been a net exporter of capital. Its central location in Europe is also advantageous. That location, along with Switzerland's multilingualism and neutrality, has induced many international organizations, such as the Bank for International Settlements and offices of the United Nations, to set up shop there. Finally, Switzerland has been involved in international banking for centuries and has developed the facilities and expertise that make it a logical center today. Its position was also boosted at the end of both world wars, from which it emerged relatively unscathed.

Perhaps most important to Switzerland's success is the favorable banking environment it offers both banks and their customers. There is strong respect for private property and noninterference in private affairs. The confiscation of private property is difficult and must be fully compensated. There are no antitrust laws, and banks can invest in companies. Nor are there any foreign exchange controls. On the other hand, Switzerland imposes very high reserve requirements, and bank interest rates are low.

Most important to many people is Switzerland's extremely strict confidentiality requirements. It is certainly well-known for its fabled numbered bank accounts. Customer's banking transactions must be kept secret except in certain very specific circumstances, and the penalties for breaches of confidentiality are severe. The exceptions to this rule involve disclosures to heirs and estate executors and administrators, and cases involving the public interest, such as bankruptcy, criminal investigations, and debt collection. With respect to criminal matters, bankers are obligated to cooperate and disclose information only if the incident in question is considered a crime under Swiss law. As tax evasion is not a criminal activity, banks do not have to make disclosures in such cases.

International banking in Switzerland is now concentrated in four cities—Zurich, by far the dominant center; Basel, which touches on three national boundaries; Geneva, the oldest banking center; and Lugano, where the Italian influence is strong.

Swiss banks are very powerful because of their importance to the economy and their reputation for conservative, stable operations. For example, they have no exposure in Latin America. Instead, most of their loans have gone to industrialized countries and to organizations such as the World Bank. Interestingly, however, they are now taking over U.S. loans to South Africa.

Most relevant in terms of international activities are the Swiss Bank Corporation, Union Bank of Switzerland, and Credit Suisse, the "big three," all of which are headquartered in Zurich. These banks offer a full range of services and have extensive representation abroad. Based on their sources of income, in the last year their portfolio management and other fee business has been expanding rapidly—and lucratively. This trend is in keeping with the policy of Swiss banks to increase this area of business in relation to borrowing and lending. Another main source of revenue was interest income, attributable to a higher volume of lending and profitable positions in bills of exchange and money market paper. Loan figures are also up in part because Switzerland now includes Liechtenstein in its domestic totals. Another big area of activity is the Swiss franc capital market, as Swiss banks are underwriters, stockbrokers, and major institutional investors, aside from being big borrowers.

Because of its location, reputation, and favorable business climate, Switzerland has attracted many foreign banks, of which upwards of 100 are represented in the major cities. They are mostly American and European, although Japan has been expanding its presence.

Another important category of bank in terms of international banking is the private bank, of which there are about 30. They play an important role in the international stock exchange and securities business and are chiefly portfolio managers.

Other banks are mainly local ones, involved with domestic business.

The Swiss National Bank is the central bank and has responsibility for regulating and overseeing the banking industry.

Asian Banking Centers

Three centers are prominent in banking in Asia: Hong Kong, Singapore, and Japan.

Hong Kong

Hong Kong, which has been a British colony since 1842, has been one of the fastest growing international financial centers in the last fifteen years or so. It is primarily a regional center that services Southeast Asia.

Hong Kong's position has not come about by accident. Established as a free port by the British, Hong Kong rapidly became a very active entrepôt in the Far East. Today, foreign trade accounts for 70 percent of its GNP. Much of the business involves warehousing and reexports, but the Hong Kong stamp can now be found on many consumer goods. Forty percent of China's trade goes through Hong Kong. This commerce has produced both a steady flow of foreign exchange in many different currencies and many opportunities for trade-related financing.

Recognizing these opportunities, and with limited possibilities for economic growth, the government of Hong Kong established as a foremost policy the development of international banking as a primary base for the economy. To implement that policy, the government has established a very favorable banking environment, with few regulations and restrictions. For example, there are no foreign exchange controls, and no distinction is made between foreign and resident investors. The cost of business is low, as is the tax rate. Banks are not subject to monetary controls except for a minimal liquidity ratio. What regulations and laws there are tend to be straightforward and less burdensome than in many places.

For these reasons, many people consider Hong Kong to be the freest investment market in the world. As a result, nearly all the large international banks have set up branches or subsidiaries there, which coexist alongside a strong network of domestic institutions. There are 115 banks in all, of which 44 are local and 71 foreign. The leading local banks are the Hongkong and Shanghai Banking Corporation and the Hang Seng Bank, both large international financial institutions in their own right. In fact, Hongkong and Shanghai Banking has a 51 percent interest in Marine Midland Bank of New York and acts as a quasi-central bank.

As might be expected, these various banking institutions offer a full range of services, such as deposit-taking, trade financing, loan syndications, and foreign exchange trading. There is an active interbank market for the Hong Kong dollar and foreign currencies, and Hong Kong is a secondary market for Eurobond trading. Hong Kong also offers a range of other financial services, such as gold trading, insurance, investment management, and commodities trading. Call and time deposits are the major business in the money market. Hong Kong has almost no public debt; as such, the government issues no securities, and there is no market in this area. However, the Hong Kong Stock Exchange is very active and volatile, with tremendous potential for profit. On the down side, Hong Kong offers a more limited range of investment instruments than is available in other centers.

Hong Kong has no central bank; instead, the functions that would normally be handled by that institution are carried out by the Monetary Affairs Branch of the government secretariat, operating through the government's Exchange Fund or a commercial bank.

Singapore

Like Hong Kong, Singapore, which started out its history as a small fishing village, became, after its capture by the East India Company in 1819, a major commercial entrepot in Southeast Asia. In 1965 Singapore gained its independence of Britain.

It is not surprising that a fairly extensive regional banking network grew up around Singapore's commercial activities. Its move into larger-scale international banking, however, occurred later than in Hong Kong, despite the presence of many large international banks, particularly U.S. ones. Much of its growth can be attributed to a conscious policy of the government to develop the banking sector, particularly its international sphere. Singapore has created and maintained the kind of stable and orderly environment and high standards demanded by the international banking community. It has also created a regulatory and tax environment favorable to banking. There are no foreign exchange controls or limits on interest rates, and the withholding taxes and stamp duties have been reduced to encourage foreign investment and the issuance of securities. Moreover, the bank licensing laws are quite liberal. Singapore is also helped by its central location in the Far East and a time zone that enables it to participate in the business days of the Middle Eastern, European, and U.S. markets, as well, obviously, as Japan's.

Not unexpectedly, the banking environment has led to tremendous expansion of both domestic and foreign banks in Singapore. Merchant banks (numbering 39) cannot accept deposits but can deal in foreign exchange and gold. The dominant banks here are West German. There are also finance companies, which make industrial loans. There are 16 of them, all subsidiaries of local and foreign banks. There is also a development bank, the Development Bank of Singapore, which is 49 percent government-owned. It offers ten-year, fixed rate loans.

Singapore offers three types of bank licenses. Full licenses allow all types of banking. Restricted licenses permit a bank to have only one branch, and it can only take deposits of U.S. $115,000 or more. Offshore licenses limit deposits to $250,000 or more and prohibit savings deposits and the raising of Singapore dollar funds.

Singapore now has 100 commercial banks and 50 offshore ones. Of the 100, 87 are foreign and have full licenses. It should be noted that all financial institutions wanting to do business in Singapore must be licensed by the government, which has been selective in its approvals. Normally it accepts only large and reputable firms with extensive and comprehensive international operations and connections and something to offer the Singapore market. It has also sought to attract a representative spread of institutions from different geographic regions.

The various deposit-taking institutions include commercial banks, Asian Currency Units, finance companies, and discount houses. They can transact business in almost any currency and some units of account. One attraction of the Singapore environment is that since 1975, banks can set their own interest rates. Given the competitiveness of the Singapore market and its links to the broader international financial community, however, the rates have tended to follow international trends.

Singapore is now a key player in the Southeast Asian financial world and in the Far East as a whole. A dominant characteristic of Singapore as a financial center is its role as a major Asian dollar market within the broader international money markets. Short-term lending and borrowing, using all convertible currencies, are major areas of activity. Singapore is also an international capital market for the issuance of medium- and long-term bonds, again in any convertible currency. These capital markets promise continued growth for Singapore's international financial transactions, given that the Asian dollar market is expanding so rapidly, even outpacing the Eurodollar market.

The key public banking institution in Singapore is the Monetary Authority of Singapore (MAS), which acts as the central bank. It is the government's banker and also serves as banker for private financial institutions. It supervises and regulates the industry, ensuring compliance with banking law. It also promotes the growth of monetary and exchange conditions that will in turn promote the growth of the economy as a whole, within the context of overall economic policy. It performs all the functions of a central bank except that of issuing currency. Banks are subject to regular inspection and oversight by the MAS, which can set operating requirements such as minimum capital balances. Finally, as banker to financial institutions, the MAS provides them with various key facilities, such as discount window and clearing services. Much of the success in Singapore's development as a financial center is the result of the MAS's efforts.

Japan

It is hardly surprising that Japan is a major international financial center, given its very extensive export business and strong economy. However, the volume of its operations is perhaps surprising, given that it is a relative newcomer to the financial world: there was no banking system at all until the Meiji restoration in 1868, and that system underwent drastic changes in 1945 during the MacArthur era. Today, however, Japan is the largest creditor country. A large part of the reason lies with its very high rate of savings—it has the highest savings in the world when measured as a percentage of disposable income.

A particularly noteworthy feature of the Japanese financial scene is the very active short-term money market, attributable to the very substantial demand for this type of financing on the part of the government and corporate sectors. Banks also generate substantial demand as intermediaries in many transactions. One explanation for that demand is the existence of huge corporate conglomerates, called *zaibatsus*, which use very large amounts of borrowing because of their size. Business in the short-term money market centers largely around call and time deposits, treasury bills and commercial paper.

Next in importance is the bond market, the second largest in the world after the United States. Most bonds, however, are issued by the Japanese government and public institutions. Corporations prefer to raise their money through equity issues and bank borrowing. While the bond market is highly regulated, the equity shares market is freer and experiences a rapid rate of turnover.

Two factors are beginning to cause a shift in the nature of business. The government-imposed ceiling on interest rates has lessened the volume of savings going into demand and cash deposits at the same time that slower growth has led to less corporate borrowing. Thus Japanese banks are having to find new ways to generate income. The major banks are now investing heavily in bigger and faster computerized cash transmission and information networks so as to participate in the international capital markets. That move has also meant that they have had to acquire new areas of expertise. The banks are also offering novel opportunities to local investors, such as money market certificates geared to higher yield assets.

There are about 78 domestic and 55 foreign banks operating in Japan. Of the domestic banks, 10 are classified as very large, of which 5 are within the top 10 worldwide. Japan has 13 "city" banks, which are comparable to England's 4 clearing banks, and a very large number of other smaller financial institutions. Beyond the major cities is a network of regional banks, numbering 64, that provide the same types of services but on a regional scale. Beyond these are mutual saving banks, credit unions, and credit co-operatives, which together constitute a network of around 1,000 institutions. Members of this latter group, which are permitted to offer slightly higher interest rates to allow them to compete with the city banks, do local business. Another major specialized institution that cannot go without mention is the Postal Savings System: with U.S. $350 billion in deposits, it is the world's largest deposit-taker. Two reasons for its popularity are that it offers slightly higher interest rates than banks do and it is structured in such a way that tax evasion is easier.

An indication of their strength is that Japanese banks are handling the financing for the second largest economy in the noncommunist world essentially alone, given the restrictions on foreign competition in the local banking scene, and they still have ample funds to lend overseas. Moreover, the overseas offices of Japanese banks are the busiest single national group in the London Eurobond market, according to *Financial Times* (May 13, 1985), handling some 25 percent of the international lending there.

As to foreign banks in Japan, of which there are 55, they are severely restricted in their operations. They cannot open savings banks; they cannot make foreign exchange loans and are restricted in terms of the conversion of foreign currencies into yen; they have to move all foreign exchange transactions through the Ministry of Finance and the Ministry of Trade and Industry; and they are very closely supervised by the Bank of Japan. Presently they are not permitted to open trust banks, although eight will be allowed to do so in 1986. In essence, then, foreign banks must operate through local banks.

As to the financial climate in Japan, while for the most part it is favorable, it is subject to regulation and constraints in some key areas. For example, the Bank of Japan administers the discount rate, or bank rate, as an instrument of monetary policy. In turn, by agreement with the banks, interest rates move with it. Thus, interest rates are effectively being managed. There are also restrictions on retail deposit interest rates that may pose problems. Because traditional savers are looking for higher rates, they are not making nearly as many deposits in cash and demand accounts. Another problem is that the government has shown a sometimes ambivalent attitude toward foreign investment in Japan, on occasion restricting nonresident portfolio investment. Another restriction faced by city banks is that they cannot provide long-term lending, as that is the province of long-term credit banks that are able to raise that type of financing through issues of debentures. Similarly, trust funds must be handled by trust banks. It is expected that at least this restriction will be eliminated in the next few years.

Despite these restrictions, Japan has in fact liberalized its banking sector considerably, and it is likely that there will be a major transformation in the next few years. An offshore banking market is likely to emerge, with a specialization in Euroyen transactions. One interesting change is that bank shares can now be traded on the stock exchange. Business has been very heavy, with some stock going up 100 percent seemingly overnight. What restrictions are retained are likely to relate to the small and specialized institutions, which up to now have been heavily protected from competition. Should the government decide to lift that protection, it is likely there will be a wave of takeovers of these smaller institutions. There is also some talk of deregulating interest rates.

Caribbean Banking Centers

Two centers are of note here—the Bahamas and the Cayman Islands.

The Bahamas

Following tourism, international banking is now the second largest industry in the Bahamas, which is now the largest banking center in the Caribbean. A number of factors have led to its emergence as a financial center. To some degree, it could be said that the Bahamas was in the right place at the right time. When the United States instituted restrictive measures with respect to overseas banking from bank facilities in America in the 1960s, the proximity of the Bahamas made it a logical offshore base for branches or subsidiaries of U.S. banks. Moreover, it is in the same time zone as New York. Nor are the islands far from London; there are now direct flights.

It is also true, however, that the Bahamian government has been opportunistic, setting up a climate that is very favorable to offshore banking. For one, the islands are a tax haven; that is, there are essentially no taxes, and the cost of opening and maintaining a bank in terms of government charges is negligible. There are no reserve requirements or exchange controls, and deposits can be made in any freely convertible currency. The legal system, based on British common law, is a familiar one, the few regulations are not burdensome, and day-to-day supervision is minimal. There are, for example, no stringent reporting requirements. Immigration laws make it fairly easy to hire foreign specialists in international banking, and there is a good-sized pool of Bahamian middle- and upper-level managers.

Another attraction of the Bahamas is secrecy. As in Switzerland, accounts are numbered. Bahamian banks by law cannot make any disclosures at all unless ordered to do so by the Supreme Court, and that does not happen easily. Usually the reason must be a strong likelihood that the money was obtained illegally. In addition, no custody fees are charged, which is not true of Swiss accounts. Finally, it is easier to make withdrawals than in Switzerland, as personal representatives can handle that transaction if the holder of the numbered account cannot appear.

The banking network in the Bahamas consists of over 400 local and what are called nonresident foreign banks, as well as trust companies, clearing houses, and the like. Nonresident banks may be either branches or subsidiaries, the latter acquired from among Bahamian banks. In some instances, the foreign bank does not bother to set up an active office but simply has an address there or operates out of the facilities of another institution. Active offices are, however, increasingly common.

The various financial institutions can and do engage in all the routine banking activities. The considerable variety in the types of business conducted stems from the different commercial reasons for establishing operations in the Bahamas. A big one has been to enter the Eurocurrency market. Nassau, the capital of the Bahamas, is predominantly a Eurocurrency center, and it has attracted $126 billion in Eurocurrency deposits. At the moment, the Bahamas is the third largest Eurocurrency center, second only to London and New York and comparable to Paris and Tokyo. This role was largely an outgrowth of the restrictive policy of the United States in the 1960s that forced banks to set up offshore operations. It should be noted that although this market in the Bahamas represents substantial assets, most of the actual operations take place outside the islands at the headquarters of the banks.

Settlements with residents of foreign countries may be made in any foreign currency or in Bahamian dollars, which are at par value with the U.S. dollar. Settlements may take place through external accounts, which are funded entirely in foreign currencies if they originate outside the Bahamas. Income on registered investments may be credited to these accounts, and the balances may be freely converted into foreign currency and transferred abroad. Government interference in these transactions is kept to a minimum. Nonresidents are allowed to operate foreign currency bank accounts outside the Bahamas. Bahamian assets may be repatriated on or prior to leaving the islands. Banks designated as nonresident may deal freely in all currencies except Bahamian dollars, so that exchange controls are not an issue.

Regulation of banking in the Bahamas is the responsibility of the Central Bank. It looks very carefully at who it licenses, with the main criteria being financial stability and an established reputation.

It is important to note that despite the success to date of the Bahamas as a center, there are clouds on the horizon. For one, the United States has been increasingly anxious about the secrecy provisions, as it believes the

Bahamas and other Caribbean locations are being used as depots for drug money and other illegally obtained funds. Scandals have racked the previous image of the Bahamas as a clean place to do business and have led to calls, mostly from the United States, for greater regulation of the banking industry. While the Bahamas is independent, it may prove hard to resist the pressures of the American government. Much of the banking business is possible because the United States has chosen not to close the loopholes that permit U.S. banks to take advantage of the breaks offered by the Bahamas. At the same time, the United States has remedied some of the domestic regulatory and tax issues that led its banks to seek offshore havens. There is also increasing competition within the region for banking business, and the costs of business in the Bahamas are increasing. An indication of where the Bahamas may be headed as an international banking center is the trend in the volume of the banking assets booked through its domiciled institutions— from $43 billion in 1981 to $30 billion in 1985, according to the *Financial Times* (May 7, 1985).

Cayman Islands

The Cayman Islands are a self-governing dependency of Great Britain. In terms of the number of banks—430—the Cayman Islands are the fourth largest financial center in the world. Like the Bahamas, the islands are blessed, as a banking center, with a location close to the United States and in the same time zone as New York. Being a British dependency, they also have close ties with Great Britain and have adopted many of its systems, including the common law.

The rapidity of the Caymans' growth as a center is clear when it is realized that there were no banks there at all until 1953 and that the boom did not really start until 1966. At that time, the Banking and Trust Law was passed, establishing favorable conditions for offshore banking. It contained a very strong confidentiality provision and numerous breaks for banks doing only international business, such as no taxes; free transfers of equity and debt capital, interest, dividends, profits, and fees; and no reserve requirements on foreign currency deposits. These conditions allow U.S. banks to offer higher rates on deposits or lower rates on loans than if the business were carried out at home. Moreover, they allow U.S. banks to offer interest on overnight deposits, a practice that is prohibited in the United States. Because of the different way the Internal Revenue Service treats domestic and foreign income, the Cayman Islands (and other similar centers) allow banks and their customers to avoid significant amounts of taxes by carefully monitoring the proportion of business they do there. The Cayman Islands also have no exchange controls. Finally, the government is constantly upgrading its communications network.

The government, as elsewhere, carefully examines applicants for banking or trust company licenses. Banks may operate through branches or subsidiaries, which are incorporated locally. Although there are 430 banks registered in the Cayman Islands, interestingly only about 50 have an actual physical presence. Supervision is handled by the Inspector of Banks and Trust Companies.

Most banks in the Cayman Islands are branches of U.S. and other major international banks. With respect to the U.S. presence, mostly it consists of shell branches. While there is a fair amount of local retail banking because of tourism, most banks engage in international activities, particularly Eurodollar transactions, although other currencies are also involved. Banks and trust companies may engage in any type of business, although generally they are required to set up separate subsidiaries to handle nonbanking business.

As with the Bahamas, the future of the Cayman Islands as a financial center is unclear. They confront the same problems as the Bahamas does in terms of competition from the United States and elsewhere, and the same pressures in terms of the secrecy provisions and the U.S. war on illegal gains sheltered offshore. In fact, in July 1984 the Cayman Islands, Great Britain, and the United States signed a novel treaty that allowed the latter limited access to information from financial institutions if there was proof of drug-related activities by customers. On the other hand, the Cayman Islands, unlike the Bahamas, have not had a falloff in business.

APPENDIX: LARGEST BANKS IN EACH LOCATION WITH THEIR TOTAL ASSETS

Bank	Assets Less Contra Accounts ($ million)
Australia	
Westpac Banking Corp.	28,140
Commonwealth Banking Corp.	20,763
Australia & New Zealand Banking Group	18,377
National Australia Bank	17,835
Belgium	
Société Générale de Banque	31,652
BBL Banque Bruxelles Lambert	20,508
Kredietbank	19,597
Crédit Communal de Belgique	17,642
Canada	
Royal Bank of Canada	65,654
Canadian Imperial Bank of Commerce	52,811
Bank of Montreal	48,885
Bank of Nova Scotia	42,841
Toronto-Dominion Bank	32,650
National Bank of Canada	13,886

Bank	Assets Less Contra Accounts ($ million)
France	
Banque Nationale de Paris	101,019
Crèdit Agricole	90,211
Crèdit Lyonnais	88,123
Sociètè Gènèrale	86,346
Banque Paribas	60,524
Italy	
Banca Nazionale del Lavoro	42,506
Banca Commerciale Italiana	39,245
Banco di Roma	34,769
Cariplo	31,701
Istituto Bancario San Paolo di Torino	31,174
Credito Italiano	29,177
Monte dei Paschi di Siena	27,471
Banco di Napoli	21,645
Banco di Sicilia	14,591
Banca Nazionale dell'Agricoltura	13,506

APPENDIX *Continued*

Bank	Assets Less Contra Accounts ($ million)
Japan	
Dai-Ichi Kangyo Bank	110,333
Fuji Bank	103,524
Sumitomo Bank	101,147
Mitsubishi Bank	98,062
Sanwa Bank	91,257
Norinchukin Bank	75,235
Industrial Bank of Japan	71,270
Mitsui Bank	67,162
Bank of Tokyo	65,021
Tokai Bank	63,172
Long-Term Credit Bank of Japan	60,327
Mitsubishi Trust and Banking	57,354
Taiyo Kobe Bank	53,186
Sumitomo Trust & Banking	52,299
Mitsui Trust & Banking	52,209
Daiwa Bank	47,137
Luxembourg	
Bank of Credit & Commerce International	12,309
Banque Internationale a Luxembourg	3,892

Bank	Assets Less Contra Accounts ($ million)
Mexico	
Banco Nacional de Mexico	10,510
Bancomer	9,855
Singapore	
Development Bank of Singapore	5,691
United Overseas Bank	4,888
Spain	
Banco Espanol de Credito	20,034
Banco Central	19,171
Banco de Vizcaya	15,078
Banco de Bilbao	14,206
Sweden	
Skandinaviska Enskilda Banken	20,351
Svenska Handelsbanken	17,677
Post-och Kreditbanken (PK Banken)	13,422
SwedBank (Sparbankernas Bank)	12,342

APPENDIX *Continued*

Bank	Assets Less Contra Accounts ($ million)
Switzerland	
Union Bank of Switzerland	52,830
Swiss Bank Corp.	48,248
Credit Suisse	35,452
United Kingdom	
Barclays Group	94,146
National Westminster Bank	87,057
Midland Bank	76,317
Lloyds Bank	55,747
Standard Chartered Bank	41,945
United States	
Citicorp	125,974
Bank America Corp.	115,442
Chase Manhattan Corp.	75,350
Manufacturers Hanover Corp.	60,918
J.P. Morgan	56,186
Chemical New York Corp.	47,789
First Interstate Bancorp	42,664

APPENDIX *Continued*

Bank	Assets Less Contra Accounts ($ million)
Continental Illinois Corp.	41,238
Security Pacific Corp.	38,613
Bankers Trust	36,952
First Chicago Corp.	34,870
Wells Fargo	26,522
Mellon National Corp.	24,199
InterFirst Corp.	21,543
First Bank System	20,420

REFERENCES

Aliber, Robert Z., *The International Money Game*, 3rd (expanded) ed., New York: Basic Books, 1979.

Angelini, Anthony, Maximo Eng, and Francis A. Lees, *International Lending, Risk and the Euromarkets*, New York: John Wiley & Sons, 1979, Chapter 6.

"Bahamas: Bank Secrecy," *The Banker*, January 1983, pp. 13–14.

"Bahamas: Move to Diversify Economy May Open New Opportunities," *Business America*, March 7, 1983, pp. 24–25.

Bank for International Settlements, *Fifty-Third Annual Report, 1st April 1982–31st March 1983*, Basle: BIS, June 1983.

The Banker, "Boom with a Guilt Complex ...," London: Financial Times Business Publishing, March 1983.

Banking in the Bahamas, New York: Peat, Marwick, Mitchell and Co., 1982.

Baughn, William H., and Donald R. Mandich, *The International Banking Handbook*, Homewood, Ill.: Dow Jones–Irwin, 1983.

Cook, Mary, *Offshore Financial Centres*, 4th ed., New York: Financial Times Business Publishing, 1981.

Dufey, Gunter, and Ian Giddy, *The International Money Market*, Englewood Cliffs, N.J.: Prentice-Hall, 1978, Chapters 1 and 3.

Faith, Nicholas, *Safety in Numbers: The Mysterious World of Swiss Banking*, New York: Viking, 1982.

Kinsman, Robert, *Your Swiss Bank Book*, Homewood, Ill.: Dow Jones–Irwin, 1975.

Miller, Robert B., "The Caymans—Offshore Banking Paradise," *The Bankers Magazine*, January–February 1981.

Mills, Rodney H., Jr., and Eugenie D. Short, "U.S. Banks and the North American Euro-Currency Market," *The Journal of Commercial Bank Lending*, July 1979.

Williams, Richard, *International Capital Markets: Recent Developments and Short-Term Prospects*, IMF Occasional Paper, no. 7, Washington, D.C.: IMF, August 1981.

4

FOREIGN EXCHANGE MANAGEMENT

As the volume of transactions involving foreign exchange has increased, the role of foreign exchange trading has become more and more important, as has the role of foreign exchange management. Initially, it was primarily companies and financial institutions that played the foreign exchange markets, both to raise certain currencies and to protect against exposures in currencies whose values were constantly changing. In the last ten years, a new group—speculators—has entered the market, seeking to exploit the opportunities presented by the volatility of today's markets—the product of the immense volume of transactions, the speed of communications, and the rapidly changing international economic and political scene.

This chapter looks at the evolution of foreign exchange management and at how the currency markets operate. Two markets are particularly important, the "spot" and the "forward," with most of the foreign exchange dealing involving them. Speculators and small investors, however, tend to frequent the newer International Monetary Market (IMM), which actually evolved in response to their demand.

Foreign exchange trading is taking place in every area of the world, a situation that makes it a 24-hour-a-day business. This chapter reviews the highlights of the different centers—Japan, Singapore and Hong Kong, Europe, and New York/Chicago. It also discusses some of the opportunities for hedging foreign exchange risk, such as Future Rate Agreements and financial options, and the difficulties involved in these transactions. A foremost one is predicting how exchange rates will move over the maturity period of a transaction. As such, the chapter also contains some thoughts on forecasting models.

BACKGROUND

Foreign exchange trading as practiced today became prominent in the 1920s. The dominant currency in those days was the pound sterling, the premier currency market London. All the markets, large and small, were characterized by the following:

- The parity rates of the main currencies were fixed against gold or silver.
- Limited communications had an impact on the type and size of transactions that were possible.
- The major purpose for dealing in foreign exchange was commercial.

The Great Depression brought foreign exchange transactions to a virtual halt. Subsequently, the world economy was beset by high levels of protectionism and the upheavals of World War II. In response to this turmoil, in 1944 the major industrial nations met at Bretton Woods in an effort to restore some stability and forward momentum to the troubled global economic scene. The highlights of the resulting agreements were:

- The creation of the International Monetary Fund (IMF);
- The creation of the World Bank; and
- The return to a gold standard, with the U.S. dollar playing a key role.

Thus, from that meeting came a new system for operating the currency markets, and the world moved onto a new order based on the U.S. dollar rather than the pound sterling.

Despite these reforms, foreign exchange transactions grew in volume only slowly, the reason being that most countries imposed foreign exchange controls in the period of reconstruction following World War II. Nevertheless, the rebuilding itself required substantial international commerce and interaction and hence foreign exchange dealing, all of which grew inexorably as countries restored their economic stability and growth. By the end of the 1950s, convertibility had been restored among the major currencies. This accomplishment, coupled with continued economic growth and technological improvements in communications, led to vigorous expansion in foreign exchange transactions. During the 1960s, certain currencies began to outperform others, notably the dollar, the Dutch guilder, and the Swiss franc. To these can now be added the deutschemark and the Japanese yen. In contrast, the French franc and the pound sterling remained weak.

To prevent wide fluctuations in exchange rates (which were being regulated under the Bretton Woods agreement), central banks undertook to buy and sell currencies so as to maintain fixed parities. This system worked for a while, but it eventually succumbed to events in the latter 1960s. In November 1967, Great Britain finally devalued the pound, which had been under pressure for some time. Moreover, for several years the United States had been financing the ever more costly war in Vietnam through monetary growth, a policy that started an inflationary trend and caused a serious loss of confidence abroad in the U.S. dollar. On August 15, 1971, President Richard M. Nixon responded by closing the "gold window," thereby eliminating the system under which the U.S. dollar could be exchanged for gold at a fixed price of $35.00 an ounce.

At this time the major European Economic Community members decided to create their own foreign exchange system. Called "the Snake," it allowed European currencies to fluctuate within a limited band, and the whole system was then tied to the U.S. dollar. However, in 1973 the United States devalued the dollar by 10 percent, thereby ending the era of fixed exchange rates. Instead, floating exchange rates became widespread in the mid–1970s.

These floating exchange rates were based on no agreement. The underlying concept was that the free market should establish the exchange rates among currencies. The main advantage to this approach was that the central banks were no longer responsible for intervening in foreign exchange markets. Nevertheless, the free market was never allowed to operate entirely freely, for the central banks still stepped in to stabilize sharp fluctuations. This system is still in effect today.

HOW THE CURRENCY MARKETS OPERATE

The Participants

There are five categories of participants in the foreign exchange markets—commercial customers, banks, brokers, central banks, and the International Monetary Market in Chicago. Here the focus is on banks, although the other participants are also discussed briefly.

Banks first became involved in the foreign exchange markets on behalf of their customers, who demanded foreign exchange services in conjunction with their business. These customers included businesses, correspondent banks, other financial institutions, and perhaps the central bank in their home country. Nowadays banks also put together financial packages for their customers through which they seek, by locking in a certain exchange rate, to ensure that changes in exchange rates will not increase the bill for goods being purchased. Often banks handle their customers' needs by assuming the risk themselves in return for lucrative fees. In addition, international businesses need to exchange overseas profits into their home currencies, another source of business for banks.

While banks still engage in foreign exchange trading for their customers, much of their involvement is now aimed at protecting their own exposures from lending and at earning profits and commissions. As banks have built up vast international investment portfolios that encompass numerous countries and currencies and that are particularly vulnerable to fluctuating exchange and interest rates, they are looking for ways to hedge against changes in exchange and interest rates.

A number of banks have also come to see the foreign exchange markets as just one more place to make a profit and are involved for that reason as well. Position-taking, as this activity is called, entails the acquisition or sale of currency unrelated to other transactions, but rather for the purpose of earning profits from anticipated changes in exchange rates.

Much of the activity of banks in foreign exchange trading is interbank—one bank to another. This interbank trading has two benefits—it affords customers good services, and it ensures the banks themselves of a deep enough market to cover the volumes they deal in.

The degree to which banks are involved in the foreign exchange markets varies tremendously. Some simply carry out their customers' transactions and get out of the market, others play the markets aggressively. About 200 banks are considered to be market-makers, although far more are involved in foreign exchange transactions.

Whatever the nature of their involvement, most banks conduct their business through specialized foreign exchange departments. A bank may have refined its operations to the extent that it has more than one department, each responsible for a different type of dealing. Generally, the actual transactions are carried out in "dealing rooms" manned by experts under the coordination of a chief dealer. Deals are made by telex and telephone, with millions of dollars or other currencies exchanged over the wires. There is no official proof of a transaction at the time it is made; rather, the whole market is based on reciprocal trust, with banks totally responsible for any agreement undertaken by their dealers. That the system works is evidenced by the rare instances of nonfulfillment of agreements.

Because of the high degree of risk in currency dealings—due to the extreme volatility of the currency market, which can adversely affect a bank's exposure in a currency where its position is unhedged, and the possibility of nonperformance on a contract by another bank or company—a bank's credit department usually assesses the risk factor and sets maximum exposures that its traders cannot exceed (these limits are called ceilings). To enforce them, each dealer must have a very efficient back office that can provide immediate figures on the bank's levels of exposure in different currencies and with particular banks. Normally the back office is located near the dealing room to enhance communications.

As for companies, they also seek to protect themselves against exposures resulting from investments involving certain currencies, as well as to make profits, in addition to meeting the routine foreign exchange demands of their international trade. Rather than carry out the transactions themselves, they may resort to their banks to put packages together for them, or work through foreign exchange brokers. The latter are in the business of linking deals among banks and other traders in the different markets around the world. Particularly because of modern communications, they are closely tied to one another in all markets, and business can be transacted almost 24 hours a day.

Central banks are involved in two ways. They must meet their countries' needs for foreign exchange, and they intervene to stabilize their national currencies. The central banks of Europe undertake that latter role as part of their obligation as members of the European Economic Community. Generally countries intervene defensively—to smooth violent fluctuations or to act when the exchange rate is moving toward a level that is unacceptable economically.

The International Monetary Market of Chicago, a fairly new participant in the game, is discussed later. Briefly, it is a speculators' market, offering opportunities for very rapid trading and profit and loss by exploiting changes in exchange rates in the buying and selling of currency futures contracts.

Types of Activities

There are two main markets in foreign exchange dealing—the "spot" and the "forward," with the former the larger of the two. Often they are separated from each other, and dealers may specialize in one or the other.

The Spot Market

The prices of currencies in the spot market are always established in terms of how many units of a currency are needed to purchase one U.S. dollar (that amount is known as the dollar spot rate). A price of DM 2.7345 means that that many deutschemarks are needed to buy a dollar. The exception to this rule is the British pound, which also has an "indirect quote," for example, £1 = U.S. $1.2345. All prices are expressed to the fourth decimal figure because of the large amounts being traded.

A typical quote for a price is expressed as follows: U.S. dollar = SF 2.3800—SF 2.3815. The first figure (SF 2.3800) is the "bid price," or the price a bank is willing to pay for each U.S. dollar, in this case 2.3800 Swiss francs. The second figure (2.3815) is the "offer price," or the price at which a bank is willing to sell. Other examples are: (a) U.S. dollar/SF spot quote = 2.2000 (bid price)—2.2215 (offer price); and (b) £/U.S. dollar spot quote = 1.2825 (bid price)—1.2835 (offer price). It should be noted that the bid price of (b) above is derived from the previous offer price and vice versa. From the figures in the second example, it is also possible to determine the price of the pound against the Swiss franc, or the cross-rate.

In everyday trading, the cross-rates are written as SF/£ = 2.8215—513 and £/SF = .3545—507.

A bank can be on the spot market in three positions:

1. Long — when it buys more than it sells of a currency;
2. Short — when it buys less than it sells of a currency; and
3. Square — when it buys and sells the same amount of a currency.

Normally, a bank's position should be square, but sometimes it is allowed to hold a short or long position for a generally brief period, as any position other than square exposes the bank to a risk. Deals are therefore typically very short term. This strategy is called "in and out" and is designed to derive a quick profit from small fluctuations in price. Sometimes only a few minutes elapse between taking and liquidating a position, although in some cases the duration can be an entire day. The delivery time period of any currency on the spot market is normally two days.

The main factors affecting spot prices are the supply of and demand for a currency. In turn, supply and demand are influenced by both long- and short-term variables. The former, which affect the market on a day-to-day basis, are related to such things as the requirements for currencies embodied in investment and commercial transactions. The key factor that determines how short-term variables affect supply and demand and hence price is the liquidity of the market. For example, on a day when the market for the deutschemark is very thin—that is, there is little trading in the deutsche-mark—a purchase of DM 100 million to repay a loan that has matured can greatly affect that day's deutschemark price. On a day of heavy trading in this currency, however, an operation like that will have little or no impact on price, since it is simply absorbed in the great number of transactions.

Long-term variables involve mainly the overall economic situation of a country, for example, its balance of payments, trends in GNP, and directions of interest rates. A key factor is the subjective perceptions of market participants, primarily the confidence they have in a country. This factor, being subjective, is largely unquantifiable and is very difficult to forecast, based as it is on personal judgments about political stability, future levels of employment, social stability, the climate for foreign investment, and the like.

The Forward Market

In the forward market, the rate of exchange is agreed to now but delivery is specified at a future date. In practice, most contracts range from one day to a maximum of one year.

The forward market involves a great deal of arbitrage (see Chapter 7), as arbitrageurs try to earn risk-free profits by exploiting the differences among spot prices and forward rates that result from market inefficiencies. Another very common type of arbitrage—interest covered—is carried out when there is a discrepancy between the interest rates available in two currencies and their forward prices.

The following example provides an illustration of arbitrage (it does not include transaction costs and taxes). Assume that the six-month interest rate for the deutschemark is 8 percent a year; for the U.S. dollar, 16 percent. Assume, further, that the U.S. dollar/DM spot price is 2.0900 and that the six-month U.S. dollar/DM forward rate is 2.0250. Given these differences, a dealer might perform the following transactions. On day 1, he would:

1. Borrow DM 2,000,000 for six months at 4 percent (8 percent divided by 2);
2. Change DM 2,000,000 into U.S. $956,937.80 (using the spot market price of 2.0900);
3. Deposit $956,937.80 for six months at 8 percent (16 percent divided by 2);
4. Purchase a six-month forward contract for $1,033,492.80 ($956,937.80 at DM 2.0250 + $76,550 interest for six months) to sell against the deutschemark, receiving in return DM 2,092,822.87 (2.0250).

On day 181, the dealer would:

5. Redeem the dollar deposit and receive $1,033,492.80;
6. Settle the forward contract and receive DM 2,092,822.87; and
7. Repay the loan in dollars.

From this operation the dealer would gain U.S. $12,822.87, calculated as follows:

From the forward contract:	U.S. $2,092,822.87
Less the loan in dollars plus accrued interest:	U.S. $2,080,000.00
Total	U.S. $ 12,822.87

These arbitrage opportunities have no risk, since all the prices are locked in at the beginning. However, recall that this operation is possible only because of a discrepancy in the forward market, which does not reflect the differential in interest rates among two currencies. The arbitrageurs must take very quick action—the discrepancies last only a few minutes, as transactions take place immediately to exploit the situation and soon restore an equilibrium.

Arbitrage is also carried out on the spot market, with the strategy to make deals that move currencies from one market to another, i.e., converting currency A into B in one market.

International Monetary Market

In 1971, a new market opened in Chicago—the International Monetary Market (IMM), a subsidiary of the Chicago Mercantile Exchange. A futures market that is possible because of the floating exchange rates, it evolved because traders felt the interbank market was not providing foreign exchange services to small investors or corporations that wanted to speculate in currency fluctuations through a daily trading strategy. Speculators are in fact the main participants in the IMM, which now operates to the tune of about $40 billion a day. More recently, commercial banks have begun to deal with various arbitrage companies that have evolved around the IMM. This link between the IMM and the interbank market ensures the liquidity of the former, and the IMM now influences the interbank market.

The main differences between the futures and forward markets are:

Futures Market	Forward Market
1. Prices are set by "open cry" bidding	Prices are set on a one-to-one basis
2. Only specific currencies can be traded	Any currency can be traded
3. The size of the contract is standardized (e.g., SF 125,000, Canadian $50,000)	No restrictions are set on the size of the contract
4. Specific standard maturity dates are set	No specific maturity dates are set
5. Specific margin requirements (both initial and maintenance) are set	Margin requirements are negotiable
6. Commissions are fixed	Commissions are negotiable
7. Limits are set on daily price changes.	Not applicable
8. The minimum price change is predetermined	Not applicable
9. Long and short positions are easy to liquidate	Positions cannot be liquidated
10. The market is highly speculative and volatile	The market is less speculative
11. The market is highly regulated.	The market is completely unregulated.

Futures markets have now opened in several cities around the world, such as London, Amsterdam, Singapore, Sydney, Philadelphia, and Montreal, and are gaining in popularity.

The Geographic Markets

The term "market" also refers to the locations at which foreign exchange trading takes place. It could be argued that a market exists wherever dealing occurs. Essentially that is wherever a telephone or telex is found, for trading today is no longer limited to dealing rooms or the facilities of companies. It can and does take place off-premises, even at home, the reason being the 24-hour nature of foreign exchange trading, given the existence of central markets the world around. While in the early days the market was essentially London, nowadays trading also centers in New York, a number of major European cities, Tokyo, Hong Kong, and Singapore, with a network of smaller secondary exchanges in virtually every country.

These markets are all interlinked, with the business from one flowing into that of another and vice versa. As one market closes, another opens up, starting with the closing quotations of the earlier market and with much of its initial business related to orders from that market. For the sake of simplicity, however, the trading day may be viewed as starting in Japan, where "the sun rises."

The Japanese market, of which Tokyo is preeminent, is high-volume, related mainly to the needs of banks' commercial customers. It involves principally U.S. dollar/yen trading because of the very large amount of commerce between the two countries. There is also a smaller amount of dealing in Japanese securities. Foreign exchange brokers are used extensively in preference to bank-to-bank transactions, especially for national transactions. Far more interbank dealing is involved in international transactions, and this type of activity is likely to increase, even for local transactions, as more foreign banks open branches in Tokyo. Unlike some markets, Tokyo closes at a set time in the afternoon, a custom that has hampered its growth.

The Singapore and Hong Kong markets open one hour after Tokyo. These centers are less regulated and more freewheeling, as both localities, desirous of becoming international financial centers as one base for their economies, have sought to establish friendly banking and commercial environments. They have been very successful in this endeavor: many banks have opened foreign branches in both centers, which now have active foreign exchange markets where many different currencies are traded. Brokers are heavily involved in local transactions in Singapore, with interbank trading characterizing international transactions. Hong Kong trading involves both. Hong Kong, because it has a somewhat smaller market, is the more volatile of the two.

Next on the circuit is Europe, as a whole the largest market, with the main centers being Great Britain, the Federal Republic of Germany, and Switzerland. European banks have no set closing time and can trade 24 hours if they choose, but generally they stop in the afternoon. Trading is both interbank and brokered except in London, where the latter predominates. A unique feature of the European market is the rate fixing. Once a day representatives of the larger banks and the central banks meet to fix the exchange rate of the U.S. dollar against local currencies and hence against one another. The fixed rate represents the balance of offers and bids and is close to what it would be internationally. However, the small discrepancy offers opportunities for arbitrage. The fixed rate is important only in that it is considered to be the legal, official rate and is often specified in contracts.

The New York market and, with it, the IMM open next, although some dealers in them may have been operating 24 hours in order to be in on the action in other markets firsthand and to avoid overnight positions. As international business has grown and more foreign banks have established presences in the United States, the volume of transactions on the New York and IMM markets has been booming. These markets are characterized by both brokered and interbank dealing. The West Coast markets are essentially tied into the New York center.

HEDGING IN THE FOREIGN EXCHANGE MARKETS

Given the scope of their international business and investment portfolios, a major concern of banks today is protection against fluctuations in currencies and interest rates. One study of 109 currencies revealed, for example, that between 1948 and 1967, 96 had been devalued at least once, making devaluation a very common risk. Thus foreign exchange management is now high on the agenda of most banks.

Two protective techniques most banks employ are to evaluate carefully the risks in all transactions involving foreign exchange before entering into them and to set ceilings on exposures in any particular currency. Another is hedging. The traditional type of hedging involves establishing a position that locks in the cost of money or foreign exchange in advance of the maturity date of the transaction. In other words, a bank establishes an obligation to deal at a particular price at a particular time. Other hedging mechanisms have evolved recently, one of them being the IMM. Even more recent is the option. Some of these techniques are standardized, while in other cases banks put together packages tailored to their own needs or those of their customers. Some of the techniques are described more fully below.

The *Future Rate Agreement* (FRA) is relatively simple—two parties, generally banks, agree to compensate each other at a specified future date for whatever shift in interest rates has taken place. Banks enter into these agreements mainly to protect themselves against interest rate guarantee packages they have put together for customers. These agreements now constitute a sizable interbank activity.

The *financial option* is a newer device to protect against changes in interest rates or changes in exchange rates. The latter has been the more important part of the business because of the active forward market for trading off and the currency risks today. The procedure is as follows. A customer buys the right—or option—to trade a foreign currency at a set rate at a specific time. The cost of the option is usually up to 5 percent of the option amount, with the actual rate linked to the likely fluctuation in the currency. The customer may later choose not to exercise the option, for example, if the exchange rate moves in his favor, of if he can benefit from the rate he has tied up with the option. Options come both standardized and tailored, with banks setting them up and charging whatever the market will bear.

The obvious attractiveness of this alternative is its flexibility, although there is a cost in exercising it. The main option markets are Chicago, Amsterdam, and Philadelphia, with Montreal and London growing as centers. The primary requirement for a market is liquidity. The trading takes place in most major currencies and now in ECUs.

There are other alternatives today that avoid the cost of options and that also give the customer flexibility, and they are now competing with the financial options market. In addition, customers are looking to reduce the cost of options by assuming more of the risk themselves, an approach similar to the use of deductibles in traditional insurance policies.

For the most part, it is the bigger banks that have been involved in the hedging business, as it requires more expertise than smaller ones have. Moreover, these markets are now increasingly being subjected to regulation, a trend that will require even more sophisticated operations.

Problems with Hedging

Hedging is a complex operation because of four major difficulties: the inseparability of financing and hedging; the unreliability of forecasts of costs; timing of the transaction; and foreign exchange controls. Timing, for example, is a major complication in the protection of cash balances in vulnerable currencies. Ideally, a dealer should hedge completely the day before any change is anticipated, and from that day onwards no coverage costs should be incurred. However, this safeguard is impossible to carry out, for only rarely is an activity's date known with certainty. Changes in governmental policy such as devaluations, as a case in point, are usually kept secret, as this measure, to be successful, must take the business community and speculators by surprise. In addition, the availability of hedging possibilities varies with time. In most cases when a government is about to impose a change, either forward exchange contracts and short-term loans simply disappear from the market or their costs rise astronomically. For these reasons, it is difficult to rely upon emergency measures just before a currency change. Yet a decision on a medium-term loan made now will affect the exposure of the lender many months hence. Even more critical is the timing of forward exchange contracts. It can only be hoped that the currency change will occur in a period when the net exposure is minimal.

As to foreign currency controls, limitations on the repatriation of profits, multiple exchange rates, and restrictions on the availability of swaps on forward exchange contracts are typical regulations that a bank has to take into account when hedging.

The most difficult and complex issue, however, is constraints on operations and decision-making. These include operational requirements, policies, and legal requirements within whose context all transactions must be carried out. Examples of operational requirements are the financial needs that must be met at any point with new funds from whatever source (receipts, local loans, swaps, or dollar loans). In addition, expenses relating to deposits and interest must be budgeted for. An example of a policy constraint is a decision to maintain minimum balances to keep lines of credit open for loans to local banks or to adhere to certain levels of financial ratios.

Foreign Exchange Forecasting Models

Banks are always looking for ways to improve the decisions they make in their foreign exchange operations. To a very large extent, the key decisions are predictions as to future trends and events. To maximize the effectiveness of their hedging, many banks are looking to the use of models for currency forecasting.

The objective of forecasting models is to minimize risk—defined as the uncertainty of the exact outcome of an event—in relation to expected costs and potential risk. Mathematically, all models are designed around the three elements discussed above: operational requirements, financial constraints, and legal issues. Each in its own way answers the question of how risk is measured. In modeling, risk is evaluated by a measure of the dispersion of the potential outcome around the expected outcome.

The first step that model builders take in solving forward exchange problems is to determine a planning horizon. Its length depends upon a large number of factors, such as project necessity, period of maturity for decisions, and reliability of the forecasts over time. After the planning horizon is chosen, an appropriate time unit—days, weeks, months or quarters—is decided on.

The second step is to forecast, for each month or period, the probabilities of a forward rate, the rate amount, and the spread of this amount. The models take into account the time parameters. There is also a margin of error factored into the monthly estimates, an important ingredient in the total risk strategy.

The third step involves the cash budget for each month in the planning horizon. It describes both the financing requirements per month prior to interest costs and the deposits required to meet those costs. Other necessary data are the possible alternative sources of financing and hedging available. The expected costs, possible spread of those costs, and expected amounts available within those spreads then have to be forecast. To some degree, the costs depend upon one another, a complicating factor. Correlation estimates of the costs of financing and hedging operations take this factor into account. Legal issues and policy are the final set of constraints.

A great many banks have taken to using state-of-the-art models to identify optimal approaches to the management of foreign currency trading. There are now some sixteen major foreign exchange forecasting services offering twenty-two models.

The performance of these services varies. One survey looked at the 16 services: Bankers Trust, Brian Marber, Business International, Chase Econometric, Chemical Bank (Fast Model and Slow Model), Citibank, Conti Currency, European American (Fast Model and Slow Model), Forex (Econometric and Technical), International Forecasting Corporation, Manufactures Hanover Trust, Multinational Corporation Model, Predex (Technical and Fundamental), Stoll (Standard, Covered, and Long-Term), Waldner and Co., and Wharton.[1] The results were inconclusive as to the best service, but did provide performance ratings. One evaluation in the survey covered relative performance in terms of three factors banks would want to predict: relative rates of change, moving averages, and momentum in price. This evaluation covered thirteen models of eight companies—Bankers Trust, Brian Marber, Chemical Bank (Fast and Slow), European American (Fast and Slow), Forex (Econometric and Technical), Predex (Technical), Stoll (Covered, Standard, and Long-Term), and Waldner and Co. These thirteen models together embody all the basic elements of a good model.

Overall, the models' recommendations were correct 57 percent of the time. The smallest cumulative losses resulted from Forex (Technical), Stoll (Covered), and Chemical (Slow). Chemical Bank (Fast) produced the highest incremental return with the lowest cost of hedging. All the models produced positive returns.[2]

The second evaluation looked at correctness in statistical terms. The purpose was to discover which services could most reliably be used by corporate managers in forward currency forecasting. The services covered included Business International, Conti Currency, Predex (Technical and Fundamental), Wharton, Chase Econometric, and Multinational Corporation Model.

The Predex (Fundamental) and the Wharton models produced significantly better results, although as a whole all the services predicted results with greater than 60 percent accuracy. On the other hand, none was able to forecast dollar appreciation adequately, a disappointing outcome. Predex (Technical) had the best record, at 55.5 percent, with Conti Currency second, at 53.4 percent. It should be noted, however, that the results were influenced by the interdependencies of the currencies used.[3]

The survey also investigated the possibility of using two or more models in combination. To do so, the models must of course be compatible in form and prediction. The results indicated that only two models should be combined at a time; using three did not yield better returns. When two models were combined, the return on capital at risk averaged 6.1 percent, as compared with 14.2 percent with individual models. The best pairing was Chemical Bank (Slow) and European American (Fast). The safest combination was Stoll (Covered) and Waldner and Co., with an 82 percent rate of profitability.[4]

As these results suggest, effective forecasting is problematical. The availability of effective methods and models has increased the confidence of speculators and thus decreased the possible profits by producing a less risky market. Changes in economic theories, policies, and events must be fed into the models constantly or the results will be distorted. Finally, most statistical models are plotted on a normal curve, whereas frequently a random chance occurrence happens that misrepresents the intentions and recommendations to the investor.

Perhaps the best policy for the foreign exchange forecaster is to use the composite approach of running several forecasting models so as to identify the best possible option under the widest range of circumstances. Although this solution is not optimal for the investor, it offers the greatest value for suboptimization.

Models are now often used for general commercial hedging and covering. Although safeguards against parity changes are not always possible through the use of models, they are increasingly important in international banking.

SUMMARY AND CONCLUSIONS

Many banks today are heavily involved in foreign exchange dealings for two reasons. One is to hedge against changes in the currencies in which their transactions are denominated. Here it is important for a bank to know its total exposure in different currencies and the maturities of its various transactions, since hedging will only be successful if pursued in the context of a bank's global operations. The second reason is to make a profit from changes in exchange rates, which today are floating rather than fixed.

Foreign exchange dealing is now a highly specialized activity that goes on 24 hours a day throughout the world. Much of today's business, however, is interbank. There are two main markets in foreign exchange dealing—the spot and the forward. Trading takes place in these markets, where bid and quote rates are given continuously. Banks normally try to achieve a square position in the spot market, as that means no risk, but they may also choose to hold a short or long position briefly to profit from fluctuations in rates. Banks use the forward market to lock in an exchange rate at some future date (for example, by purchasing an option), or to arbitrage so as to earn risk-free profits. To satisfy the desire of speculators to exploit these markets, in 1971 a new futures market—the International Monetary Market—emerged in Chicago. It has been followed by others elsewhere in the world.

Given the importance of foreign exchange management, banks are always looking for ways to improve this operation. Clearly a vital part of these dealings is being able to predict how exchange rates will move over certain periods of time. A number of banks and companies have developed forecasting models as one tool. While none is perfect, some offer a fairly high degree of reliability; their use has resulted in ongoing profits from foreign exchange dealing. One suggested approach is to apply more than one model and to use the common results from their runs.

As to the future of foreign exchange dealings, clearly they will remain integral to a bank's operations. In fact, they have now emerged as even more important, as banks try to boost their capital by engaging more in off–balance sheet transactions and less in traditional lending. How long that trend will last is uncertain. However, as banks gain more sophistication in this area and are assured of reasonably consistent profit-taking, it is likely to remain a steady business.

NOTES

1. S. Goodman and R. Levich, "Two Technical Analysts Are Even Better Than One," *Euromoney* (August 1982).
2. Ibid.
3. "How the Rise of the Dollar Took Forecasters by Surprise," *Euromoney* (August 1982).
4. Ibid.

REFERENCES

Booth, L. D., "Hedging and Foreign Exchange Exposure," *Management International Review*, 22, January 1982, pp. 26–42.

Dufey, G., and R. Mirus, "Forecasting Foreign Exchange Rates," *Columbia Journal of World Business*, 16, Summer 1981, pp. 53–61.

Enzig, P., *The History of Foreign Exchange*, New York: St. Martin's Press, 1962.

George, A. M., *Foreign Exchange Management and the Multinational Corporation*, New York: Praeger, 1978.

Goodman, A., "Technical Analysis Still Beats Econometrics," *Euromoney*, August 1981, pp. 48–49.

Goodman, S. "Two Technical Analysts Are Even Better Than One," *Euromoney*, August 1982, pp. 85–96.

Kahnamouyipour, K., "Foreign Exchange: Hedging, Speculation, or Swap?" *Accountancy*, 91, October 1980.

Naider, G. N., and T. S. Shin, "Effectiveness of Currency Futures Market in Hedging Foreign Exchange Risk," *Management International Review*, 20, December 1981.

Ruck, A., "Understanding Foreign Exchange Trading," *Euromoney*, April 1981.

Soenan, A., and E. G. Van Winkel, "Real Costs of Hedging in the Foreign Exchange Market," *Management International Review*, 22, January 1982, pp. 53–59.

Stokes, H., and H. Neuburger, "Interest Arbitrage, Forward Speculation, and the Determination of the Forward Exchange Rate," *Columbia Journal of World Business*, 14, Winter 1979, pp. 86–98.

5

COUNTRY RISK ASSESSMENT

As international bankers have increased their lending to less creditworthy countries, they have had to pay more attention to the potential for loss. Nowadays, loss does not necessarily result from problems with the operations of a company borrower. Instead, it is the result of factors exogenous to the company, factors related to the political, social, and economic environments in which the borrower is operating. As a result, the concept of country risk has emerged, and with it, the practice of country risk assessment.

Originally, the purpose of country risk assessment was to identify those risks that could affect a borrower's ability to repay according to the terms of the loan. Today, some banks have gone a step further and have integrated country risk assessment into their daily operations as one tool in such tasks as strategic planning, marketing, and evaluation of the performance of their international portfolios. The appropriate term here is "country risk management," a practice of which country risk assessment is but one element.

DEFINING COUNTRY RISK

Country risk, as seen through the eyes of the international banker, is the potential for a loss of the assets (money) a bank has loaned across borders in a currency other than that of the host country. The cause of the loss would be an event or condition that leaves the borrower unable to meet the terms of the loan. (Also at risk, from the perspective of some banks, are physical assets such as branch offices; they are not discussed here.) The borrower may be a host country government, a local firm, or a multinational corporation of yet another country. Whatever the case, the loan is booked according to the country of risk, that is, the country from which the re-payments will flow.

Types of Country Risk

Country risk, as stated above, relates to the political, economic, social, and natural environment in the country in which the activity for which the loan is made will take place. The risks are ones over which private companies or individual borrowers have no control; instead, they are under the control of the host country government, either in terms of prevention or in terms of amelioration. Examples of country risk by their broad categories are:

Political events—confiscation/expropriation of the assets of the borrower; occupation by a foreign power; civil disorder; ideological conflicts (often closely linked with religious differences); changes in government (both planned and peremptory); regionalism/tribalism in terms of the internal balance of power; inequitable distribution of income related to ethnic rivalries; unwillingness of a government to honor its obligations; changes in policy that affect the borrower's cash flow; and increasingly today, terrorism.

Social events—civil war, riots, labor union strife, religious conflict, socioeconomic differences in living standards that result in tension or instability.

Economic conditions—recession; strikes; increases in the cost of imported inputs and foodstuffs; drop in the price of the main or key exports; inappropriate policies and development strategies; increased local taxes on earnings; restrictions on the transfer of remittances out of the country; devaluation/depreciation of the exchange rate and other controls; ceilings on interest rates.

Natural disasters—drought, flood, earthquakes, pests.

Some of these are clearly exogenous factors over which a government would seem to have no control. Such an event becomes a country risk if the government is able to mitigate or ameliorate the effects of the event. For example, while it is obvious that a developing country government cannot control a worldwide cyclical recession, it can implement adjustment policies that ensure the continued ability of the borrower to repay the loan. As such, country risk is involved.

When a risk occurs that impairs repayment, the bank faces, in order of seriousness: default; repudiation of the debt, that is, a decision not to repay; renegotiation of the loan on terms generally easier for the borrower and less advantageous for the bank, such as longer maturities, smaller periodic payments, and lower or fixed interest rates; rescheduling of the repayments, but with the terms remaining the same; moratorium on repayment; and temporary restrictions on remittance earnings. These risks are the focus of country risk assessment—determining the probability that an event or condition will arise during the terms of the loan that will result in one of the above situations.

Another type of risk in international lending should also be noted. Rather than directly affecting the ability of the borrower to repay, it affects the ability of the lender to assess and predict the likelihood of risk adequately. This type of risk includes the absence of data on key indicators, such as the actual extent of a country's external debt or debt service obligation, government manipulation of data or information, and the inherent difficulty of predicting the potential for certain events, such as a coup or the extent and duration of a cyclical economic trough. Furthermore, the data may be obsolete and therefore misleading and useless.

Country risk is often confused with other categories of risk that are usually a subset of country risk. To clarify the distinction, it is worth reviewing these other categories:

Sovereign risk applies specifically to the creditworthiness of governments as borrowers. As such, it is similar to commercial risk, except that, because of the nature of a government, sovereign risk involves more factors than just commercial ones. At the same time, it is narrower than country risk, in that it does not include many of the social, political, and nature-related factors that enter into country risk.

Political risk refers specifically to political factors that might impair a borrower's ability to repay. Again, it is a subset of country risk.

Credit risk refers to the ability (or in some cases the willingness) of the borrower to repay the lender. The term is virtually synonymous with country risk but is more relevant to "business" risk, i.e., the profitability of the investment.

Indigenous risk refers to transactions solely involving local loans and funds in local currencies.

Sectoral risk refers to a change in economic policy that might affect an activity in one sector in such a way as to impair the borrower's ability to repay. It is embodied in country risk.

Other risks are the exchange rate, liability, foreign direct investment, and the like. All are specific risks that also fall under the broader country risk.

Transfer risk, a term heard with greater frequency today, refers specifically to the possibility of nonpayment by a commercial borrower because the host country restricts the transfer of foreign exchange out of the country. It is one type of country risk.

The Nature of Country Risk

Before discussing how country risk is determined and what is done with the information, a couple of points should be noted by way of context. First, country risk is not static or absolute. Rather, it is dynamic, changing constantly in response to changing domestic and international conditions. And it is relative—it is a risk only to the extent that it impairs repayment, a possibility that in turn depends on the nature of a particular country, the timeframe, the purpose and nature of the loan, and the borrower. For example, a coup may not be a risk from the perspective of an international banker if it removes from power a leader pushing an inappropriate development strategy that has led to a balance of payments crisis, or it may constitute a risk only in the short-term period of transition. Country risks are also relative across countries. By way of illustration, two countries may have similarly negative current account deficits. However, one country may be deemed more creditworthy because it has a diversified export base that has significant potential for generating foreign exchange and is pursuing a basically sound economic strategy, whereas the other relies heavily on one primary product subject to recurrent price fluctuations and follows inappropriate industrial policies that have led to serious structural problems. So risk is relative to the broader timeframe and to other countries. Both points are important, as they dictate to some degree the nature and focus of country risk assessment, as discussed later.

THE EVOLUTION OF COUNTRY RISK ASSESSMENT

What led to the emergence of the concept of country risk and its assessment? As in so many areas of life, it was born of necessity. When the Eurocurrency market was established in the early 1950s, it eliminated one of the major constraints on lending across borders—restrictions on the transfer of funds out of a country that hampered repayment of international loans. The result was a rapid and extensive expansion in international lending. Initially, the borrowers were creditworthy institutional customers from reliable, stable industrial countries. In other words, the risks involved were the traditional commercial ones bankers were used to dealing with. However, by the second half of the sixties a new trend had emerged—massive borrowing by the governments of less developed countries. This borrowing raised all sorts of new issues. First, the borrowers were not traditional commercial ones, and creditworthiness could not be evaluated on traditional commercial terms. These borrowers, after all, could themselves alter the very conditions affecting the likelihood of repayment. Moreover, banks here were operating in a domestic and international sphere far more complicated and intertwined than that of traditional borrowers. The ability of a borrower to repay depended on the entire economy of a country and particularly on its ability to earn and transfer foreign exchange. In turn, that economy was intimately linked to the worldwide economy.

The Emergence of Sovereign Risk Assessment

Because of the particular nature of governments as borrowers, the concept of sovereign risk arose. It was soon evident that risk assessment had to be very broad, covering political and social as well as economic factors, or the entire environment of a country. By the early 1970s the banking community was familiar with the term "country risk." Having a label was one thing; however, what to do with country risk was another. How was it to be assessed? What kinds of things affected a country's debt-servicing ability and how? There were no clear-cut answers, and too often bankers found themselves resorting to "headline banking." In making decisions, they automatically responded negatively to lurid headlines of disorder and political upheaval, or positively to news of the discovery of the greatest known reserve of a rare but vital mineral. They did not consider the impact of the event in terms of productive capacity, on which debt servicing hinged. While civil war might seem inherently risky, its impact could be minimal if it were short-term and did not affect the area and facilities involved in the investment. In fact, if it were in the end to bring an otherwise divided citizenry together or at least result in effective political control over the entire country, civil war might even be positive from the perspective of the lender.

In one other way, the banker's approach to sovereign risk missed the mark. There was a tendency to focus on past performance in assessing potential risk. A more appropriate method is to use as the timeframe the period of the loan or investment and to consider the probability of events occurring within that period, with past performance just one factor. Given the rapidity of change and the degree to which most countries are linked to a dynamic world economy, past performance could not be expected to provide the answers. Similarly, because of the constancy of change, it was soon clear that country risk assessment could not be a one-shot deal.

Another point that also became clear was that sovereign risk varied even within a country: it depended on such factors as the purpose and maturity of the loan and on the type of borrower. Risk assessments needed to be carried out for each of those categories. In a country with an unstable leader, a company providing a vital export might be a more secure investment than the government. If there were a coup, the new leader might be tempted to repudiate the obligations of his predecessor, whereas he might not want to tamper with a key source of foreign exchange. Within the private sector, a bank might be a better risk than a company—the former could count on assistance from the central bank. Lending for a project that would ultimately increase the country's productive capacity was seen as less risky than financing current government consumption.

With little experience in this type of lending, banks looked initially to multinational corporations for guidance and information on how to handle sovereign risk. While the analysis of the multinational corporations was helpful in some respects, the banks found themselves facing different issues and concerns and requiring greater analysis. As such, they had to develop their own approaches. At first they relied for their country assessments on standard, short fact sheets prepared by their economics departments. These were mainly historical in nature, with only brief evaluations of debt-servicing ability. There was a heavy emphasis on numbers and quantitative analysis. Moreover, each factor was looked at independently of the others. Before long, however, it was realized that each factor interacted with the others. The methodology employed by banks became increasingly sophisticated and consistent.

Initially, the banks used the assessments primarily to evaluate individual loans and to set exposure limits for different countries. Moreover, the tendency was to loan only to low-risk countries, a practice that produced very lopsided portfolios. Eventually, more forward-thinking banks saw merit in applying country risk assessment to such tasks as balancing their portfolios by achieving greater diversity in terms of geography, purpose of the loans, and liquidity. On the other hand, country risk analysis still seemed to serve as a brake on lending, rather than as a means of identifying marketing opportunities.

The Concept of Country Risk Management

The move toward more sophisticated methodologies and uses of country risk assessment received a boost as a result of the failures and near failures of banks in 1974 and 1975, which occurred largely because of their international operations. It directed attention to the quality of the international loan portfolio as a whole and its relation to the solvency of the bank. Soon bank supervisory agencies began to see a need for country risk assessments in order to monitor and advise banks. Some asked to look at the banks' assessments; others carried out their own.

Today country risk assessment is still in evolution. It was not until the beginning of the 1980s, for example, that the important link between country risk and a country's institutional and regulatory framework was recognized, as well as the necessity to factor in the timeframe of a loan. Whereas the typical approach to assessment was quantitative, many institutions are now favoring mixed approaches, even accepting the subjective opinions of experts as a critical input. Increasingly, country risk assessment is seen as a management tool, and not just as the basis for deciding individual transactions. But there is still no standard way to carry out the analysis, nor any set pattern for its application. Implementation is still hindered by serious gaps in the data base, and there will always be those factors that defy prediction.

ASSESSING COUNTRY RISK

As noted, there is no standard procedure for assessing country risk. Nevertheless, there are certain general approaches that are the most common, and there are certain indicators that are typically looked at. And there are certain principles to be followed, whatever the approach.

The Principles

The focus in a country risk assessment is on trends, rather than on past performance and immediate conditions. Similarly, it is on structural and institutional factors and on underlying forces, rather than on short-term, temporary conditions. Of interest are only those events that might have an impact on the ability or willingness of the borrower to repay the loan, and the real issue is to determine the probability of that event or condition occurring, when it is likely to happen, and what is the probable outcome in terms of debt service.

The context of a country risk assessment is broad and comprehensive— it addresses not only political, economic, and social factors, but also a timeframe that covers both past performance and one to five years in the future, the common term for bank lending. It means considering not just the country itself, but also its links to the rest of the world and likely trends there in terms of their impact on the host country's economic status. And it means looking not just at the country as a whole, but at key elements within it, such as certain economic sectors or geographic regions.

As mentioned earlier, country risk assessment is not a static, one-time effort. It should be an ongoing process, with the frequency and scope of periodic assessments dictated by the nature of the country and the loan. A poor, newly independent country beset by ethnic tension, with a leader whose power is uncertain, will require more frequent monitoring than one which is internally cohesive—that is, one in which the transfer of power by tradition proceeds in an orderly way and whose policy is not likely to change dramatically.

An assessment is only as good as the resources applied to it, particularly human and informational. It is important to use experts who are familiar with the different disciplines involved and with the country being studied. It is advisable to have them visit the country periodically to bring themselves up to date. They must also be versed in the bank's objectives, needs, and operations.

These experts will need good data and other material to work with. Ideally, they should have access to both quantitative information—statistics and ratios and the like—and the qualitative opinions of people close to the country and knowledgeable about world trends. Again, in light of the dynamic nature of economics, a bank will need to have an ongoing system of information gathering and dissemination. (Certain key sources of information are listed in the next-to-last section of the chapter.) Finally, assessments should be retained for evaluation in light of actual events in order to improve the process.

A relative perspective is needed. Although certain standards are available against which to measure some indicators, in reality they are not very helpful. The key is the specific features of a country, such as its potential resource base, and what that says about its ability to service debt of different levels and terms. Other relative factors involve the nature of the debt—whether it is soft or hard, its maturity, grace periods, interest rates, etc.

Inasmuch as country risk assessment is to a large extent a comparative process—that is, risk in one location relative to another—it is important to develop a consistent approach that permits comparisons.

The Factors for Review

In looking at the factors that are typically analyzed in assessing country risk, two broad categories can be identified: economic and noneconomic, with the latter broken down into political, social, and natural environmental factors. It is important to remember, though, that noneconomic factors frequently reveal themselves in economic terms, and that all factors need to be analyzed in relation to one another, given their close interaction in real life.

Economic Factors

To reiterate, the focus is on identifying the factors that bear on a country or borrower's ability to repay its loan in timely fashion. As such, lenders look at certain determinants of a country's economic strength and likely ability to make repayments (such as its resource base, government policies, quality of economic management, and financial restrictions), and at certain economic indicators that relate to current performance: economic growth, foreign exchange balance, exports, and external debt and its nature.

A key economic factor is a country's resource base, which includes not just raw materials, but human resources, infrastructure, industry, finances, especially savings, agricultural output, and whatever else has a bearing on a country's productive capacity and ability to earn foreign exchange. Particularly important are the diversity and exploitability of those resources. Bankers will look for a diversified base or a strong export such as oil for which demand and prices are less subject to fluctuation. Manufactured exports are preferred to primary commodities because they, too, are somewhat less subject to the vagaries of the marketplace. Also important is the extent to which the resource base can satisfy domestic demand, particularly for foodstuffs and industrial inputs, as these are two key reasons for imports and hence the outflow of hard currency. In terms of risk assessment, the issues here are both existing and potential resources and the government's plan for exploiting them.

Government policies, both short-term and long-term, are an obvious influence. Among the issues here are the degree to which trade is free and the economy is allowed to operate without distortions, particularly with respect to pricing and exchange controls; agricultural versus industrial policy; the appropriateness of the development strategy; the government's attitude to foreign business; taxation; degree of commitment to provide the infrastructure or other support for economic development; and willingness and ability to make unpopular adjustments in times of economic downturns. Again, it is not just existing policy, but future policy, that must be addressed. Moreover, it is not just economic policies per se that are important. Equally decisive for stable economic growth are social policies insofar as they affect such factors as a sense of nationhood, social calm, education, training, work permits for foreigners, transportation, and labor relations not only in terms of pay, but also in terms of fringe benefits, retirement, insurance, and the like.

Increasingly, bankers are focusing on the quality of economic management. A number of factors are important here, but broadly they relate to policy formulation and implementation and to personnel. Among them are the appropriateness of the development strategy (does it relate to a country's comparative advantage, focus on output growth, provide for balanced growth, pay due attention to the agricultural sector, and tie in with the country's factor endowment?); the soundness of the government's borrowing practices (is borrowing for the expansion of productive capacity or for budgeted consumption or balance of payments purposes?); the government's willingness and ability to implement economic reforms, such as those called for by the IMF, or adjustments required because of cyclical conditions (here public response to austerity measures and the government's ability to withstand it are the key factors); willingness to address structural issues (the principle of optimum intervention); the competence, expertise, stability and numbers of the core economic team; and the adequacy of communication and coordination among those managing the economy. Also important is the quality and timeliness of the data available to the government for input into its planning and economic monitoring. Clearly, an absence, for example, of data on the extent and nature of external debt will reflect badly on the quality of management and in turn on the borrower's creditworthiness. Other signs of bad economic management are a prolonged balance of payments crisis, inflation, high rates of unemployment, unnecessarily high imports of food, low import cover, constant turnover among economic staff, uncoordinated planning or an absence of long-range development strategies, excessive borrowing, and a debt service burden out of line with the country's receipts of foreign exchange.

Many countries face financial restrictions that in turn impinge on their creditworthiness. A country whose current account is in deficit and which has an unfavorable debt service burden will have a lower credit rating if those conditions are ingrained rather than the product of a cyclical downturn. The current account depends on the growth rate of domestic demand, the competitiveness of the exchange rate, the prices for exports, and the diversity of exports. The debt burden refers to the percentage of foreign exchange required to pay the principal and interest on the debt. One factor that should be included in financial analysis but that is very difficult to determine is private nonguaranteed external debt. Another important element in a country's external financial position is its ability to draw on IMF funds and to tap commercial banks.

Within these broad categories, there are some specific economic indicators that bankers typically look at. One is the ratio of the current account on the balance of payments to GNP (GDP). It is a truism that most developing countries are net borrowers. The question has always been how large a current account deficit a country can run relative to GNP. Once more, there is no standard. Rather, the level depends on the prospects of the country and its economic base.

Another key indicator is the ratio of national savings to GNP (GDP). Domestic savings are the source of investment funds, and to the extent that they fall short, the country and its investors must resort to external borrowing. Thus this ratio is an important indicator of both the country's potential for continued economic growth and its likely external financial needs and debt burden.

A number of indicators relate specifically to the country's external financial position. The important broad measures are long-term economic growth with reasonable price stability, a function of the expansion of the productive capacity to export; and the availability of foreign exchange, a function of the receipts from exports of goods and services, net transfer receipts, and imports of capital. Ratios of certain macroeconomic indicators are used to assess long-term economic growth, with the focus on investment and savings. Ratios involving the balance of payments show the likelihood of a trade deficit, which affects the ability of the country to repay its loans. Here it is important to look at whether the deficit is likely to increase or decrease over the period of the loan. Ratios of external debt relate trends for GNP and the balance of payments, showing the level and burden of external debt, its structure, and the availability of foreign exchange.

There are a great many individual ratios within each of these categories; only certain key ones are addressed here specifically. One is the debt service ratio—the required debt payments relative to the availability of foreign exchange, as determined by exports of goods and services. The import cover of official reserves indicates how long a country can continue production requiring imported inputs in the event of a falloff in foreign exchange earnings. The rule of thumb is a reserve equal to three months' supply of imports. However, the terms for many imports are longer than 90 days, so this measure is not necessarily relevant. Moreover, a high level of reserves may be the result of heavy external borrowing, in which case this measure is extremely misleading, while a low level could reflect a temporary cyclical downturn. Finally, the terms of debt—the ratio of scheduled debt service payments over a given period relative to debt outstanding—is a key indicator, although it has the serious drawback of excluding private nonguaranteed debt. Moreover, while the overall amount of debt is important, a country can sustain a far larger amount if the terms are soft. The key elements here are the level and nature of the interest rate (fixed or floating), the maturity of the loan (long, medium, or short) and the repayment schedule relative to the country's cash flow, present and future.

Sometimes these factors are weighted. Weighting is tricky, however, particularly in that the factors may not be uniform across countries.

It is important to note some of the limitations of the key ratios. None alone or in combination is sufficient to predict a country's future debt servicing capability, as they leave out certain important qualitative aspects such as the nature of economic management, discussed above, the quality of debt management, political stability, etc. Moreover, a government can alter the underlying data to reflect better conditions than exist; after all, it is the source of most data. Some ratios conceal key information, such as timeframes, or the dynamic element. Finally, there is no standard interpretation as to whether the level of a ratio or other indicator is in fact high or low, as the answer always depends on the size of the country's economy, the level of economic development, the structure of the economy, and similar factors.

Noneconomic Factors

These factors encompass the legal and social environment of a host country, with the main consideration being political risk, especially political stability. The issue is the possibility of changes that shift the rules of the game that underlie the decision to invest and affect the ability to repay. It is important to remember that political risks are not inherently negative, and, moreover, their actual impact may vary depending on the timeframe. Many people feared what would happen in Yugoslavia when Marshall Tito died, and his increasing age and illness caused considerable uncertainty and tension. At the time of his death, political risk was a paramount concern. For example, would his successors choose—or be able—to maintain a relatively open door to the West? In the long run, the transition was smooth, and the basic premises on which investors had based their decisions remained stable. Similarly, external political threats can be destructive, or can pull a divided nation together in a spirit of cooperation and sacrifice.

With respect to the political system, specific issues include the following: How is a change in leadership handled? Has the country had one autocratic ruler, and what will be the effect of his departure from office? How does the political system handle change? Does the executive leadership have the strength to impose its will on the legislature? Is there a sense of nationhood, or is the country an uncomfortable union of antagonistic ethnic, religious, and tribal entities? And is there conflict between older and younger gen-erations? Finally, there is the matter of political geography: Does the central government have control over the entire country? What holds the different regions and countries together? What are relations with neighboring coun-tries—are there territorial disputes, affinities of social groups split by arti-ficial boundaries established by colonial powers? And what role do the major powers play?

As to social factors, such as culture, habits, and environmental charac-teristics, they are particularly pertinent to areas of the world that fall in the moderate- and high-risk category, such as Africa and the Middle East. One important aspect of a country is traditional values: what they are, the extent to which they are influential, and the tension between them and more mod-ern values. Certainly a dominant value has been religion, which has emerged as a critical and very explosive force in many developing regions.

Finally, there is the question of natural environmental factors, again a prominent issue in many of the low- and moderate-risk countries, which seem to be in danger zones and are less able to deal with disasters. While drought is a problem even in the industrial world, its impact there is far less because of the diversified economic base of most countries and their better external financial position that allows the import of foodstuffs with-out serious economic repercussions. In countries closer to the margin of economic survival, a drought can cut off the sole source of foreign exchange earnings and drain foreign exchange reserves as foodstuffs have to be im-ported. In countries afflicted by prolonged drought, where large segments of the population, especially young people, are facing chronic malnutrition, there is concern about the development potential of the human resource base and its effect on future economic growth. Again, natural disasters are not per se negative from the perspective of the international banker. It depends on who and what are affected, when and where the disaster hap-pens, and how long it lasts.

CARRYING OUT COUNTRY RISK ASSESSMENTS

As noted, several general approaches to country risk assessment have evolved over the last three decades. The initial one was largely selective and qualitative—the gut feelings of those familiar with a certain location. How-ever, institutions soon moved to a far more quantitative and objective ap-proach, facilitated by advances in computers and econometric techniques and spurred by the mystique of numbers as the source of all answers. More recently, there has been a trend back toward more qualitative input, but this time on a more formal and systematic basis and in combination with quantitative analysis. One reason for the shift has been the obvious difficulty of reducing the human factor to meaningful numbers. Moreover, it proved difficult to come up with valid universal scales for the softer factors, so that comparisons were difficult. Finally, numbers can be misleading.

Resource Requirements

One difficulty with country risk assessment is its cost in terms of time, manpower, and money. Even the largest banks cannot carry out full assessments for each country in which they do business. Therefore, banks employ assessments of different scope and are selective in terms of the countries reviewed. Generally, the approach is to categorize countries broadly into high-, moderate-, and low-risk. The last group, which includes the industrial world, is subject to very little review, while the first does not figure prominently in private bank lending. Most of the attention is therefore on the middle group, which includes mainly developing countries. Even this category includes too many countries for complete assessment of each one, and typically banks focus the most intensive scrutiny on those areas where their exposure is greatest or where there is a particular risk that needs tracking. The others will be subject to shorter, briefer reviews.

For the most part, assessments at banks are carried out in the economics department by specialists on the country concerned. However, they collaborate closely with other experts on aspects such as politics or social issues. Frequently they solicit input from bank staff on location or from local experts. Upon occasion, and where the bank does not have the internal resources, outside experts will be hired. In fact, one approach—the Delphic— is to get opinions from a number of outside experts. One advantage to going outside is that it provides a check on any internal predispositions to lend because that is the bank's—or a bank branch's—business. Qualitative information can also be obtained from local publications (these sources are described in a later section of this chapter). Multiple sources of outside information are a good idea in order to provide a well-rounded analysis reflecting divergent viewpoints. For example, the Overseas Private Investment Corporation (OPIC), which wants to sell its services, may paint a more favorable picture than an objective economic analyst.

Methodologies

As noted, for a long time banks and companies were very secretive about the methodologies employed. Even today, although techniques are publicized, there still seems to be a reluctance to piggyback on one another's assessments, despite the cost and time involved. However, there is now substantial information on the more common approaches and techniques banks use.

Two aspects of the assessment will have to be decided in advance. One is the overall methodology to be used, the other the variables to be the focus of the review. To some extent, the choices will be a function of economics and time.

The basis of most country risk assessments is the country study. At one extreme is the lengthy, in-depth, comprehensive review that covers all of the key topics and issues that might affect loan repayment. It involves substantial primary research, with a timeframe of three to five years, the maximum term of most loans. Generally, it includes numerical as well as qualitative analysis. At the other extreme are quick, rough reviews that rely entirely on secondary sources of information, contain little number crunching, and focus on the near term. In between are assessments of varying scopes and complexities.

Many banks employ checklists as a framework for their assessments, with a numerical rating for each factor. The end product is a set of ratings for each risk. If used consistently for all countries studied, the checklist will also yield a set of comparative risk ratings. Another approach is to develop and apply a simple, relevant paradigm as the basis for the analysis. One starting point is an analysis of the resource base for production, including natural, human, and financial resources. The next step is to look at the economic policies directed at exploiting that base, with the focus on how the country uses and manages its resources. Finally, the external financial position is investigated. It is in turn closely linked to the resource base and economic policies.

Another approach, popular because of its relative simplicity, is based on the monetarist theory that if domestic money creation exceeds domestic demand, there will be excess borrowing abroad, and the balance of payments will deteriorate, with the reverse also true. The focus is on the total credit provided to the economy by banks as a measure of the domestic supply of money, and changes in the supply as a result of government actions, which will in turn affect the total credit to the economy and the amount of external borrowing and so on. This approach, because it requires just a few variables, seems easy to apply. However, it relies on assumptions about the relationship of the supply and demand for money that in turn are based on conditions that do not pertain in many developing countries, which are the target of most country risk assessments.

Whatever the techniques employed, the end result should be a good understanding of the key indicators and their trends and prospects, particularly in terms of structural characteristics, and a set of ratings for each country and the various risks. It should give some indication of the relative risks within the country as a whole by breaking out certain sectors or areas by type of borrower, loan, and timeframe. Frequently the analyst may posit several alternative future scenarios and develop a set of risk ratings for each.

Finally, all this information must be made available to decision-makers in a form that encourages its use. The report should be brief, clear, and directed toward decision-making. For example, it should anticipate the kinds of questions that will be asked and provide answers. Following are some guidelines for the preparation of reports on country risk assessments to be used by bankers:

• Comprehensive, timely information on key issues and topics, and avoidance of obvious or irrelevant material (the assumption is that the reader has familiarity with the subject and country);

• Consistency among reports as to basic assumptions about key indicators and trends so as to facilitate comparisons;

• Conciseness, with careful attention to the summary and conclusions;

• Highlighting of key trends, issues, and conclusions in a box (e.g., political outlook, economic policy, trends and prospects, balance of payments, external debt position, and outlook for debt service);

• Provision of clear answers or information on which to base decisions;

• Integrated economic and political analysis;

• Elaboration of the causes for developments and events—what matters is why something happened;

• Support for facts and evidence for projections, conclusions, and recommendations; and

• Small, concise tables, with text references.

COUNTRY RISK MANAGEMENT

There has been a tendency for the literature—and for many practitioners—to limit their discussion and use of country risk assessment to decisions on individual loans and perhaps to setting country exposure limits. Increasingly, however, attention is being paid to country risk assessment as one element in the broader concept of country risk management. More recent literature points out the wider usefulness of risk assessment in many daily operations. Thus there are two respects in which to look at country risk assessment: (1) how it is used for loan decision-making; and (2) the degree to which it is part of, or integrated into, daily operations, particularly strategic planning, marketing, portfolio monitoring and evaluation, setting price policy, setting short-term exposure guidelines, and performance evaluation.

Loan Decisions

With respect to actual lending decisions, the risks identified in the assessment should dictate to some degree whether to make the loan and on what terms. For example, if the political situation is unstable, the implication is that a loan should be short-term. On the other hand, if the opposition espouses basically the same policies and promises more effective leadership, then the political risk, if any, is likely to be short-term, to be followed by more favorable conditions. A record of a certain type of recurrent problem with projects in the country—the government's failure to provide the necessary infrastructure or personnel—may indicate that the borrower would do well to obtain certain guarantees or insurance. The assessment might lead to the inclusion of some contingency clauses providing for certain changes in loan terms in the event of new but specified conditions. For example, hurdle rates can be used where political risk is likely to vary. That is, a bank will identify in advance new interest rates that will pertain if certain political changes occur, thus ensuring that it receives its desired rate of return on investment. Similarly, the capital budget for a project can be based on the level of risk—if it increases, the amount of the capital budget will be decreased. If the capital budget cannot be altered—some projects, such as a major capital facility like a steel mill, do not permit it—then the bank may ask the host government to agree on some kind of political risk guarantee, such as reducing its tax rate. Finally, the bank may seek to structure the loan in such a way as to lessen the chances of certain political risks by increasing their cost to the government. Including other international lenders such as the World Bank or other governments in the project may discourage the host country from a step such as expropriation. The bank could also indirectly retain control of the sale of the output. For example, it could include a private sector supplier in the project who would obtain long-term supply contracts for the output of the project. Should the terms of the loan be abrogated, the supplier would have the right to meet its contracts from other sources, thus denying the project an immediate outlet and shrinking its revenue. To summarize, a bank will seek to maximize its leverage against certain risks by the terms of the loan and by the structure of participation.

Country Risk Assessment and Bank Management

As noted, country risk assessment is viewed today as a tool that has other functions besides that of guiding loan decisions. It also has a clear role in a bank's strategic planning. It is an excellent tool in the development of the overall international portfolio that provides optimum return with minimum risk and with adequate liquidity to deal with adverse changes in the balance of assets and liabilities. That is, it can be applied in structuring a bank's portfolio so that its exposure is not so great in any location or type of loan or borrower that a borrower's inability or unwillingness to comply with the terms of the loan affects the bank's overall profitability materially. When used in this way, country risk assessment goes beyond a review of conditions in individual countries and should result in a comparable set of ratings across the entire range of countries—and potential countries—in which a bank is doing business.

Country risk assessment also yields invaluable information on potential areas of lending; thus it is also a marketing tool. This latter use has been recognized by some institutions but as a rule is not a role being pursued.

Clearly, such applications require ongoing knowledge of conditions in the host country. A key element of daily operations is monitoring loans, and here, too, country risk assessment is very useful, particularly if designed with that use in mind. The initial assessment can provide the framework for monitoring by identifying the key variables that need to be tracked over the life of the loan. It might also indicate how frequently the routine updating of variables should be and trigger points at which an assessment needs to be instituted, say, when an indicator or measure exceeds a certain level. Depending on the outcome of the reassessment, the bank will then need to decide whether and how to cut its losses or whether to institute contingency clauses. Some banks, as a part of their assessment, prepare a number of scenarios in advance and plan their responses to those conditions. As the time of reassessment, they may determine which scenario most closely fits actual conditions and use the planned responses to guide actual decisions.

Clearly, prior use of country risk assessment in international portfolio management requires an established system for the continuous collection of information—and for its dissemination to the key parties. The latter element of an information system is frequently overlooked. To ensure that the information is used, it must be relevant to the analyst's needs and of manageable size. At the same time, analysts and decision-makers need to be trained in the usefulness and application of country risk assessment to their operations.

Another important application of country risk assessment is portfolio evaluation. The quality of the loans must be assessed in terms of spread, maturity, and country risk. One evaluation technique is a competitiveness index—that is, how the bank's lending compares with Euromarket lending. This task involves a comparison of a ratio of the index of the volume of new term lending to the index of Euromarket lending. Another index is that of loan quality.

SOURCES OF INFORMATION

As noted, country risk assessment requires a permanent, up-to-date pool of information, some of it qualitative, some of it quantitative. This section looks at the sources of information other than that derived from the personal experience and knowledge of experts and bank personnel.

The Information Base

Before looking at the types of sources, it is worth reviewing some characteristics of a good data/information base. For one, it is important to make available consistent data—that is, to use data series with consistent definitions, periods of collection, timeliness, comparable variables, and the like, both in terms of individual countries and across countries.

Since country risk assessment deals heavily with trends, it is also important to have access to time series, again, consistent within and across countries to the extent possible. Timeliness of the data and information is also imperative. Any caveats about the quality or quirks of the material should be provided to the user. The information made available should cover a range of viewpoints. Of particular interest is material that provides a sense of the attitudes and concerns of the host country toward foreign lending and investment.

A system should be set up whereby trip reports or other firsthand information obtained by operational staff makes its way into the information base. One step is to alert personnel to the types of information that are needed. For example, what is the current political situation, who is involved, what are their economic and political ideologies, and what are the likely trends? What is the labor situation, for example, number, strength, and coverage of unions and history of militancy, and attitude of the government toward strikes? What is the economic status of the population, the distribution of income, and the attitude of the average citizen to his economic situation? Staff may be asked to acquire statistical and business information that might not normally be available, supplemented by conversations with businessmen, foreign and domestic. Of particular interest are opinions as to the quality of economic management (planning, policies, program implementation, attention to structural issues, and adjustment capacity) and the confidence of the economic community in the country. One ongoing concern is the lack of information on private nonguaranteed debt.

Finally, it is important that users be made aware of or be able to find out easily what is available.

Information Sources

Many banks have in-house information bases and may also have access to an outside data base. Much of their material may be primary, that is, may have been compiled by their own staff. Smaller organizations may rely heavily on data banks and resort mainly to secondary material. As to useful secondary sources of information, certain categories of information routinely provide certain statistical information. International and regional development agencies, such as the World Bank, United Nations, and Asian Development Bank, issue regular publications covering a comprehensive range of topics and data. As a rule, the material is well-annotated in terms of definitions, omissions, and other characteristics. Individual sources are usually relatively consistent and offer time series, but there is often inconsistency across sources. International banking institutions such as the International Monetary Fund, the Bank for International Settlements, and the World Bank provide routine, periodic data on lending, borrowing, external debt positions, and the like.

Most countries publish their own national statistics, generally the basis for the material put out by the international development agencies. Many times they will make the material available. However, it should be used cautiously, as frequently its quality is unknown, and the data may have been manipulated and are not always timely.

Newspapers and periodicals are important sources of both quantitative and qualitative material, particularly the latter. Statistical information is generally derivative of that put out by the international agencies but frequently is in a more concise and usable format. Aside from the documents themselves, many of the larger publishers have their own data banks to which banks can subscribe for a fee.

Many international business and trade associations such as the International Energy Association issue regular publications in their spheres of interest. Generally they offer both quantitative and qualitative material.

Finally, many of the large banks with extensive international operations publish both statistical information and qualitative analysis.

Among the key publications are: the *Financial Times* and the *Economist*, both of London; IMF documents such as *IMF Survey, International Financial Statistics*, and *Balance of Payments Yearbook*; several World Bank documents, such as *World Debt Tables* and *Borrowing in International Capital Markets*; the Bank for International Settlements' *International Banking Developments; World Financial Markets* of Morgan Guaranty Trust Co. of New York; *Euromoney* and many Euromoney Corp. publications; the series of *Business* periodicals of the Business International Research Society; OECD publications such as *External Debt of Developing Countries* and *Financial Market Trends*; UN publications such as *Monthly Bulletin of Statistics* and *Yearbook of International Trade Statistics; International Aid and Loan Bulletin* of Lloyds Bank Ltd.; and the International Energy Agency's *International Energy Statistical Review*. Other useful publications are put out by the Foreign Broadcast Information Service (FBIS) of the U.S. State Department, which provides summaries of material from foreign media, and the British Broadcasting Corporation (BBC). For opinion and analysis, particularly of political and social trends, but also of business and economics in general, the *New York Times, Wall Street Journal*, and *Le Monde* are excellent sources. For information on commodities, there are *Futures Market Service* of the Commodity Research Bureau of Jersey City, New Jersey, *World Commodity Report, Financial Times* of London, and *Metals Week* by McGraw-Hill of New York.

For background and historical information, the following are helpful sources: *Europa Yearbooks*, put out by Europa Publications Ltd. in London, with worldwide coverage; *Keesing's Contemporary Archives* of Keesing's

Publications Ltd., in London; the *Area Handbooks* of the U.S. Department of Defense; and two publications of the U.S. Central Intelligence Agency, *The World Factbook* and *Handbook of Economic Statistics*.

Finally, it is important to be aware of the limitations of the data, many of which have been alluded to. Particularly with developing countries, the quality of the data is often uncertain, and frequently the information is not very timely. The data issued by the international organizations may be based on extrapolations from outdated censuses, say, ten years old, corrected by other trends and the subjective analysis of country experts. Some areas of information are not available at all; among the key ones are private non-guaranteed debt, the maturity structure of commercial bank lending by country in terms of original maturities, short-term debt, and commercial lending.

THE OUTLOOK FOR COUNTRY RISK ASSESSMENT

There is no question that country risk assessment—or as it is more appropriately termed, country risk management—will increase in importance. The flow of cross-border private credit will continue to expand, particularly with respect to countries that fall into the moderate-risk category. This trend is already underway—as the availability of soft financing from international development agencies has been declining, the volume of private commercial credit has been climbing. Moreover, in general the record of repayment, at least until recently, was quite good. In addition, banks are becoming increasingly sophisticated at minimizing their exposure, spreading the risk, and guaranteeing their assets, thereby reducing their potential for loss. Finally, banks are in the business of lending and making a profit, and international lending is a large, expanding, and lucrative market. Nevertheless, the type of international lending being undertaken today, which involves large amounts of money, complex operations, and returns that depend on a host of political, social, and natural factors in addition to the usual economic ones, requires careful planning and implementation. A foremost tool will continue to be country risk assessment and management.

As international commercial lending increases, country risk assessment will become more and more important and more and more sophisticated. It is likely that institutions will see its various uses and begin to apply it not just to decisions about individual loans, but to the other areas of portfolio management, such as strategic planning and performance evaluation. To some extent, banks are being pushed in that direction whether they like it or not. As a result of the bank failures and near failures in the 1970s, much of it occasioned by injudicious international lending, public supervisory agencies such as the U.S. Comptroller of the Currency are scrutinizing banks much more carefully. One tool they are using to evaluate international portfolios is country risk assessment, and that scrutiny is forcing many institutions to be more careful, systematic, and comprehensive in their lending practices. A logical tool is country risk assessment.

SUMMARY AND CONCLUSIONS

International lending has increased dramatically in the last 25 years. The problems experienced by banks recently have brought to the fore what was increasingly evident anyway—that international lending can be a risky business, particularly in developing countries. One tool that banks resort to more and more is country risk assessment, that is, an evaluation of the risks a country poses over time that might affect the ability of the borrower to repay, as well as the likelihood of their occurring. It also looks at what the probable impact of an inability to repay is, that is, the ultimate risk, which ranges from delayed payment to default.

Country risk assessment addresses the political, economic, social, and natural characteristics of a country. Ideally, the analysis should cover the period of the loan or transaction, as all risks are dynamic. In addition, risk assessment involves a relative perspective, in the sense that a possible event may pose a threat to one sector but not another, or may be long-term or short-term. Similarly, what constitutes a risk in one country might not be so in another.

There are no standard risk assessment methodologies, but certain techniques and approaches are commonly used. The assessments focus on trends, starting with the past and running into the future. They tend to be as comprehensive as possible, covering economic, political, social, and environmental factors. They look not only at the country and project, but also at the global context, since what happens elsewhere in the world will affect the project. Ideally, an assessment will include both quantitative (number-crunching) and qualitative (expert opinion) analysis. Finally, the assessment must be ongoing over the life of the transaction.

Country risk assessment requires substantial resources in terms of staff, information, travel, and time. Clearly, it is not possible to carry out full-scale assessments for each loan. Therefore a bank will have to decide on the scope of the assessment that should be carried out and the frequency. Generally, complete assessments need to be carried out for loans to high-risk countries, particularly where the transaction is large. The frequency of ongoing assessments will again vary depending on the riskiness of the loan, its size, and events at a particular time. For example, if there is social unrest in a country, it may require closer monitoring.

Whereas initially country risk assessment was used solely in conjunction with decisions as to whether to make a loan, banks are now coming to view it as a broader management tool. It is, for example, increasingly being applied to overall strategic planning of investment and loans, to evaluation of the bank's global investment portfolio, and to such operations as marketing.

As to the future, given that the risk involved in international banking is, if anything, increasing, banks should continue to hone and apply country risk assessment to a great many of their operations and management tasks. This likelihood is reinforced by the insistence of regulatory agencies on sounder banking practices and better portfolio diversification and strength. In fact, many regulators are using country risk assessment in their own examinations of bank operations. As such, country risk assessment is likely to become a routine management tool at banks with extensive international operations.

REFERENCES

Abbott, G. C., *International Indebtedness and the Developing Countries*, London: Croom Helm, 1979, p. 312.

Beek, David, "Approaches to Country Risk Analysis Adopted by Other Official Financial Institutions: A Comparison and Evaluation," Federal Reserve Bank of New York *Research Memorandum*, January 11, 1977.

Bench, Robert, "How the U.S. Comptroller of the Currency Analyzes Country Risk," *Euromoney*, August 1977, pp. 47–57.

Brakenridge, Bruce, "Country Exposure, Country Limits, and Lending to LDCs," *The Journal of Commercial Bank Lending*, July 1977, pp. 3–13.

Brown, Collin, "The Problems of Provisions Against Sovereign Debt," *The Banker*, February 1983, pp. 35–41.

Carvounis, Chris, "The LDC Debt Problem: Trends in Country Risk Analysis and Rescheduling Exercises," *Columbia Journal of World Business*, 17 (1), Spring 1982, pp. 20–27.

Cline, William R., "External Debt: System Vulnerability and Development," *Columbia Journal of World Business*, 17 (1), Spring 1982, pp. 4–14.

Dale, Richard S., "Country Risk and Bank Regulation," *The Banker*, March 1983, pp. 41–48.

Dean, James, and Ian H. Giddy, "Six Ways to World Banking Safety," *Euromoney*, May 1981, pp. 128–35.

Dizard, J., "The Revolution in Assessing Country Risk," *Institutional Investor*, international ed., 111, October 1978, pp. 65–76.

Ensor, Richard, ed., *Assessing Country Risk*, London: Euromoney Publications, 1981, p. 172.

Feder, G., R. Just, and K. Ross, "Projecting Debt Servicing Capacity of Developing Countries," *Journal of Financial and Quantitative Analysis*, 16 (5), 1981, pp. 651–69.

Fishlow, Albert, "Latin America's Debt," *Columbia Journal of World Business*, 17 (1), Spring 1982, pp. 35–46.

Frank, C. R., and William R. Cline, "Measurement of Debt Servicing Capacity: An Application of Discriminant Analysis," *Journal of International Economics*, 1, 1971, pp. 327–44.

Friedman, Irving, *The World Debt Dilemma: Managing Country Risk*, Philadelphia: Robert Morris Associates, 1983, p. 239.

Goodman, Stephen, "New Eximbank Country Rating System: An Interim Report," *Eximbank Memo*, June 3, 1976, p. 9.

Haegele, Monroe J., "The Market Still Knows Best," *Euromoney*, May 1980, pp. 121–28.

Haner, F. T., "Rating Investment Risks Abroad," *Business Horizons*, April 1979, pp. 18–23.

Kabus, Irvin, "You Can Bank on Uncertainty," *Harvard Business Review*, May–June 1976, pp. 95–105.

Llewellyn, David T., "Avoiding an International Banking Crisis," *National Westminster Bank Quarterly Review*, August 1982, pp. 28–39.

Lomax, David, "Sovereign Risk Analysis Now," *The Banker*, January 1983, pp. 33–39.

Mathis, John F., "Developing Countries' Foreign Debts: Lessons from Recent Experience and the Risk Outlook," *The Journal of Commercial Bank Lending*, July 1982, pp. 38–46.

Mueller, Ronald, et al., "Assessing Country Exposure" (panel discussion), *The Journal of Commercial Bank Lending*, December 1974, pp. 28–43.

Nagy, Pancras, *Country Risk, How to Assess, Quantify and Monitor It*, London: Euromoney Publications, 1979.

———, "The Use of Quantified Country Risk in Decision Making by Banks," in Richard Ensor, ed., *Assessing Country Risk*, London: Euromoney Publications, 1981, pp. 103–10.

O'Brien, Richard, "Assessing the Credit Risks of the Developing Countries," *Euromoney*, October 1975, pp. 16–21.

Seck, D., "The Assessment of Country Risk in LDC International Lending: Critical Review of the Literature," Theory Paper no. H–80–04, Ecole des Hautes Etudes Commerciales, Montreal, December 1980, p. 92.

Senkiw, Roman I., "Using Country Risk Assessments in Decision Making," *The Journal of Commercial Bank Lending*, August 1980, pp. 28–36.

Shapiro, Harvey D., "Monitoring: Are the Banks Biting Off More Than They Can Chew?" *Institutional Investor*, October 26, 1976, pp. 140–42.

Short, Genie D., and Betsy B. White, "International Bank Lending: A Guided Tour Through the Data," Federal Reserve Bank of New York *Quarterly Review*, Autumn 1978, pp. 39–46.

Thomson, John K., "The Poor Man's Guide to Country Risk," *Euromoney*, July 1981, pp. 182–89.

Westerfield, Janice M., "A Primer on the Risks of International Lending and How to Evaluate Them," Federal Reserve Bank of Philadelphia *Business Review*, July–August 1978, pp. 19–29.

Wilson, John Olivier, "Measuring Country Risk in a Global Contest," paper presented at the 53rd annual Western Economic Association Conference, Honolulu, June 22, 1978, p. 12.

6

MULTINATIONAL BANKING SERVICES

The variety and volume of international business and investment by both banks and their clients have necessitated the development of an equally diverse and highly sophisticated system of financial and banking services. Developed over decades, first for import and export financing and later for an extensive range of other financial endeavors, these instruments are specifically designed to help deal with the complexities of international trade and other transactions. The various instruments, while in essence assuring the seller of payment and the buyer of receipt of the merchandise, also involve two other important functions: (1) a means of financing transactions, and (2) protection against foreign exchange risk (by guaranteeing the availability of payment in a specified currency).

This chapter looks at some key instruments involved in financing—letters of credit, drafts, bankers' acceptances, securities underwriting, shipping loans, and leasing facilities—and at their application. It also reviews the key documents involved in international trade transactions.

FINANCING INSTRUMENTS

Letters of Credit

The letter of credit, one of the most important instruments issued by banks to facilitate international trade, is separate from the sale/purchase contract between two parties. It is a financial agreement whereby the issuing bank extends its credit to a beneficiary (the seller) on behalf of an applicant (the buyer); it authorizes the beneficiary to draw drafts on the bank—or one of its correspondent banks—under certain conditions stipulated in the letter. The letter of credit usually includes only the amount of the credit and its expiration date, the shipping date and the documents to be presented on arrival, a brief description of the merchandise, and the tenor of the draft.

The bank deals only with the documents relating to a letter of credit; it is not responsible for the merchandise itself. However, it usually wants proof that the goods are insured for added protection. It makes no actual outlay of funds until a draft and documents are presented, but has to be prepared to make payment at any time during the life of the letter of credit.

There are both import and export letters of credit, with the difference between them the status of the buyer and seller in the agreement. However, the basic form is the sight import letter of credit.

The letter of credit allows transactions between a buyer and seller to be conducted with less risk of noncompletion by either party. The bank's risk is restricted primarily to the creditworthiness of its customer, since it is agreeing to pay based on rigid conditions specified in the letter, and not against the merchandise. Moreover, banks can, to some degree, hedge against foreign exchange risk and can eliminate the possibility of the buyer's and seller's funds being tied up during the time of shipment of the merchandise. However, all parties to a letter of credit must be diligent in preparing and examining the documentation on their own behalf. And they must ensure that all conditions have been met in accordance with the specified obligations. Any discrepancy found by one party that cannot be remedied could lead to that party's not having to fulfill its obligations, although the others will still have to meet theirs.

Revocable and Irrevocable Letters of Credit

Letters of credit can be revocable or irrevocable. However, the majority are irrevocable, which means that they cannot be cancelled or changed without the consent of all parties. A revocable letter of credit, which is intended to serve as a means of arranging payment and not as a guarantee of payment, can be cancelled or amended at any time prior to payment.

With an irrevocable letter of credit, the bank's sole obligation is to produce payment to the seller upon delivery of the stipulated documents, which represent title to the imported goods. The burden is therefore on the buyer to ensure the integrity of the seller apropos the quality of his merchandise. The issuance of the letter of credit does not compel the seller to make a shipment, and the obligation is on the importer to investigate the reputation of the seller from whom he wishes delivery.

With an irrevocable letter of credit, the bank's main risk is that the credit standing of its customer—the buyer—might change, even before shipment of the goods, as the bank will still be responsible for paying the seller when the latter meets the specified terms. To provide itself some protection, the bank usually stipulates that the bills of lading for shipping the goods be drawn up in negotiable form, with the goods specified as collateral for the bank in the event that the importer is unable to pay his debt.

Confirmed and Unconfirmed Irrevocable Letters of Credit

Irrevocable letters of credit can be confirmed or unconfirmed. Typically, a deal is transacted through a second bank in the exporter's, or seller's, country. If the second bank adds its guarantee of payment to that of the issuing bank, the letter of credit is classified as confirmed. On the other hand, the second bank may only act as an agent for the seller in checking and accepting the required documents. In that case, the letter of credit is unconfirmed. That is, the second bank bears no indebtedness.

Negotiable Letters of Credit

Either because of locale or rapidly changing rates of exchange, it is not always convenient for the seller to present the documentation to a specific bank. In these instances, the straight letter of credit can be replaced by a negotiable letter of credit, which can be presented to any bank willing to act as payor.

Time Letters of Credit

If an exporter wishes to extend credit to the importer, it may use a time letter of credit (also called a deferred-payment letter of credit), whereby the issuing bank promises to pay at a specified date after the presentation of documents. The exporter may provide more lenient credit terms than the bank would but is still guaranteed payment by a major bank. With this instrument, the payment may be due more than six months after sight or date, that period being the maximum allowed under the Federal Reserve Act for eligible bankers' acceptances in U.S. dollars (to be discussed later).

Letters of Credit Payable in Foreign Currency

A letter of credit that is expressed in a foreign currency transfers the risk of fluctuation in the exchange rate from the seller to the buyer. Here the foreign bank pays drafts drawn under the issuing bank's credit without requiring simultaneous equivalent balances to cover. As such, the issuing bank's customer is obligated to purchase the necessary foreign exchange to cover the draft. If the sight draft is denominated in the currency of the buyer, the foreign bank will pay out in the local currency at the rate of exchange at the time of presentation.

Transferable Letters of Credit

Normally a letter of credit may only be used by the account party, but in some instances this party may be an agent who wishes to transfer the letter of credit to the actual seller. Here the issuing bank can make the letter of credit transferable in entirety or in portions to another seller or number of sellers. The letter can be transferred only once, however; the new beneficiary cannot do so again. This provision is particularly useful for businessmen on buying trips, as they can take a letter of credit in their own names and transfer portions of them to sellers as they arrange for purchases.

Revolving Letters of Credit

When the value of a single import of certain goods is greater than the amount either the bank or the buyer is willing to have outstanding, a series of identical shipments can be arranged in conjunction with a revolving letter of credit. This procedure has the advantage of requiring only one letter of credit, as it can be amended to reinstate the same amount after the completion of each transaction. It also serves to regulate the size of shipments. Revolving credits can be cumulative or noncumulative.

Red Clause Letters of Credit

When the need arises for cash advances for the purchase of goods, particularly by an agent, a red clause can be included in the letter of credit. In this case, when the merchandise is shipped, the documentation reflects the amount due to the seller as the difference between the invoice amount and the cash advance. A variation on this letter of credit is the green clause, which is not used frequently. It allows for cash advances to the seller, but requires that the goods be stored and shipped under the bank's control. Only when the bank has all the documentation does the agent receive his commission.

Back-to-Back Letters of Credit

When an agent acts between a buyer and seller and uses the buyer's credit as his own, two letters of credit, called back-to-back letters of credit, can be issued with identical documentary requirements except for the price of the merchandise. The difference between the amount of the draft and that of the invoices is the agent's profit. Any bank issuing the second letter of credit in a back-to-back transaction should carefully evaluate the deal and all the parties and ensure that there are no discrepancies between the two documents.

Standby Letters of Credit

The standby letter of credit allows the seller to draw on the issuing bank if the clauses in the contract are not met. Standby letters of credit stand in place of performance or bid bonds and are often used when money is tight to enable bank clients to borrow from other private and institutional lenders. However, the risks to the bank are high, and abuses of these types of letters of credit have forced U.S. regulatory agencies to place restrictions on them.

Drafts

A draft is a written order to pay a beneficiary a specific sum of money at a stipulated time. It is the document that, when presented, generally results in the final payment.

Clean Collection Drafts

Used to negotiate the terms of an export sale, these instruments are drawn in favor of the exporter on the buyer. In the case of a sight draft, the buyer will honor the draft when presented after shipment of the merchandise. The two parties may also agree on a later payment date. In this case, a time draft or usance draft will be drawn that the buyer accepts on presentation as an acknowledgment of his obligation to pay the draft at maturity.

Documentary Collection Drafts

A documentary collection draft is accompanied by invoices, bills of lading, insurance papers, and consular and other specified documentation. Before the buyer is provided with the other documents, which represent title to the goods, the buyer has to honor the draft by paying it or accepting it. In turn, the seller will not be paid if all the documents are not in order. This system provides safeguards to the three parties involved: the buyer, the seller, and the bank.

Bankers' Acceptances

A banker's acceptance is another important financial instrument through which banks provide credit to customers without using their own funds. Drawn in the form of a time draft, this instrument amounts to an acceptance on the part of the issuing bank to pay a third party a particular amount at a stated time. Bankers' acceptances are fully marketable by the holder. As such, a seller in a trade negotiation can hold the acceptances until maturity or sell them at a discount to an investor in order to receive the cash immediately. Bankers' acceptances are frequently sold through brokers.

Bankers' acceptances are attractive to short-term investors, who then become secondarily liable for guaranteeing payment to the holder at maturity. One source of their appeal is that they are generally issued by primary commercial banks, and their yield is usually slightly higher than that of U.S. Treasury bills. For the borrower, the main advantage is the interest rate: as short-term obligations, the rate for acceptances is usually lower than the prime. Even after paying the acceptance commission to the issuing bank at the time of acceptance and the market discount, the cost to the borrower is usually less than that of a promissory note from a bank. As for commercial banks, the greatest advantage occurs when money is tight and the demand for loans is greater than their supply of funds. By using bankers' acceptances, banks use the funds obtained from investors to make the loans.

Eligible Bankers' Acceptances

With certain stipulations, bankers' acceptances used to finance specific types of commercial transactions (usually related to foreign trade) are eligible for a discount at the Federal Reserve Bank, a provision that protects the issuing bank. These same acceptances, drawn in accordance with Section 13 of the Federal Reserve Act, are also eligible for purchase by any Federal Reserve member bank. The criterion for eligibility is that the financing must be used for goods currently under shipment between countries or within the United States, or for goods in storage. In the latter case, the goods must be secured by a warehouse receipt. Moreover, the acceptance can run no more than six months. However, so long as the market is active and mature, there is no need for the Federal Reserve Bank to discount or purchase bankers' acceptances.

Ineligible Bankers' Acceptances

Banks may create bankers' acceptances that are ineligible for discounting because they are for purposes other than those stipulated in the Federal Reserve Act or because they run for longer than the six-month maximum permitted by the act. The bank may choose to use these instruments instead of a promissory note. In effect, then, it is making the loan using its own funds. Ineligible acceptances are, however, still marketable to investors and are therefore a means of making loans at rates lower than the prime. If the acceptances are discounted, the creating bank incurs a reserve requirement as a result of which it charges borrowers a higher rate than is applied to eligible acceptances.

Shipping Loans

Ship financing is an area of international banking that has many pros and cons. The reason is that shipping, obviously a key element in trade, is a capital-intensive and very cyclic industry. Particularly in today's market, the supply and demand for tanker tonnage versus cargo is in constant flux. Consequently, freight rates are subject to large fluctuations, as are revenues to shippers. With careful management and planning, shipowners can offset losses in slack periods with high yields in boom periods. They can also enter into long-term charters at fixed rates that, during slumps, sustain the rest of a fleet that is operating on "spot" (short-term) contracts. The shipping field is highly specialized in terms of types of ships and cargo capabilities. The focus here is mainly on the tanker trade.

Despite the endemic problems of the industry, ship financing is still very attractive to many banks. Not only are shipping loans larger and longer than most other loans, but they also carry somewhat higher spreads. Ship-owning is also heavily concentrated in a few locations and in the hands of a small number of companies and groups. That feature increases the accessibility of a shipping portfolio to those willing to accept the risks.

A lender making a ship loan has three potential sources of repayment. One is the general corporate strength of the borrower, the second is the vessel's income stream, and the third is the collateral value of the vessel itself. Lenders therefore investigate these three factors carefully.

The character and capacity of a borrower should be investigated through charterers, insurance underwriters, brokers, banks, and other industry sources. An understanding of the legal system under which the borrower is operating is also vital, as is its corporate structure. Frequently shipowners establish individual corporations for each vessel they own in order to isolate each ship from the liabilities of the others. These individual corporations are often placed under the umbrella of a holding company. Moreover, ships are frequently incorporated offshore and in countries that provide attractive tax environments and less stringent operating regulations than in other countries. Liberia is one example. Thus, a lender will need to find out who is responsible for maintaining the vessels (the lender's collateral) in sea-worthy condition, for the ship under charter, and for the availability of excess liquidity when needed. It is imperative that the lender become acquainted not only with the performance potential of the specific vessel and its collateral value, but with the entire shipping conglomerate. Only a complete fleet analysis and investigation of the market, as well as of the borrower, will enable the lender to make a sound decision about a shipping loan.

Multinational Leasing

In an era of credit scarcity and interest rate volatility, leasing has become an attractive alternative to ownership. Given that in the international arena lease agreements often provide for eventual transfer of ownership (at known and often nominal cost), sometimes with accounting and tax advantages, leasing is in effect a worthwhile alternative to borrowing.

Leasing includes many forms of financing that are tied directly or indirectly to asset financing. Leasing is often considered attractive for the acquisition of equipment or other assets, particularly where the equipment is likely to become obsolete. Here a short-term operating lease is an excellent alternative to an outright purchase. Vendor discounts on installment sales have also become more and more appealing as an alternative to a single vast outlay of capital.

The working capital necessary to sustain a multinational corporation can also be manipulated through lease arrangements. The large capital demands created by financing the sale of products from within can be alleviated through leasing. Moreover, additional working capital can be generated by selling existing assets and then leasing them back, with added tax benefits.

The full-payout finance lease with a nominal purchase option at the end of the term is the most commonly used form of lease financing. U.S. accounting standards require that the lessee capitalize this financing as a debt. The majority of the payout is considered a repayment of principal, and only a part of the charges is considered an interest expense. In many other countries, however, these agreements are treated as off–balance sheet financing for the borrower, and in most instances the payments are fully tax-deductible under local law. This situation is known as a true lease. When entered into by a U.S. subsidiary, it is considered as such by the subsidiary but as a finance lease by the U.S. parent.

A simpler form of leasing is single investor tax leasing, in which the lessor provides 100 percent of the equity and consequently receives the full amount of the cash flow generated by the investment tax credit and depreciation. The lessee simply pays rent to use the equipment.

Leveraged leasing is used most commonly as complementary financing for the export subsidy programs offered by most industrialized countries. This type of tax lease involves three parties: the lessee, the lessor (who contributes 20 percent or more of the purchase price), and a long-term lender, who contributes the remainder of the purchase price. Used predominantly to finance high-cost equipment, it allows the lessor to offer attractive financing rates, as the equity is highly leveraged, and to receive the full benefits of ownership. Thus this leasing provides a quick return on investment.

With increasing financial and political instability in many regions of the world, as well as escalating costs for parent companies of multinational operations, these vendor programs are becoming increasingly popular, particularly for manufacturers of heavy equipment. The advantages include the greater expertise of the lessor in assessing the creditworthiness of customers and the obviously smaller investment exposure of lessees in foreign countries.

Leasing therefore is not only attractive to companies looking for medium-term financing, but also to parent companies looking for greater liquidity or reduced risks abroad.

KEY DOCUMENTS IN TRADE FINANCING

Various documents in foreign trade convey ownership of merchandise, facilitate the movement of goods, and enable the countries involved to compute the impact on their balance of payments. They are also the means by which international banks become involved in trade transactions. As such, proper documentation is vital.

Commercial Invoices

The commercial invoice, which goes from the seller to the buyer, states what has been sold, the price, and other information, such as the dates of the order and of shipping.

Consular Invoices

Customs officials at ports of entry for imported goods require one or more export documents to clear the merchandise. Some nations require a special document known as a consular commercial invoice, which must be stamped by the consulate of the importing country domiciled in the exporting country. U.S. officials also require a special customs invoice that is used to compile trade and balance-of-payment statistics. For the same purposes of control, all merchandise being exported from the United States must be included in the shipper's export declaration.

Bills of Lading

The bill of lading is a means of conveying title to the goods shipped and is therefore considered the most vital document in international trade financing. Prepared by the shipping company and given to the exporter, it specifies receipt of the goods by the shipper, the terms and conditions of delivery, the weight and dimensions of the cargo, and the shipping marks of the crates.

The bill of lading also states who is to receive the merchandise at the designated foreign port. If the goods are consigned directly to the buyer, the document is known as a straight bill of lading and cannot be transferred. More typically, however, the seller will instruct the shipping company to consign the goods to the order of the shipper. Termed an order of negotiable bill of lading (and endorsable by the shipper, now the exporter), it requires that evidence be presented at the port of unloading as to ownership of the merchandise. As such, the bill of lading becomes the evidence against which the shipper will release the goods to anyone who has it in his possession.

In receiving the cargo, the shipping company issues a clean or foul bill of lading, depending on the condition of the merchandise it receives. Frequently all parties agree to insure the goods during their passage. It is important that these documents be transferable and that they be written by a reliable company.

Some of the other documents required for specialized merchandise transactions and needs of a buyer are: a certificate of origin, which governs tariffs control; a weight list and/or packing list; and an inspection certificate, which may be required for some goods, for example, plants, to ensure they are not contaminated.

INVESTMENT BANKING

A primary area of business for many multinational banks today is investment banking, with the main activities being securities underwriting and advising companies on ways to raise capital. This field of endeavor has become popular for several reasons. For one, it offers substantial income in the form of fees and commissions, frequently with little outlay of capital. For another, these activities are off–balance sheet, an important point nowadays, as banks are trying to boost their gearing ratios. Where the transaction does involve the acquisition of assets, the rate of return is double that from commercial banking. In addition, securities underwriting offers excellent opportunities for arbitrage.

As always, there is also a downside. The market is very volatile, and exploiting the opportunities requires a substantial capital base, strong expertise, and good management. The competition is now intense and promises to become more so as more banks enter the market at the same time that many customers have become increasingly sophisticated and able to negotiate good terms. Therefore profit margins have declined dramatically. Finally, an important part of the traditional market has not only disappeared, but it is now competing directly with bond issues by banks—i.e., corporations have found that they can raise their own capital, and get better rates, by issuing commercial paper themselves. IBM, for example, pays a lower rate on commercial paper issued in the Euromarket than does the U.S. Treasury. Finally, at present investment banking is a cloudy field for U.S. banks. Many have been entering the field through the back door in ways that, while legal, may not always be consistent with the intent of the law, which is changing in any event, but without any clear outcome or timetable right now.

The Securities Underwriting Business

Two of the most prominent instruments used in international banking are bonds and syndicated loans (the focus here is on bonds, as syndicated loans are the subject of Chapter 9). The underwriting and sale of bonds by foreign governments and businesses has in turn become one of the principal functions of the international divisions of banks.

There are two types of international bonds: foreign and Eurobond. The former are issued by a foreign borrower in a national capital market and are underwritten by an international banking syndicate in the lending country. They are denominated in the currency of the market country and are underwritten in accordance with local securities laws. The largest foreign bond markets are in the United States (Yankee bonds), Switzerland, Japan (Samurai bonds), and Great Britain (Bull Dog bonds).

Eurobonds emerged in 1963 when the United States imposed the Interest Equalization Tax. Companies then needed an international capital market where long-term bond issues could be floated by international borrowers for worldwide investors. Unlike foreign bonds, Eurobonds are underwritten by an international syndicate that is not subject to the securities laws of any one country. They can be denominated in any major national currency or even in an artificial currency unit such as the Special Drawing Right (SDR). The U.S. dollar, the deutschemark, and the Kuwaiti dinar are some of the currencies used most often. London, Amsterdam, Brussels, Dusseldorf, Frankfurt, Luxembourg, New York, Paris, Zurich/Geneva, Singapore, Hong Kong, Kuwait, and Abu Dhabi are the major marketplaces with the technical facilities to channel these funds.

Eurobonds are generally issued in denominations of $1,000 or its equivalent and, unlike bonds in the U.S. domestic market, are in bearer form. Payments are made through banks located in the country of the currency denominated on the bond. Except where the bondholder is a national of or a resident of the issuer's country, the payments are invariably free of withholding taxes at the source.

Over the years, the Eurobond market has developed a strong institutional framework and has become partly self-sustaining in terms of the supply of funds. Moreover, Eurobonds are very liquid because of an increasingly active and strong secondary market. So-called market-makers—dealers who actively buy and sell bonds as principals rather than as agents or brokers—are the foundation of this secondary, over-the-counter market. By contrast, very little trading of these issues takes place on the stock exchanges, although most Eurobonds are listed on one or more of them. Defaults on Eurobonds have been extremely rare, and they are considered a fairly risk-free and prestigious investment.

The Euromarket, besides offering short-, medium-, and long-term securities, also offers what is known as floating rate notes (FRNs). These are securities with quarterly or semiannual interest rates linked to a short-term rate such as the London Interbank Offered Rate (LIBOR). Maturities range from medium- to long-term; issuers include corporations, banks, governments, and agencies. (FRNs are discussed further in Chapter 7.)

The Roles of Multinational Banks

Banks play two basic roles in securities underwriting: lead manager and participant. The former involves managing the bond issue; the latter, investment in the issue. Lead management is the prize, as it generates lucrative fees and prestige. Twenty-five years ago, Morgan Stanley turned down anything short of the lead role. Today, competition for this role is severe.

A lead manager carries out several tasks in conjunction with an underwriting. First, the bank designs a suitable issue of bonds, that is, it advises the customer on the appropriate amount, currency, interest rate, and maturity. It must make sure that the issue meets all legal and regulatory requirements; in U.S. terminology, it must exercise "due diligence." It must also be able to guarantee the availability of the funds on time. As such, it must find the participants and distribute the securities. In some cases, a bank may have to provide short-term bridge financing until the issue is sold. In the old days, the entire process of underwriting a bond issue took a leisurely few weeks. Nowadays it is effected in a few hours.

Clearly, this business is not for all banks. For one, it requires a big capital base. The bank must have a cushion on which to fall back when profits are under pressure; the business is risky; the bank may have to buy the securities on its own account or provide bridge financing; and the transaction is expensive. The bank must also have a broad-based, efficient distribution network so that it can distribute the issue quickly and profitably. Contacts are paramount. Finally, it must have top-quality people and comprehensive, up-to-date information.

SUMMARY AND CONCLUSIONS

As the needs of customers have expanded, banks have found it necessary to provide a wider array of services. Alongside the traditional trade-related credit and payment facilities, such as letters of credit, drafts, and bankers' acceptances, bankers now provide leasing arrangements and securities underwriting, primarily for bonds and syndicated loans. The latter activities, which fall under the category of investment banking, offer substantial off–balance sheet income from fees and commissions, frequently with little capital outlay.

Opportunities in the field of investment banking are likely to increase substantially in the years ahead for U.S. banks, as the restrictions imposed by Glass-Steagall will probably be modified, if not removed. That same process has also been occurring in other countries. It is also highly likely, given the competitiveness in multinational banking, that customers will be able to demand an even greater range of tailored services as banks vie with one another for business. At the same time, all but the largest banks are likely to find that they will need to define their markets more clearly and to specialize in certain fields, in large part because the cost of being a global financial supermarket is beyond most of them. In addition, profit margins in most transactions are now very slim, and steady income may depend on high-volume, specialized business.

REFERENCES

Eiteman, David K., and Arthur I. Stonehill, *Multinational Business Finance*, 3rd ed., Menlo Park, Calif.: Addison-Wesley, 1982.

Rodriguez, Rita M., and E. Eugene Carter, *International Financial Management*, 3rd ed., Englewood Cliffs, N.J.: Prentice-Hall, 1984.

7

ASSET AND LIABILITY
MANAGEMENT

Banks are in the business of making money. Very simplistically, banks do so by taking advantage of profit-making opportunities, maintaining a positive and optimal gap between assets and liabilities, and exercising sound management that ensures solvency and liquidity. At one time, these requirements were relatively easy to meet. Banking business involved a limited range of transactions and services, operations proceeded at a reasonable pace, the volume of business was far smaller, the participants in the marketplace were more familiar and easier to monitor, and so forth.

International banking today is dramatically different and more perilous. Asset and liability management is no longer straightforward, as such events as the collapse of the Herstatt bank of West Germany and the problems of the 1980s have shown vividly. One reason is that the volume of international banking has grown tremendously, and with that trend has come close interdependence among banks in every country. Bad management no longer threatens just the individual bank, but rather the entire system.

The banking environment today and the ongoing problems confronting the industry have led to renewed attention to proper asset and liability management by banks, or the balancing of assets and liabilities so as to optimize profits while remaining solvent and ensuring the liquidity needed to cope with short-term changes in conditions and deposits. This chapter looks at the nature of international banking in terms of the risks and opportunities with which assets and liability management must deal and at what constitutes good management within that context. It also reviews a few of the key management tools available to banks today.

THE INTERNATIONAL BANKING ENVIRONMENT

There are several aspects of today's banking environment that are particularly noteworthy in terms of achieving profits and good management. For one, the types of activities in which banks engage have become far more numerous and complex; banking, particularly international banking, has become a highly specialized business. Two forces have led to this change: investors and borrowers are always on the lookout for new sources of funds and the cheapest money, as are banks, which are also looking for ways to hedge the risks they face. Their efforts have led to the design of an ever-widening array of transactions. At the same time, because of modern-day communications, the speed with which these transactions occur—indeed, have to take place lest opportunities be lost—is extremely rapid, requiring instantaneous decisions. Those same technological advances permit the conduct of business virtually 24 hours a day, with the focus of activity shifting around the world in keeping with the business day in each time zone. And the volumes of business today are vast—many types of deposits must be made in excess of $1 million, loans to a single borrower can run hundreds of millions of dollars, and interbank transactions worldwide amount to hundreds of billions of dollars *daily*. Finally, the market has become increasingly competitive, with the effect of reducing the profit margin on some activities, particularly lending, to minimal levels. While many banks are trying to increase their income from fees for activities of the service type, even here the competition is fierce and the opportunities are limited.

The Risks

While today's market offers enormous flexibility and opportunity for profit, it also poses enormous risks. These can be classified as diversifiable, or nonsystematic, and nondiversifiable, or systematic. The former are ones over which banks have direct control, the latter are ones over which they have no control and whose effects they can only mitigate by proper management and action.

Diversifiable Risk

Within the former category is lending, once a relatively simple transaction. In an effort to maximize profits, many banks, particularly U.S. ones, now borrow in the short-term market (three to six months) in order to make loans that frequently have maturities of one year or longer. That practice poses all sorts of pitfalls. The mismatch in maturities constitutes a funding risk—banks must be assured of a steady, adequate source of short-term funds to cover their medium- and long-term loans. Normally, this is not a problem except when the money markets are tight, but then it can be a serious problem for banks that have less access to funding sources.

Another feature of today's international banking also makes for funding risk. International banks do a lot of their business with one another, a situation that has led to the evolution of a very active and large interbank market. Thus, among a bank's depositors are a small number of primary ones, located in just a few countries, whose individual deposits run into the millions of dollars. Banks often use these deposits as a source of funds to lend or to redeposit in other banks, perhaps in another country, in an effort to earn more money. The withdrawal of just one of those large deposits can have serious repercussions on a bank's balance sheet and profitability. To guard against that possibility, banks need to have diverse sources of funds and safe levels of liquidity.

Another risk relates to borrowers that are foreign, be they governments, institutions, or individuals. A bank may face a risky mismatch between the source of its funds and a loan to a foreign borrower, given the potential for problems with foreign transactions. The bank may not be familiar with the foreign customer or with conditions in his country; neither may be as credit-worthy as a domestic transaction might be. However, that additional risk permits the bank to charge the customer a risk premium and therefore to reap additional profits.

The interbank market (discussed in more detail below) poses yet another risk, what many call the ultimate nightmare. Throughout the course of the day, banks are making payments on behalf of other banks without requiring that they have the money in their accounts (this situation is known as a daylight overdraft). They do so based on the assumption that that bank will settle its accounts by the end of the day. Hundreds of banks are linked through this chain of payments, and at the end of a business day, these overdrafts can amount to over $100 billion. At points over the day, a bank can owe $3 billion more than it has received. The nightmare is what happens should one of these banks default—will there be a ripple effect that ulti-mately brings down the entire banking system? That was the fear when the Herstatt bank collapsed in 1974. Although the system did survive, and has continued to do so, the risk is still present.

Yet another risk relates to the profit margin on transactions, defined as the difference between the cost of borrowing and the yield from lending. Because of the competitiveness of the market, interest rate spreads have shrunk, while maturities have lengthened. These and other factors have reduced the average profit margin to only one-eighth to one-fourth of a percentage point. Several factors are omnipresent threats to that slim dif-ference. One is changes in interest rates, in terms of both their levels and their conditions. With banks borrowing short at one rate and lending long at another, often with a very narrow spread, even a small shift in interest rates where maturities are mismatched can result in a negative yield. As is known only too well, interest rates these days are extremely volatile; they can change 100 basis points overnight.

A similar problem exists with exchange rates. Transactions for the most part are denominated in the U.S. dollar, pound sterling, Swiss franc, deutschemark, or yen, but may take place in any currency or currency unit (such as the Special Drawing Right, or SDR) or may involve more than one currency. Exchange rates also tend to fluctuate substantially, and it is difficult to predict what the level will be five years hence, or even three months hence, when a payment becomes due, relative to that rate on the day a transaction was entered into.

The risks inherent in a single transaction are relatively easy to manage. However, banks are making hundreds of transactions of different types subject to different conditions and involving different countries every day, and have in place thousands more. Each requires a separate agreement and has its own terms. All this activity takes place within a market that is extremely volatile on a day-to-day basis. And all these transactions must be managed as a whole, virtually simultaneously.

Nondiversifiable Risk

Compounding all these risks is country risk—encompassing a host of factors within a country that could affect repayment of a loan, the assets used as collateral, or the guarantee or other conditions on which a transaction was based. These factors include friendly or unfriendly changes in government, modifications in government policy or regulations that might affect the flow of funds between countries or exchange rates, nationalizations or expropriations, social unrest, and the like (these risks are discussed in greater detail in Chapter 5). Similarly, there are other broad risks, such as inflation and global recession, that a bank faces. And there is the risk of natural disaster, a possibility that seems most prevalent in some of the riskier regions, such as Latin America (earthquakes and drought) and Africa (drought and flooding). These are factors over which a bank has no control, although it can minimize and manage them.

The Interbank Market

Much of the nature of today's international banking environment can be seen in the microcosm of the interbank market. It embodies all of the forces at play in international banking; indeed, it is an outgrowth of the search by banks to deal with and profit from some of those forces. As such, it is both part of the banking environment and a tool that banks have created to facilitate their operations and to manage their assets and liabilities. At the same time, the nature of the interbank market—the way it links a large number of banks and facilitates very rapid and diverse transactions worldwide—creates or exacerbates the very risks that banks must guard against. Since it is such a major force in international banking—based on figures of the Bank for International Settlements, the daily volume of business in the interbank market in 1984 was over $1 trillion—it is worth looking at in some detail, even at the risk of repetition.

Interbank Business

Banks carry out the bulk of their lending and borrowing with each other—a practice called wholesale banking—in the interbank market. This market, which links over 1,000 banks in more than 50 countries, has greatly increased the availability, depth, and liquidity of funds, as well as the flexibility and variety of investment in terms of transactions, currencies, and conditions such as maturities, interest rates, and credit risk. It does so in part by serving as intermediary among savers, investors, and borrowers in different countries. It also offers constant liquidity and reasonable prices, even in the event of a market squeeze, because of the continuous buying and selling by banks. At the same time, the interbank market has also reduced the cost of business and the risk of international transactions in terms of maturity transformation.

The interbank market exists wherever there are telephones and telexes, although the focus is the dealing rooms at banks. Certain large banks—about 50 of them—act as market-makers, with the rest following their lead. That is, the market-makers determine the bid and offer rates for funds. (Not all of the interbank market rests with banks per se. Brokers are also very active, providing their customers with swift, anonymous access to a number of banks. The focus here, however, is on international banks.)

Although the interbank market is diverse, activity centers around certain primary locations. London is the major one, but there are other centers—for example, New York, the various Eurocurrency markets, Tokyo, and the Bahamas. Thus the interbank market operates 24 hours a day, shifting from time zone to time zone.

Most trading in the interbank market takes place in the five major currencies (U.S. dollar, pound sterling, yen, deutschemark, and French franc) and involves large sums, generally in excess of $1 million. Other currencies may be involved, depending on the requirements of the borrower and the related needs of the lender. The use of a particular currency is limited only by the volume of trade, any governmental exchange control restrictions, and whatever internal exposure limits and constraints a bank imposes on itself. Maturities are generally short—from overnight to six months. Participating banks characteristically engage in two-way trade, quoting both bid and offer rates. Because of the competition, the spread is usually very small, averaging one-eighth of one percentage point. The rate varies (rate tiering), however, because of the increasingly large number of banks involved in the market, all of which represent different credit risks and volumes of business. Not surprisingly, the largest banks pay the lowest rates in the tier. These primary international banks have been able to use this differential as one more source of profit-making. Smaller banks, on the other hand, suffer from it, particularly in tight markets.

Sources of Funds

International banks have access to a multitude of different types of funds—demand and time deposits, federal funds, repurchase agreements, bankers' acceptances, commercial paper, foreign exchange, and Eurodollars held by corporations, governments, and individuals. Primarily, however, they use standard time deposits or negotiable certificates of deposits. The latter, by far the most common source of funds, comes in three forms: tap, tranche, and SDR. The first two are usually medium-term in maturity. *Tap CDs* have varying interest rates that are based on the maturity, with longer maturities receiving higher interest rates. This pattern conforms to the usual yield curve: interest rates rise with maturity, a pattern that allows banks, which are borrowing short-term, to lend at a profit. However, there have been periods when the yield curves have been negative—that is, the curve has sloped downwards, with longer maturities receiving lower interest rates than shorter ones. Banks cannot sustain negative yield curves for long.

Tranche CDs, which are usually denominated in Eurodollars, are issued in amounts of $10 million or more, typically the latter, with many running $15–30 million. This CD is made up of various portions, or tranches, that the depositor is entitled to liquidate individually. The interest on the balance of deposit varies according to the liquidations. Tranche CDs are a point of contact between the Eurodollar and Eurobond markets, as they fall in between the short-term Eurobond and regular money market instruments.

SDR CDs (as well as European Currency Unit, or ECU, CDs, which are actually more common than SDR ones), because they are denominated in terms of a basket of currencies as opposed to individual ones, provide the depositor a hedge against fluctuations in currencies. The theory is that a change in one currency in the basket will be offset by opposite changes in the others, so that the value of the currency unit as a whole remains more or less constant. The conversion rates are those that exist on the date of original issue of the CD and the date of maturity. As noted, CDs are negotiable, that is, they can be sold before maturity. There is an active secondary market in London. Once sold, the seller loses all contingent liability.

The most common CDs are Eurodollar and U.S. domestic ones. The former emerged in 1966, during a period when the market was tight, to meet the needs of investors for marketable paper. Eurodollar CDs have a higher yield than U.S. domestic ones—about 35 to 75 basis points more, with the spread even wider if money is tighter or maturities longer. One reason is that Eurodollar CDs are not federally guaranteed, and many are issued in London by unknown banks. Because of their greater risk, investors can demand a risk premium, known as the London premium. In addition, Eurodollar CDs are less liquid than U.S. ones, in part because technically they are only payable at the London branch of issue (in practice, however, they are handled elsewhere). Thus investors demand a rate premium as well.

The additional yield from the two premiums seems to outweigh the potential risks in the minds of investors: most CDs are still issued in London, with over 100 banks handling them. Moreover, they are extremely liquid, with active trading in the secondary market in London. These CDs are very popular with institutional investors, for which they may be the only means of raising cash.

Aside from issuing CDs to raise money, banks may trade them as a way to manage the interest rates of their assets and liabilities. This transaction does not affect a bank's balance sheet.

Settlements in the Interbank Market

Most transactions among banks are settled via five electronic payment systems, of which two are predominant. The Fedwire is owned and operated by the Federal Reserve, where all member banks have an account. More than 2,000 banks use it. In mid-1985, it was handling about 166,000 payments a day at a volume of $366 billion. The Clearing House Interbank Payments System (CHIPS) is a privately owned system based in New York. It involves 138 banks, both U.S. and foreign agencies. Of these 138, 22 are settling banks—that is, they clear all transactions of their own and of the other 116 banks in the system at the end of the day. Twelve of the 22 are in New York. If a bank is not part of CHIPS or the Fedwire, it must use a member bank as a correspondent. CHIPS handles about 91,000 payments per day, for a volume of around $277 billion. Perhaps the most remarkable indication of the volume of business, however, is the amount of the weekly transfers on these two wires—$3.9 trillion.

Both wire systems settle all accounts the same day, the Fedwire immediately, the CHIPS at the end of the day at 5:45 P.M. The Fedwire may be kept open until 6:00 P.M. should a bank need more time to settle its accounts. CHIPS banks settle their accounts, including any shortfall, through the receipts they get each day and through normal overnight borrowing of what are called federal funds (as these funds are available at any bank that has excess funds, the term "federal funds" is a misnomer). Generally, big banks are net buyers of federal funds, small banks net sellers. The banks return these overnight borrowings the following morning at the opening of business.

The major difference between the two systems is that the Fedwire guarantees payment of all transactions it receives, whereas CHIPS agrees to pay only provisionally—when it receives the funds from the sending bank. However, CHIPS has not yet failed to settle its accounts.

The other two wire systems are Cashwire and CHESS, both in Chicago. Together they handle 1,000 payments a day worth about $1 billion. There is also the Automated Clearing House (ACH), which handles 2 million small transactions a day equalling about $5–10 billion. The main advantage of the ACH is its cost—one-tenth that of the Fedwire. However, it does not have an on-line system that shows each bank's exposure.

The Risks

As is so often the case, the benefits of the interbank market do not come free; there are also risks. Many are the same ones discussed in the earlier general discussion on risks and opportunities. In addition, the interbank market has an Achilles' heel: the absence of a lender of last resort. As noted, there is a great deal of redepositing of deposits among banks in the market. Should one bank fail to honor its liabilities, it could provoke a disastrous chain reaction throughout the banking system, with no guarantee of a government bailout. This weakness was painfully revealed in the Herstatt collapse. As described below, however, both the regulatory units and the banks themselves recognize this weakness and are taking steps to deal with it.

ASSET AND LIABILITY MANAGEMENT

Asset and liability management must be viewed within the context of the goals of profitability and solvency on the one hand and the risks and opportunities posed by the international banking environment today on the other. Thus the objective of management is to achieve maximum profits while avoiding the risks that might threaten solvency and hence survival.

Asset and liability management can be viewed as consisting of two primary parts: the internal policy and structure of a bank relating to management, and the tools available for management.

Internal Policy and Practice

Some of the same principles that apply to sound bank management in general also apply to assets and liabilities management: the need for qualified personnel; the existence of an efficient, modern department devoted to the specific task of assets and liabilities management; a capacity for effective, comprehensive, ongoing risk analysis; adequate diversification in terms of sources of funds, borrowers (by type and location), and end-use of lending; clear policy and operational guidelines; and competent supervision. At the same time, the nature of international banking adds some specific dimensions to these traditional management concerns, as well as some unique requirements.

Resources

Because of the highly specialized nature of banking transactions and the speed with which they need to be carried out, a bank has to have a team of specialists who understand the full range of opportunities and attendant risks and who have the creativity to come up with new alternatives. They must be empowered to make rapid decisions, within overall guidelines. For example, interest rate arbitrage (discussed below) must be exercised within a few minutes, as that is the duration of the opportunity.

Given the risks—in particular, the very small profit margin of many transactions—the work of the specialists has to be supported by very accurate and current risk analyses. Moreover, many of the hedging positions a bank takes are based on the reliable prediction of certain conditions in the future. Hence, asset and liability management depends on a strong capacity to predict the future movement of interest and exchange rates with a reasonable degree of accuracy.

Finally, the specialists must have access to the bank's overall asset and liability position at all times, since every transaction will have immediate consequences for the overall balance sheet that may require further action. A critical element in assets and liability management is the balance between interest rates, currencies, exchange rates, maturities, and risks on both sides of the balance sheet. Traditionally banks focused almost solely on their assets; now, however, they look to both assets and liabilities and at the relationship between them, virtually 24 hours a day. One reason is that the sources of funds, which constitute a bank's liabilities, have become increasingly important. This was brought home in early 1980–81, when many banks experienced negative yield curves. Moreover, given the small profit margins, it is important to minimize the costs of liabilities. Finally, liabilities in the form of money market instruments offer opportunities for making money. In keeping with this new approach, some banks have established asset and liability management committees that review such factors as foreign exchange positions, funding strategies, level and composition of assets and liabilities, and liquid reserves within the context of the bank's global operations.

The Assets and Liabilities Gap

There are three categories of assets and liabilities: matched, variable, and fixed. *Matched* means that the assets and liabilities are always balanced: the sources and uses of funds are the same, interest rates and terms are the same, and the maturities are predetermined. Thus the bank is assured of a reliable, known positive profit margin. Funds with matched rates typically are federal funds, bankers' acceptances, and Eurodollars flowing through the interbank market.

Variable assets and liabilities have interest rates that fluctuate with general market conditions. The problem that bankers must guard against here are gaps in interest rates, or downward yield curves. Certificates of deposit, federal funds such as Treasury notes, short-term loans, floating rate notes, and repurchase agreements (repos) are generally characterized by variable rates.

Fixed rate assets and liabilities are somewhat easier to manage because the key variables are known in advance. Nevertheless, as described earlier, because a bank also has variable assets and liabilities with varying conditions, it must constantly ensure that the balance between the two—including both fixed and variable—is favorable. The funds in question here are usually long-term debt, capital and reserves, long-term investments such as leases, and Eurobonds.

Based on the results of its ongoing analysis of the asset and liability gap, a bank is constantly fine-tuning the balance to optimize profits and hedge against new risks. In effect, assets and liability management is like a juggling act.

Capital Adequacy and Liquidity

Two other concerns in asset and liability management are capital adequacy and liquidity, in large measure because outsiders base their confidence in a bank on those measures. Here again, the traditional standards no longer pertain in today's banking environment. For example, traditionally, capital has been calculated on the basis of common stock, capital surplus, and retained earnings. Many bankers today believe that that definition is too narrow and should instead include preferred stock and long-term debt, that is, debt with maturities of ten years or more. Moreover, the true test of a bank's capital adequacy is now seen as the ability to remain solvent and profitable while keeping suitably liquid. There must be adequate capital to protect depositors, absorb losses, and cover operations. Suggested measures of capital adequacy include capital to total assets, capital to risky assets, and capital to deposits. There is no standard for capital adequacy; it varies based on the characteristics of each bank.

As to liquidity, if not properly managed, it can reduce the efficiency of a bank's transactions and reduce its earning power. The task as defined by banks is to determine and maintain the right equilibrium between liquidity and profitability. Too much liquidity reduces profits, while too little interrupts the ability of the bank to conduct business.

Traditionally, liquidity has been viewed as an isolated balance sheet item at a certain point in time, or as the ability to convert short-term assets into cash without great loss. Thus it has been measured by such factors as the ratio of cash assets and short-term government securities to total assets, or cash assets and treasury securities and federal funds sold to total assets. Today's international banker, however, measures liquidity in a more dynamic context—that of a bank's ability to acquire short-term funds quickly and efficiently from both domestic and world financial markets in order to smooth out volatile deposit withdrawals and loan demand. As such, the traditional measures have proven inadequate. Instead, more dynamic ones are needed that focus on the asset and liability gap. Liquid investments today are characterized by low risk, easy marketability, and reasonable yield.

Interbank Relations

Because of the importance of interbank activities, particularly in terms of access to funds, maintenance of good relations with other banks is imperative. Often those relations make the difference between gaining access to funds in times of a tight market, and not. For example, many banks seek to enter into standby facilities with other banks with whom they do business regularly; these facilities essentially guarantee funds on call for the duration of the facility. Close relations also afford the information required to identify and exercise some of the tools of hedging and profit-making, for example, swapping, which is discussed below.

Safeguards for Solvency

As mentioned, the system of payments that ties international banks poses a unique risk—that default by one bank on its payments will set in motion a domino effect throughout the banking system. While the likelihood is considered slight, to guard against it, the Federal Reserve has called on the banks to take certain voluntary precautionary measures. The term "voluntary" is somewhat misleading, as the Fed has stated it will not allow any bank that does not institute the measures to use its settling facilities. Without them, the private wires could not function. Despite this element of coercion, banks have shown an interest of their own in setting up safeguards.

One of the measures is for banks to set overall global limits on the amount of uncovered payments they have outstanding at any time. This precautionary measure is called sender net debit caps, with the level related to the specific characteristics of the bank. This limit reduces the total loss a bank could incur in the event of a breakdown in the system. Similarly, some banks have imposed overall and daily limits on the amount of uncovered payments they will make on behalf of any other bank. This practice is called bilateral net credit limits, and they, too, vary based on the creditworthiness and other characteristics of counterpart banks. This measure is designed to limit the amount of loss that would result from the default of a single creditor. Some banks have also set limits on the amount of any mismatch between assets and liabilities in the form of rollover credits. Reserve requirements are also set higher now and have been extended to include certain off–balance sheet items; banks are also holding larger loan loss reserves. In addition, banks have begun to treat funds in the interbank market much the same way they do their other credit lines.

Types of Transactions

A final point relating to internal assets and liabilities management involves the choice of transactions a bank undertakes. Traditionally, international banks have tried to provide a range of services to all customers. Several interrelated factors now mitigate against that approach—the shrinking profit margins on many activities; the competitiveness of the banking industry; the cost of business; and the emphasis on sound management and greater capital adequacy and liquidity.

These factors are producing, and will continue to produce, major changes in the way banks do business. For one, many banks, especially the smaller ones, are now moving away from lending; not only are the profits small unless the volume of transactions is high, but they also affect a bank's balance sheet at a time when it must boost its gearing ratio. Lending in the future is likely to be the domain of predominantly larger banks, and even they will restrict their lending to better risk borrowers such as large corporations or industrial countries. This pattern will be particularly true of syndicated lending. Moreover, in that particular area, banks will vie hard for the lead management role and will try to minimize their own participation. The effort of banks to boost their capital has led to more emphasis on off–balance sheet transactions, which run the gamut from arbitrage and services for fees to the sale of physical assets, with the proceeds being assigned to the capital base. Greater attention is also being paid to operating costs, with several results. For one, services that once were offered free, such as checking accounts or advice on foreign markets, are now likely to carry a charge. Some activities will be eliminated altogether. Banks may shrink their network of branches and other presences in foreign countries. Finally, all but the largest banks are likely to specialize more in terms of the markets they serve and hence the facilities they offer. Again, the intent is to improve the return on assets, to boost profits, and to ensure adequate capital and liquidity.

THE TOOLS OF ASSET AND LIABILITY MANAGEMENT

In their effort to maximize profits and guard against risk, banks have devised a number of tools beyond internal policy and practice with which to implement the objectives of assets and liability management. These include greater use of the floating rate note, arbitrage, swaps, and various option hedges, such as liability, reinvestment, portfolio, and balance sheet hedges. These are discussed in more detail below.

Floating Rate Notes

The floating rate note, or FRN, is an international money market instrument that first emerged in the 1970s following a period in the 1960s during which the medium- and long-term markets were very tight. The use of FRNs grew slowly until 1975, when commercial banks also began to use them as a source of funds. They provide an appropriate mechanism to shift interest rate volatility risk to the depositor/borrower.

The FRN is a negotiable bearer note issued in denominations as low as $1,000, but in overall amounts and longer maturities than is possible with conventional floating rate currency credit. The conventional floating rate CD, for example, generally runs only up to six months or a year. The interest rate on FRNs varies at a fixed margin above LIBOR for a specific period, generally six months or one year, or is set as the mid-rate between the bid and offer rate. FRNs are actively traded in the secondary market.

FRNs have become one of the primary sources of medium-term Eurodollar funds. They are particularly attractive to smaller institutions that lack the credit standing to purchase regular Euromarket funds at decent rates or in the minimum amounts available. Moreover, as mentioned, they are highly liquid. Because of that characteristic, investors tend to view them as a short-term money instrument rather than as a long-term bond, whereas the issuing banks lean more toward including them as long-term funds.

Eurodollar Arbitrage

Even though the Eurodollar market is independent, it has been closely integrated with the U.S. banking system since U.S. capital controls were lifted in 1974. Not only are the assets and liabilities in the two markets nearly identical—bank deposits and loans denominated in dollars—but since 1974 Eurodollar and domestic interest rates have been close. However, there has always been a differential between the two, the reason being that there is always a small difference in the bid-offer spread. Further, Eurodollar reserve requirements apply only to inward arbitrage (see below).

Exploiting Market Differentials

Since 1980, the differentials between the U.S. and Eurodollar markets have been wider, with substantial fluctuations. While some have claimed that that pattern proves the independence of the Eurodollar market, in fact the divergence has forged a new link that has brought the two markets even closer together. Never ones to lose sight of an opportunity, banks (as well as nonbank depositors and nonbank borrowers) have seized on that differential as a way to make money. When banks arbitrage, they borrow cheap in one of the markets and then relend the funds in the other, where they can charge higher interest rates. Typically, banks issue CDs as the source of their funds, so that arbitrage is tied to the rates for CDs. The reason for this preference is that the CD market is larger and more liquid. Banks may, however, also use commercial paper. Banks also arbitrage by shifting funds among different liability categories, a way to balance their assets and liabilities.

The Direction of Arbitrage

Arbitrage can go in two directions: U.S. banks can buy cheap in the U.S. market and relend in Eurodollar market, or vice versa. The first flow is called outward arbitrage, the second inward arbitrage. The determinant of the direction of arbitrage, that is, whether it is outward or inward, is the effective cost of money in the respective markets. Effective cost in turn is based on several factors. The effective cost of funds in the U.S. market is determined by the nominal interest rate less the cost of the Federal Deposit

Insurance Corporation (FDIC) premium, which is equal to one-twelfth of one percent, or 0.037 percent, of *all* deposits, and the cost of the cash reserve requirements. However, because the FDIC issues annual credits or dividends, the actual cost of its premium is actually one twenty-seventh of one percent, and that is the figure banks use to compute the effective cost of funds. Another important point is that the FDIC does not include borrowing by offshore branches in computing its fee. Banks may also charge a risk premium when calculating the effective cost of domestic funds. The reason is that outward arbitrage expands the balance sheet (the acquisition of funds abroad constitutes a liability, the relending an asset). Given the condition of the international financial markets today, banks consider many loans to be risky. The risk premium may run from ten to fifty basis points and can push the cost of Eurodollar funds beyond the point of feasible arbitrage; the actual premium varies with each bank's perception of the risk. Finally, each bank has its own internally imposed constraints. Of late, these have been a substantial concern, as banks try to shore up their now-tarnished image of sound management and act to meet the tighter requirements of regulators.

One set of measures that banks use in determining whether to arbitrage is the financial ratios that measure capital adequacy and profitability, for example, the capital/assets ratio the bank adheres to in its balance sheet. Outward arbitrage is the big factor here, as it affects the capital/assets ratio, presumably favorably. At the same time, arbitrage can affect another measure of a bank's performance—its overall rate of return on assets. Because arbitrage yields only three to six basis points, far less than other transactions, it can pull down the overall rate of return, even though the activity is profitable. A risk premium may further narrow the margin.

A final cost factor is any capital controls imposed by governments, for which there is no set figure. These controls may prevent a bank from lending abroad or limit the size of transactions.

There are also constraints on the liability side. Banks do not have unlimited access to domestic funds at a reasonable cost. Excessive issuance of domestic CDs for arbitrage in the end will simply raise a bank's interest rate and lower its creditworthiness, a price that may not be justified relative to the return. Since 1980, banks have gotten around this problem to some extent by issuing CDs in the Eurodollar market.

It should be noted that the cost of money varies by category of arbitrageur, as each is subject to different regulations and costs, and hence so does the direction in which funds move. Here the focus is on arbitrage by U.S. banks.

How Arbitrage Works

Since 1980, conditions in the U.S. market and the Euromarket have been such that U.S. banks on the whole have found it most profitable to borrow cheap in the domestic market and relend at the higher rates available in the

Eurodollar market. Thus the norm has been outward arbitrage. By way of illustration of how this process works, take the following example. Assume that the three-month CD rate is 10 percent, that the three-month Eurodollar bid rate is 12 percent, that the FDIC premium is 0.037 percent, and that the CD cash reserve requirement is 8 percent. The effective cost of domestic money is therefore 10.89 percent (10 percent plus 0.037 percent divided by [1 minus 0.08]). Since the Eurodollar bid rate is 12 percent, a bank can make 111 basis points (that is, 12 percent minus 10.89 percent).

Inward arbitrage, by contrast, involves the acquisition of funds from external sources that may offer cheaper funds, again generally using CDs. Inward arbitrage is generally exercised as a means of liability management and, as noted, does not expand a bank's balance sheet. Again, the choice of inward arbitrage is related to the relative effective costs of money. Here, the effective cost of foreign funds is equal to the nominal interest rate on Eurodollar deposits adjusted for the Eurodollar reserve requirement.

As an example of how inward arbitrage works, assume that the three-month CD rate is 10 percent, the three-month Eurodollar offer rate is 10.3 percent, the FDIC premium is 0.037 percent, the CD cash reserve requirement is 12 percent, and the Eurodollar cash reserve requirement is 6 percent. The effective cost of domestic funds in this case is 11.41 percent (10 percent plus 0.037 percent divided by [1 minus 0.12]); the effective cost of external funds is 10.96 percent (10.3 divided by [1 minus 0.06]). Even though the nominal cost of Eurodollar funds is 30 basis points higher than the nominal cost of domestic funds, the effective cost is 44 basis points lower than the effective cost of domestic funds. Therefore U.S. banks will have an incentive to obtain Eurodollars from their offshore branches in lieu of issuing CDs. This shift will put upward pressure on the CD rate (10.61 percent) until the effective costs are equalized (given those rates, at 11.29 percent). Thus the differential between the Eurodollar and domestic rates will have widened from 30 to 71 basis points as a result of bank arbitrage.

Clearly, the effective costs of money vary over time in every market and will affect the desirability and nature of the arbitrage. For example, there was downward pressure on Eurodollar rates during the oil shocks of 1973 and 1979, and upward pressure during the Herstatt and Franklin National Bank crises.

Note that three assumptions are implicit in this arbitrage: (1) the external return is greater than the effective cost; (2) the external return is greater than the domestic return; and (3) the bank can raise money through CDs or commercial paper (notes payable). When one of these assumptions no longer holds, arbitrage activity will cease.

Banks have also used the Eurodollar market to make the changes in their assets and liabilities that result in the optimum balance and maximum profit. A bank may issue new domestic CDs in order to replace some interbank Eurodollar liabilities. This arbitrage is less usual, however. Doing so requires a major change in the operations of a branch, and that would run counter to the substantial autonomy that branches have in running their operations.

The major multinational banks now engage in arbitrage every day in large volumes. The opportunity, while frequent, is also fleeting. Arbitrage quickly narrows the differential between domestic and Eurodollar interest rates; in fact, it serves to establish the upper and lower limits. (It does not, however, in and of itself determine the level of interest rates.) The speed with which the gap closes requires that banks move fast.

Either because of arbitrage or other conditions, the spread in rates may not be large enough to justify the transaction; that range is called the arbitrage tunnel. It depends mainly on the level of domestic interest rates and of the reserve requirements on CD and Eurodollar liabilities.

Swap Financing Techniques

Swap financing is an instrument that involves an exchange between two parties of certain elements of their assets and liabilities, such as currencies or interest rates, so that each party ends up with more desirable elements. International banks, for example, make the following swaps:

From	To	Currency
Fixed interest	Floating interest	Different
Floating interest	Floating interest	Different
Floating interest	Fixed interest	Same
Fixed interest	Floating interest	Same
Floating interest	Floating interest	Same (LIBOR vs. prime)

How Swaps Work

Swaps always involve a counterparty—another institution with equal but opposite needs that wants to exchange positions. For example, company A may have a bank loan in dollars with a floating interest rate set at the LIBOR plus 3.4 percent, whereas it wants that debt at a fixed cost for five years (that is, to have a fixed interest rate for five years). Bank B, by contrast, wants to generate long-term floating rate funds that it can relend for five-year periods, rather than financing that lending by tapping the short-term interbank market. Thus company A and bank B have equal but opposite needs.

The two institutions can enter into an agreement to swap interest rates as follows. Bank B issues a five-year fixed rate bond, in return for which company A agrees to pay a fixed amount of interest (to cover the coupons on the bond), with the rate set at the LIBOR plus x percent. In this transaction, only the interest changes hands, not the principal, as only the interest is actually paid. Thus in practice the payments are netted (that is, only the difference between the two is paid).

Usually the notional amounts involved in swaps run from $5 million to $500 million, the maturities from one to twelve years. The floating rate indices are the LIBOR, Treasury bills, commercial paper composites, the prime rate, CD composites, federal funds, etc. The floating rate reset period may be daily, weekly, monthly, quarterly, semiannually, or annually. Settlements may be set as monthly, quarterly, or semiannually. The payment bases are gross and net.

Swapping can also occur when one party with an interest rate advantage in one market exchanges it for an advantage that another party has in another market, again to the mutual benefit of both.

Banks also engage in currency swaps to reduce the cost of borrowing and to hedge against the exchange rate risks inherent in longer-term transactions (maturities of one year or more). Currency swaps provide a long-term hedge cover against the risk of exchange rate changes by adding liquidity and contributing to the development of the long-term forward market in the major trading currencies. Currency swaps have developed particularly rapidly of late because the volatility of interest and exchange rates have both created new investment opportunities and enhanced the need to hedge the risks of international transactions. At the same time, the rapid expansion of the international capital markets offers excellent opportunities for currency swapping.

Generally, a currency swap involves two borrowers with complementary needs for the currencies to be swapped. For the most part, borrowers are looking for nondollar currencies, as those interest rates generally are lower. The swap works as follows. Assume the two currencies to be used are Swiss francs and U.S. dollars, with an exchange rate between the two of 2 to 1. The interest rate for Swiss francs is 7 percent; that for dollars, 14 percent. Assume, further, that a potential borrower has good access to dollars, but limited access to Swiss francs, the currency it wants. This situation may occur if an investor is saturated with one company's paper in a particular market and would have to pay a premium to raise funds in that market. The borrower obtains a bond for $50 million for five years, with annual coupons equal to $7 million in interest for four years. The total liability—the amount owed on maturity—is $57 million.

The borrower then enters into a swap contract with another institution that has access to Swiss francs but wants dollars. Thus the borrower indirectly is borrowing Swiss francs at 7 percent by using its access to the dollar market and then engaging in the currency swap.

Once again, there are risks to this transaction. The dollar borrower is still obligated to repay the dollar loan on maturity, regardless of whether the counterparty repays it the dollars. And the borrower has no guarantee that the value of the dollar will not change unfavorably in relation to the

Swiss francs in the period of the loan. To hedge against the latter risk, the borrower can enter into a long-term forward exchange contract that ensures the availability of the required dollars at the due date of the loan in exchange for its Swiss francs. As to the possibility of default by the counterparty, the only option is to run a thorough credit check.

In the case of a fixed rate currency swap, assume that company A has an outstanding Eurobond issue denominated in deutschemarks that it wants to swap into dollars. Company B proposes that it issue a fixed rate dollar bond and swap it into deutschemarks. Company A then sells its deutschemarks on the spot market to company B against its dollars. Five years later the two companies reverse the transaction at a prearranged rate, which may or may not be the same rate as that of the original transaction. In effect, over the life of the transaction, the two companies exchange only amounts calculated as though they were interest on the dollar or deutschemark amounts swapped initially. Diagrammatically, the transaction appears as follows:

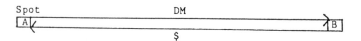

Spot   DM

Notional interest settled annually:

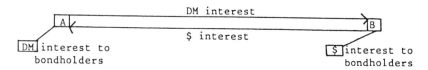

Exchange at final maturity:

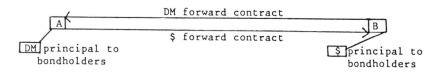

There are also long-term swaps. In these instances, one party will approach a bank and ask it to serve as intermediary in finding it another party with mutual interests with which it can make the swap. The two parties will not be aware of one another's identity. It is acceptable for the bank to bring together two institutions both of which have Baa ratings. Combining a Baa and an AAA rating is not, however, acceptable. A distinguishing feature of long-term swaps is that the bank assumes the credit risk. Otherwise the swap proceeds as usual.

Banks earn healthy fees for arranging swaps and assuming the credit risk: from 25 to 50 basis points. Citibank has developed particular expertise in long-term swaps and is considered the lead bank in this area. Other banks that earn major income from this type of transaction are Morgan Guaranty, Paribas, Bankers Trust, Salomon Brothers, Goldman Sachs, and Credit Suisse–First Boston.

From the perspective of the swappers, it is obviously important to choose a good intermediary. Desirable characteristics are: the ability to match reliable counterparties; expertise in structuring the transaction; assurance of confidentiality; capacity to absorb the credit risk of the counterparty; and flexibility and speed of response. Also critical is an ability to manage large temporary risk positions in a variety of currencies when there is no immediately available counterparty.

The Participants

As the popularity of currency swaps has grown, so has the range of participants. Initially this activity involved only multinational corporations. Now, however, it encompasses commercial banks, financial institutions, and organizations such as the World Bank. In fact, the bulk of the swaps today involve financial institutions and banks.

Since 1981, the World Bank has been engaging heavily in currency swaps. As the Bank funds most of its activities by borrowing, it has a massive need for funds. It is always looking for ways to broaden the scope of its lending and to diversify its markets. Clearly, it wants to obtain its financing at the lowest possible cost. At present, interest rates on such currencies as the deutschemark, yen, and Swiss franc have been far lower than those for the dollar. However, access to those currencies has been constrained for the World Bank, and it has therefore resorted to currency swaps.

The initial opportunity involved several major U.S. corporations that wanted to hedge or cover themselves against changes in exchange rates in nondollar currencies in which their long-term loans were denominated. To do so, they were seeking to convert to dollars. They found a willing partner in the World Bank. Both parties thus obtained the desired currencies without having to resort to any capital market.

The World Bank's aim is to borrow 30 percent of its funds in nondollar currencies through currency swaps. Interestingly, since it has used this instrument, the average cost of its borrowing has dropped from 10 percent to 8.72 percent. The reason is that it has used this instrument to obtain currencies for which nominal interest rates are low, such as Swiss francs and yen. The savings per swap have ranged from 25 to 100 basis points. The Bank does not feel that exchange rates will move sufficiently over the term of the forward contracts to wipe out or exceed the gain from the lower interest rates.

One advantage to the currency swap is its greater certainty and lower cost in comparison with other alternatives. A further point is that the currency swap also offers an opportunity for arbitrage. That opportunity exists at one level because equally creditworthy borrowers, such as the World

Bank and major U.S. corporations, still pay markedly different interest rates in the same markets. These counterparties can swap their respective lower-cost borrowings to mutual advantage. Arbitrage opportunities have also grown up around the funding activities of non-dollar-based commercial banks that want cheap floating-rate dollars. They engage in swaps with other foreign banks looking for fixed rate deutschemarks or Swiss francs.

As with everything, there are limits on swaps. Although they are commonly thought to be driven by interest rates, in fact they are driven by differentials in creditworthiness within markets, not between them.

Option Hedges

A *liability* hedge can be used to protect against changes in interest rates where a bank is borrowing short-term and lending longer-term. If the funding source is a CD, the bank can lock in the cost at the appropriate time by selling, or taking a short position, in CD or Treasury bill futures, with delivery months corresponding to the CD maturity. Should the rates increase, the bank will profit from its futures position, a benefit that will substantially offset the higher funding costs. Should the rates decline, even though the bank has to pay additional margins on its futures position, it will have a corresponding savings on its funding costs.

The *reinvestment* hedge is used in cases where a bank can benefit from a fixed rate of return on a future loan or investment, as opposed to a floating rate. For example, if a bank has a bond or other investment security that is about to mature and prevailing rates are attractive, it may wish to lock in that currently available yield for reinvestment of the proceeds. It can do so by buying, or taking a long position, in Treasury bills, Treasury bonds, or domestic CD futures, with a delivery month matching the maturity date of the investment security. It can pursue the same strategy in issuing a loan commitment at a rate to be fixed in relation to market rates in the future. The long futures position in effect serves as a temporary substitute for the future loan and locks in a return that preserves a profitable spread between the liability cost and the expected loan yield.

The *portfolio* hedge provides cover against sustained periods of high interest rates, which can have a drastic effect on the value of bonds and other fixed rate assets. To protect its assets portfolio against this situation, a bank can sell, or take a short position, in financial futures. If interest rates rise, the bank obtains profits in the futures market that offset the losses in the value of portfolio assets.

The *balance sheet* hedge is used to cover the net interest rate risk that results from mismatches between maturity dates and rate sensitivities of all assets and liabilities on the balance sheet. As part of overall asset and liability management, the bank measures the gap between maturity dates and interest rate sensitivities of its assets and liabilities, and then establishes a futures position to offset the net exposure to rate fluctuations. By way of example, if a bank has a gap consisting of long-term fixed rate assets unmatched against fixed rate liabilities, the appropriate hedging strategy is to take a short futures position to fix an offsetting liability cost.

SUMMARY AND CONCLUSIONS

The international banking environment today is far more risky than in the past. The reasons include the high volume of operations and low profit spreads, the close interlinkages of banks worldwide, the amount of speculative transactions, the sheer speed with which business takes place, and the variety of activities in which banks engage around the world. This riskiness became all too apparent in the early 1980s, when a number of developing countries found themselves unable to meet the repayment terms of their loans. That crisis is still continuing, and banks have found themselves with a massive amount of problem loans.

Both their own concern about the soundness of their operations and the scrutiny of regulators have led banks to pay close attention to assets and liabilities management, or the maintenance of a positive gap between the two sides of the balance sheet in terms of interest rates, currencies, and maturities, along with adequate liquidity to withstand sudden changes in deposits, problems with loan repayments, or other adverse conditions. Basically, the focus is on fixed and variable assets and liabilities.

Many of the principles underlying good management in general apply to assets and liabilities management as well, for example, the need for highly qualified personnel, good information, and clear guidelines and policy. Other features are distinct: the importance of ongoing analysis of a bank's overall, or global, assets and liabilities position at any time of the day, the need constantly to fine-tune the balance sheet, and the necessity to maintain adequate capital and liquidity. Banks have also been establishing safeguards that would limit their potential loss should certain events take place. For example, they have set ceilings on the amount of uncovered transactions they will carry overall or for another bank; they are imposing similar ceilings on mismatches between assets and liabilities in terms of such conditions as interest rates; and they are defining maximum loan limits on the lending to a particular customer, country, or region. They have also begun to favor transactions that generate fee income or commissions and that do not affect the balance sheet.

Banks are also looking to protect themselves by hedging against certain risks. The various tools not only offer a chance to protect a bank's position over the long term against changes in interest and exchange rates, but also offer chances to make off–balance sheet profits. Hedges work in three basic ways: (1) they allow a bank to lock into a certain interest rate or value of a currency at a specific future date (currency options); (2) they involve two parties swapping advantages or desired financial conditions that each has and the other wants (interest rate swaps); and (3) they involve taking advantage of differentials in interest rates and currency values (by borrowing cheap in one market and lending at a higher rate in another). Several common tools are FRNs, Eurodollar arbitrage, swaps of interest rates or currencies, and option hedges.

REFERENCES

"Asset/Liability—Management Systems Available to Financial Institutions," *Mid-Continent Banker*, August 1983, pp. 40ff.

Baker, James V., *Asset/Liability Management*, Washington, D.C.: ABA, 1981.

Bank Administration Institute, *Asset/Liability Management at U.S. Commercial Banks*, Rolling Meadows, Ill.: BAI, 1982.

Clifford, John T., "A Perspective on Asset-Liability Management: Part I," *Magazine of Bank Administration*, March 1975.

Davis, Steven I., *The Management Function in International Banking*, New York: John Wiley & Sons, 1979, Chapter 7.

Dew, James Kurt, "Which Asset-Liability Management Model?" *American Banker*, February 14, 1984.

Gardener, E. P. M., "Balance Sheet Management—New Tool for an Old Problem?" *The Bankers Magazine*, July—August 1983, pp. 58–62.

Goodman, Laura S., and Martha J. Langer, "Accounting for Interest Rate Futures in Bank Asset-Liability Management," *Journal of Futures Markets*, Winter 1983, pp. 415–27.

Howard, D. S., and G. M. Hoffman, *Evolving Concepts of Bank Capital Management*, New York: Citicorp, 1980, pp. 7–27.

Lastavica, John, "Three Rudiments for Asset/Liability Managers," *ABA Banking Journal*, October 1983, pp. 104ff.

Lindsey, Paul, et al., "A Plain English Guide to Asset-Liability Management," *Northwestern Banker*, Part 1, September 1984, pp. 34–36; Part 2, October 1984, pp. 13–14ff; and Part 3, November 1984, pp. 26–30.

McPherson, Edward R., "Asset/Liability Management: A Practical Approach," *The Journal of Commercial Bank Lending*, May 1983, pp. 17–20.

Moskowitz, Warren E., "Global Asset and Liability Management at Commercial Banks," Federal Reserve Bank of New York *Quarterly Review*, Spring 1979, pp. 42–48.

"Putting Asset/Liability Ratios in Better Balance at Community Banks," *Mid-Continent Banker*, January 1984, pp. 42–44.

Rohlwink, A., "How Asset and Liability Management Improves Performance," *The Banker*, March 1984, pp. 41–42ff.

Stigum, Marcia L., and Rene O. Branch, Jr., *Managing Bank Assets and Liabilities: Strategies for Risk Control and Profit*, Homewood, Ill.: Dow Jones—Irwin, 1983.

Ugeux, Georges, *Floating Rate Notes*, London: Euromoney Publications, 1981.

8

PROJECT FINANCING

An oil company in an industrial nation is interested in developing petroleum resources in a poor third world country to ensure a relatively cheap and reliable supply of oil for its domestic industry. Because the resources are in a remote, undeveloped region of the country with a largely unskilled pool of manpower, building and operating the facility will be extremely costly. Complicating the situation is that the oil company recently embarked on another major project that has pushed it to the limit of its credit. Moreover, it is concerned about political conditions in the country, and certainly any lender, if such is found, would also be concerned. Given the intense competition for commercial financing these days, private sector lenders might not be very interested in this petroleum project.

At the same time, the host country wants badly to exploit those resources. Doing so would serve a number of national objectives. One would be to meet the legitimate demands of that remote region for assistance in economic and social development. That objective is doubly vital in that a neighboring country has been trying to foment unrest in order to invade and seize the resources, which it has long claimed are in territory illegally taken from it. The petroleum would also provide a vital source of energy and petroleum inputs to the country's incipient industrial base at a time when external supplies are erratic and constantly changing in price. It would also become a major source of badly needed foreign exchange. Until now, the host country has been unable to exploit the petroleum for lack of funds and expertise. The former is clearly the more serious problem—it has been unable to meet its payment schedule on some large commercial loans and has been ranked as high-risk. Fractious domestic political conditions have made it impossible to implement reforms demanded by the IMF that would also satisfy commercial lenders. Therefore access to funding from international development organizations and commercial lenders is restricted.

The mission of the area development bank in the region is to assist countries below a certain per capita income, such as the host country. However, its hands are tied because of the country's credit situation. Similarly, the development agency in the home government of the oil company sees advantages in helping the country. Not only would that assistance be in keeping with its mandate—and simultaneously silence a legislature very interested in helping this strategically placed third world nation—but it would also augment its own country's energy supply at reasonable rates. Furthermore, the developing country is—or was, until its balance of payments deteriorated so badly—a good customer of agricultural products. However, the development agency cannot finance such a vast undertaking by itself and must be assured of host country participation, a condition that is unlikely to be met, given fiscal conditions there.

This scenario, while fictitious, is not unlike many encountered in the world today. The same types of opportunities—and constraints—are faced by project owners, sponsors, lenders, and governments. In fact, they have given rise to a creative approach to lending and borrowing known as project financing. While project financing can take a multitude of forms—as many as there are creative minds to fashion them—it is characterized by the willingness of the lender to be repaid out of the proceeds of the project once operational, as well as by the participation of several different parties in the transaction in different capacities. As with other lending, there is, of course, a requirement on the part of the lender for security, and the borrower will need to provide the lender strong assurances of repayment.

Project financing offers a number of advantages. Foremost is that it makes financing possible by pooling the resources, reputations, and experience of multiple organizations. Second, it allows the risk to be spread over several parties. The package can be structured to include parties, such as the World Bank, that can provide leverage against certain risks, such as nationalization of project assets. Often the inclusion of a third party can ensure access to an area that otherwise might be closed to a second party. Those institutions involved in the project financing may also structure the deal in such a way as to reap tax and other benefits. From the perspective of a host country for the project, this type of financing package may be the only way to raise the revenue needed to support a desirable development project. As to banks, they have an opportunity to become involved in a potentially profitable endeavor that might have been too large for them to undertake alone. It is also a good way for banks to enter new fields in which they will want to operate independently at a later date.

It should be emphasized that project financing takes a variety of forms, and there is no standard package. The players and their objectives vary, the type of funding varies, the structure of the package and hence of the project itself varies. The goal is to identify the needs of the project and the goals of the parties involved, and then to find a package that best meets those requisites. The two most fundamental issues are, however, coming up with the desired amount of funds on terms acceptable to all parties, and, from the perspective of the lender, obtaining, or, from the perspective of the borrower, providing, the maximum amount of coverage against risk.

Before looking at the options, it is worth reviewing who might be involved and what their goals are in terms of the project itself and the project financing.

THE PARTIES TO PROJECT FINANCING

Four parties to project financing can be distinguished, although any one of them can play more than one role.

The Project

The project itself may be an entirely new entity, such as a corporation, or may be part of an existing entity, such as a subsidiary. Its goal may be simply to make a profit; or to provide the parent corporation a supply of an input or a market for an output; or to obtain for the parent corporation certain fiscal objectives, such as tax advantages; or to enable a parent to develop operations in a certain location that might otherwise be closed to it. The structure of the project can take a number of forms that are, to a large extent, dictated by the goals of other participants and the resulting nature of the financing package. Clearly, the project's immediate goal is to obtain the funds it needs to become operational, and at the best possible terms, which means a fixed low interest rate, long maturity, minimum equity contribution, and minimum potential liability.

The Sponsor

The sponsor may be the project itself or another party that wants the project implemented, such as the project owner. Frequently there are multiple sponsors. An example of the latter case would be a parent company requiring a reliable supply of an input or service, a government wanting to exploit a resource, and an international development agency looking for an optimal project to which to channel funds. Reasons for multiple sponsorship might be for one party to avoid certain regulatory or legal restrictions that it might be subject to on its own, particularly in terms of further borrowing or of operating in a certain location, or to avoid constraints that might be the result of poor relations with the host country or its labor force. As to the financing itself, the sponsor is also looking for adequate financing at fixed, favorable terms, with a minimal capital outlay and liability. It will also be looking for financing that has a finite cost budget. In addition, it wants no-recourse lending, that is, lending that does not affect its own credit standing or subject it to any borrowing restrictions and that does not show up on its balance sheet. Most likely is is also interested in obtaining maximum tax benefits (generally, these are less income tax, certain tax credits for investments, depreciation and depletion allowances, and interest deductions), which are to be achieved by structuring the financing package a certain way. And it wants to minimize its personal liability.

Third Parties

A third party might be involved in a number of ways. One would be to serve as a conduit for or to facilitate the financing. It might be an existing entity or be set up solely to meet the requirements of the financing package. Or it might guarantee the credit by committing itself to purchase the project's output. The third party might be looking for a profitable investment, a market for its own products, a source of inputs for its own operations, achievement of certain economic and social objectives, in the case of a government or international development agency, or certain tax advantages. In terms of its project financing goals, they may be as limited as the security of its investment of whatever type, or they may be similar to those of the sponsors.

The Lender

The lender, depending on who it is, may be interested in the project's implementation in the most cost-effective manner (the case with the project owner) or in purely risk-free profit (a syndicate of banks). Commercial lenders are not interested in equity or venture capital risk; they want credit risk. Moreover, they are increasingly interested in short-term maturities and want a floating interest rate. A very major concern is the security of their investment, and consequently they will require a range of guarantees and assurances against the various types of risk their investment might be subject to (discussed later). Typical lenders are banks, government agencies, international and regional development agencies, export credit agencies, leasing companies, interested third parties, sponsors, insurance companies, and pension funds.

Clearly, there may be a lot of overlap among these parties and who is involved. At the simplest extreme, the package might be just the project and a parent company. At the other extreme, it might involve a project, several sponsors with varying degrees and types of participation, several lenders, such as a syndicate of banks, an area development bank, and one or more governments, a nominee corporation set up to be the recipient of the loans, and a casualty insurance company. The lender may be the sponsor, while the sponsor might also be a third party with another organization acting as lender.

The factors that determine the nature and number of parties involved are mainly the sources of financing available, the way in which the various risks are to be covered, and the desire of the sponsor and/or project and/or third parties to obtain the maximum tax advantages and to isolate themselves from any risks or liabilities the project might incur.

THE LENDING OPTIONS

Having dealt with the parties that might be involved in project financing, the next step is to consider the types of financing. They are equity contribution; debt (straight loans); capital (owner's); stock—common or preferred (notes/debentures, bonds, commercial paper); leases (operating, capital, leveraged or unleveraged); sales, acquisitions, and mergers (straight undertakings on ABC, ACB or ABCD undertakings); and advance payments.

Equity contributions can be dealt with quickly. As with other investments, with few exceptions the sponsor or owner of the project will have to make an equity contribution to qualify for debt. While the proportion varies, a rule of thumb is 40 percent owner equity.

Debt consists, as noted above, of loans. These may be secured or unsecured, but generally fall into the former category. In project financing, the facilities, equipment, real property, and other resources may serve as collateral, or the parent company may have to provide the security on the basis of its assets. Other options are unconditional take-or-pay contracts, in which some party guarantees to make set payments on a prearranged schedule for the output of the project, regardless of whether there is delivery. Generally, the amount of the payments is equal to the periodic debt payments (principal, interest, commitment fees, and other costs, plus an amount to cover contingencies). Production payments involve the guaranteed assignment of a certain amount of the proceeds of the project to the creditor. An unsecured loan is backed by the general credit and reputation of the borrower, but typically it has ratio covenants attached to it, as well as provisions that accelerate repayment or that trigger certain contingency arrangements. Covenants may be written that preclude the borrower from incurring any further obligations or from making any other investments until the loan is repaid. Commercial lenders provide only the most creditworthy customers with unsecured loans, although a project owner that is also the lender may choose to do so.

The other important aspect of a loan is its maturity. As noted, commercial lenders generally offer only short-term loans (one to six or seven years). By contrast, certain international financing organizations and development banks offer only long-term loans (ten to fifteen years). The implications are several. First, the project financing package might have to involve various lenders of different types so as to cover the desired loan period. Second, as is evident, the medium term is not covered at all. In fact, only a few institutions make funds available for this period. Among them is the Private Export Funding Corporation (PEFCO), a medium-term financing organization set up by a consortium of over 60 banks and export companies. It can raise capital and receives indirect guarantees from the U.S. government.

An increasingly popular form of project financing, particularly in the United States because of the tax advantages it offers, is *leasing*. It can cover both equipment and services. Its main advantages are that someone else has to make the equity payments, the fees are fixed over the life of the lease, it is equivalent to 100 percent financing, it may be the only source of financing available because of restrictions on other types of or possibilities for borrowing, payments come from pretax earnings and can be coordinated with the cash flow, it permits the project or sponsor to retain its capital for use elsewhere, and it may offer better terms. On the other hand, there is no residual value to show for the payments at the end of the lease, the project has less flexibility in terms of maintenance, servicing, and use of the equipment or service, the lease is a senior fixed obligation against the project, and the project loses the prestige of ownership. Moreover, the tax breaks that make leasing popular in the United States may not be available elsewhere. Finally, where leasing is used in the United States, it must take a form that the Internal Revenue Service accepts for tax purposes. For example, it must be a true lease, that is, ownership of the equipment must rest with the lessor at the beginning and end of the lease, a requirement that precludes, for example, a lease/purchase plan.

A more obvious source of financing is *sales of assets, acquisitions, or mergers*. In the first case, a key question is whether the revenue from a sale invested in the new project will yield more than the existing operation. It should also be remembered that the return on a sale is not just the sales revenue, but also the expenses and manpower saved from running their operation.

Acquisitions and mergers are ways to acquire assets often more cost-effectively and with little lead time. They are particularly useful where a sponsor does not have a borrowing capacity itself. Through these approaches it may acquire resources needed for the project (equipment, technology, labor, and management), as well as capital and credit capacity.

Finally, there is the *advance payment*, similar in many ways to the production payment. Here a lender, usually a company that uses the output of the project, makes a cash payment to the project, in return for which the project assigns it a set share of the output from its operations and the right of the lender to purchase all the output it wants.

Export credit facilities are also available for partial funding as well as for guarantees of loans or insurance. Most countries have export credit agencies whose purpose is to promote exports. Generally, these agencies offer low-interest (subsidized) loans, loan guarantees, or insurance. They may also offer marketing services, information on trade matters, and technical assistance.

RISK COVERAGE

From the lender's perspective, this aspect of financing is critical—no loans will be made if the risk of forfeiture or loss is too high. It is important to note that the risks a lender will consider go well beyond the potential soundness of the project or creditworthiness of the sponsor(s). They include:

1. The viability of the project in terms of:
   - Its ability to operate according to the specifications of the agreement, that is, a certain output at a certain price beginning at a certain time,
   - The reputation of the construction contractor,
   - The project's ability to handle contingencies, such as cost overruns, delays in start-up, worldwide recessions,
   - The reliability of the market for its output, and
   - The reputation of the technology being used;
2. The political environment of the host country, especially its stability and the likelihood of expropriation (country risk);
3. The labor environment in the host country; and
4. Currency issues such as devaluation or a freeze on the transfer of funds into and out of the country.

There are a number of ways a borrower can cover these risks to the satisfaction of the lender; they can be categorized as insurance, guarantees, cross-default clauses, and nature of the participants in the financing package. An important point about most risk coverage techniques is that they do not require any out-of-pocket costs unless, of course, the provisions of a risk agreement have to be met.

Insurance

The best known type of risk coverage is insurance, although it is not available for most of the risks described above. For the most part it covers only casualty losses. Some government agencies, however, provide coverage against political risk, such as the U.S. Overseas Private Investment Corporation (this organization is dealt with in Chapter 10).

Project Participation

Political risk is also frequently addressed by structuring participation in the project financing or the project itself in such a way as to increase the consequences of delays, defaults, or increased costs attributable to actions by the host country. For example, a major international financing or development group may be asked to join the project or the lenders. If that institution is providing loans to the country beyond the project, its participation affords considerable leverage against political risk. That leverage can be reinforced by including a cross-default provision, in which failure to repay the project loan means the sponsor is in default on all other loans from the same institution. In some cases the loan can go through a development bank that then sells a portion to a commercial syndicate. This approach both retains the leverage of the development bank's participation and facilitates access to the commercial market. Where the host country is involved as a lender, the borrower may also seek to have the participation of the World Bank, for example, with the understanding that decisions relating to its participation will require a majority vote of its directors. That approach provides balance in decision-making, so that no single participant can bias the project in its favor. Another technique is to include local businesses, banks, the host country's central bank, or another agency in the project. Similarly, involvement by the project sponsor's government may serve as a deterrent, for example, where the Export-Import Bank of the United States (Eximbank) is lender and guarantor. In some cases a host country government may be asked to provide a letter stating its intention not to interfere with the project.

Guarantees

The most common type of assurance falls in the category of guarantee, which can take many forms. Under the relatively straightforward direct guarantee, the sponsor or a third party directly and unconditionally guarantees it will assume the debt of the borrower or project in the event of default.

There is also a category of indirect guarantees. The most important of these is variously called a take-or-pay, hell-or-high-water, or throughput contract (the latter where the project involves an oil pipeline). Here the guarantor agrees to make set payments beginning at a set date for the output of the project, whether or not delivery is made. Usually the payments are large enough to cover the debt service and contingencies that might arise. Frequently even these contracts are backed by an agreement to transfer the assets of the project to the lender. Other indirect guarantees include such things as price supports for the output, afforded by the host country government; contingency contracts, in which the borrower or the guarantor agrees to take a certain action in the event that some other condition arises; payment carve-outs, in which the project agrees automatically to pay the lender a certain portion of the proceeds from the operation; and comfort letters, in which a creditworthy, reputable sponsor or borrower states in a letter its intention to monitor the project closely, to allow it to use its reputable name, and to do all it can to ensure the project's success (other reassurances may also be included at the borrower's request). Conversion rights—the right to assume ownership of the project and its assets—may often be attached to any of the guarantees.

Implied guarantees are more informal. They involve the reputation of the sponsor and its desire to maintain it by ensuring the success of the project; the importance of the project to a strong sponsor, for example, because it will yield a reliable supply of some input (this guarantee is called economic necessity); the importance of the project to the host country government; and the association of a reputable name, for example, that of the sponsor, with the project.

Completion Contracts

Clearly, many of these guarantees assume that the project becomes operational. In fact, perhaps the most critical time in the life of the project is that of construction and start-up. It is in these stages that there is the most likelihood of things going wrong and of costly delays and overruns being incurred that can affect subsequent cash flow and profitability. As such, many lenders require completion contracts, which guarantee that the project will operate according to specifications (a set output of a certain quality at a certain price) by some date and for some designated period of time. Depending on the nature of the project, the contractor may handle the completion contract; otherwise it must be handled by the sponsor or a third party.

Guarantors

Guarantors include: the project owner; third parties such as suppliers to the project, e.g., U.S. or foreign manufacturers that provide inputs; sellers; users of the project's output; interested governments and international or regional development groups, such as the Eximbank or the International Finance Corporation; and any party with an equity interest in the project, such as a foreign government or its central bank.

THE STRUCTURAL ALTERNATIVES FOR PROJECT FINANCING

As noted, there are many ways to structure a project financing package, with the driving force being the desire of each participant to meet its objectives, as outlined above. To recap briefly, from the perspective of the project sponsor, the objectives may include tax and other financial advantages; no-recourse borrowing that does not affect its credit standing; minimum capital expenditures; arrangements that are not limited by any covenants or restrictions it faces in terms of borrowing or financial obligations; avoidance of restrictions and regulations that might pertain to it but not the project, if properly structured; a pooling of the resources (manpower, financial, experience, and technological) available from other organizations; spread of the risk; and distance from the potential liabilities of the project. The priority assigned these objectives will vary from project to project and among the participants in the project financing, and juggling them requires creative and skillful designing and negotiating. From the lender's perspective, the main concern is to maximize the return on the loan and to minimize the risk of loss.

The options, with the reminder that several of these may be present within the same financing package, include: an independent corporation; a subsidiary; and joint ownership or control, with the main forms being partnerships, trusts, joint ventures, leasing companies, captive financing companies, turnkey operations, and management contracts.

The Corporation

The corporation is used in two different ways. For one, the project itself may be set up as a corporation, with the financing going through it with the support of sponsors or third parties. While this option does establish distance from the sponsor, it generally precludes others from getting any tax advantages and may, depending on the nature of the risk coverage, leave the sponsor or third party still liable. In many cases, corporations are also set up between the project and the sponsor. Called nominee corporations, they are undercapitalized entities composed of trustees with nominal ownership of the project. The financing goes to this corporation. Clearly, however, it must be supported by other institutions.

The Subsidiary

The subsidiary offers a way to obtain tax advantages and may, if the sponsor is strong, implicitly be backed by an implied guarantee. Subsidiaries can be restricted—limited to certain operations—or unrestricted.

Joint Ownership/Control

Joint ownership/control is a popular structure. It allows interested parties to share the cost, risk, and management of the project; it can be organized so as to afford the participants maximum tax advantages; it can facilitate launching a project at a certain location if one participant is local or has extensive experience and a good reputation there; it allows the participants to pool their resources; it may have the least impact on the credit standing of individual participants; and it frequently allows optimal borrowing terms to be obtained.

Partnerships

Partnerships, one type of joint ownership, can be general or limited or a combination of the two. In the general partnership, the partners have unlimited liability for the entire project, and all their personal assets are attachable. In a limited partnership, each partner is liable up to the limit of his investment or a prestated amount. In a mixed partnership, a dominant partner such as the corporate sponsor may be the general partner, while the individual investors are limited partners. Partners are bound by a legal contract that clearly spells out their rights, obligations, and liabilities.

Partnerships can operate a project, hold property, and enter into financing arrangements on their own. One way to address the issue of liability is to set up a subsidiary to the partnership that enters into an agreement with the partnership to operate the project as a joint venture (see below). Partners can also negotiate with the lender that it have limited recourse to the assets of the partnership and project, although the lender in turn may require take-or-pay contracts or the like. Partners may also require that each obtain the approval of the others before entering into any other loan agreements or financial obligations, with cross-indemnification of the partners or the parent partnership. Finally, there is the option of insurance coverage.

Trusts

Trusts involve joint ownership without a formal partnership contract. Rather, the participants are bound by an informal agreement. Frequently the trust is set up just for the construction phase of a project, during which time it holds title to the project. A trust may own facilities jointly or solely and can in turn lease the project to an operator or operators. Generally an independent, nominally capitalized corporation or financial institution acts as trustee, with limited discretionary authority. The rents are usually guaranteed by the users, the trust's parent, some responsible source of credit, or take-or-pay contracts. The trust, for example, may borrow short-term to finance the construction against an unconditional take-out guarantee of the sponsors, who may need to guarantee the short-term debt. While the trust offers tax and management advantages, it can be a very cumbersome way to do business.

Joint Ventures

The joint venture is a contractual relationship whereby the participants minimize their individual duties and obligations by sharing them. It is set up for a limited period and with limited objectives and is covered by an operating agreement. If one party forfeits, the others can sell its interests, but sometimes they are also liable for its obligations. The participant with the most experience usually becomes the manager, or the parties can appoint a corporation to act on their behalf. Parties to a joint venture do not have general agency for one another, but are only liable to the extent of their investment and advances to the project; they hold property as tenants in common, with undivided interests (that is, the property cannot be divided); and they can sue one another for breach of contract. As joint ventures are not legal entities, they have difficulty borrowing for themselves, but each party can borrow against its interest, pledged as security, or on its own account. Joint ventures may also resort to leasing, with each party a co-lessee with an undivided interest in the joint venture. This structure is often used with mining projects and gas and electricity utilities using a common source of energy.

Leasing

The advantages of leasing were discussed earlier. Leasing may go through an existing leasing company, which may or may not be connected to one of the sponsors, or a leasing company may be set up specifically for the purposes of the project.

Captive Financing Companies

A less common structure is the captive financing company. It is an organization used by corporations that frequently sell merchandise on credit. The captive financing company buys the purchase contract from the parent company and assumes responsibility for collection. It may borrow against its accounts receivable. As such, it can also be used in project financing. If a sponsor has an existing captive finance company, it may use that one, or one may be set up specifically for the project, with capital in the form of accounts receivable and whatever is necessary for start-up.

Turnkey Operations

In turnkey operations, a company, frequently multinational, sets up a project and then turns over (sells) the operation to another company or entity or has someone else manage it. The advantage to the ultimate owner, of course, is its lack of involvement in the tricky construction stage and the easier financing requirements. As to the developer, it will have to arrange the financing itself, with one option a project financing package.

Management Contracts

Finally, there is the management contract, under which a third party runs the project after completion. In this case, the manager assumes much of the risk in terms of the operational requirements, freeing the sponsor from a lot of the potential liability.

PUTTING TOGETHER THE PROJECT FINANCING PACKAGE

Given these building blocks, how does a project financing package come together? This section describes that process mainly from the perspective of the commercial lender. In doing so, however, it will also clarify what a potential borrower must do in order to persuade the lender to provide the financing.

One point is worth noting at the outset. While it may seem as if the lender is in the driver's seat, borrowers do have some leverage. First, the lender will not make any profits without making loans; that is its business. Somewhat risky projects offer more profitable investments in many instances, and the risks can be minimized. Second, a lender may have some hidden agendas that may make it more inclined to lend. For example, it may be interested in expanding into new areas of lending—mineral resource development, for example—or into a new geographic region. It may be interested in developing better relations with a third world country where it is currently operating, but where the government feels it is not doing enough in the national interest. These kinds of factors may give the lender greater incentive to come to terms. Finally, a well-prepared proposal that addresses a lender's concerns is a persuasive tool.

The Criteria for Project Financing

What is a lender looking for in a project? First, it wants to be sure the project will be viable, since repayment is to come from the proceeds of the project. It will want to see that the project sponsor has:

- Specified clearly and concretely the nature of the project and its goals.

- Carried out careful, independent, reputable feasibility studies that look at the economics of the project, the contingencies and the potential risks and problems (particularly cost overruns, delays in project completion, and changes in financial conditions on which the assessment of feasibility is based, such as local taxes, availability of infrastructure, and prices of inputs); reliability of the supplies of inputs, at certain prices, of transportation for inputs and output, and of markets and purchasers; stability and friendliness of the host country government.

- Prepared a plan for the acquisition of equipment and materials, especially if export credit facilities are to be part of the project financing.

- Identified and obtained a commitment from a reliable, reputable contractor.
- Described the availability and experience of the managerial staff and of any specialized labor needs, including during start-up; and presented a valid management and operational plan.
- Described and justified the technology to be used, which typically should be a proven commercial one.
- Indicated how risks are to be handled, both operationally and financially, and where the risk burden lies.
- Presented a carefully designed financing plan, which should include: the availability and source of the required equity financing; strong backing in terms of credit/guarantees; the sources and tentative commitment of additional financing and other support, with any contingency requirements by potential lenders and how they will be met; the financial and credit standing of any sponsors and third parties providing guarantees or other support; and the proposed repayment plan, which should be designed realistically in terms of the project's cash flow and operating expenses and any contingencies that result in additional costs, and the range and nature of any risk coverage.

    Note that commercial lenders are not interested in equity or venture capital risk; therefore the loan request must involve credit risk. Recall, as well, that there is a wide range of options in terms of designing the financing plan. The key is to understand the objectives of the different parties and their priorities and then to choose options that best meet those needs. It is also helpful to show whether the plan has been used elsewhere in the same area of activity or in another one.
- Indicated the value of the assets of the project, which should have reasonable worth.
- Showed project compliance with local laws and regulations and the required government approvals.

Risk Analysis

Once the lender has this information in hand, it will proceed with its own feasibility study and risk analysis of both the project and the country (see Chapter 5 for more detail on country risk analysis). It may request additional information of the borrower and project or may pose additional questions based on its studies. The lender may, if it is, for example, a large bank with multinational operations, conduct its own assessments. It also may choose, and most likely will do so if it is small, to hire outside experts, an approach that also has the value of independent judgment.

Negotiating the Project Financing

If the lender is satisfied that the project is feasible and that the loan is relatively secure, it will proceed to the stage of negotiations. It will want to have all the terms and obligations of all parties spelled out as clearly as possible. The negotiating team is likely to include a lawyer highly experienced in project financing, as well as loan officers and other experts. Among the items to be negotiated will be provisions for lender action given certain contingencies such as nonpayment or delays in payment. The agreement may also spell out a method of conflict resolution, such as arbitration, a commonly used method.

Where the lender is a syndicate, there will also be negotiations among the syndicate as to the rights and obligations of each party. The lender will develop a plan for monitoring and auditing project implementation and for the collection of funds. Further, it will identify the events that could trigger the contingency provisions.

It should be clear from the above description that project financing is not a rapid process. From the lender's end, its review and the negotiations frequently take a year or more. To that must be added the time required for the project sponsor to undertake its own feasibility study and project planning.

WHEN PROJECT FINANCING FAILS

Sometimes the best guide to any activity is to look at the failures and the reasons behind them. By way of concluding this chapter on project financing, it is worth looking at what commonly causes losses in project financing:

Delays in project completion and start-up. If adequate plans have not been made for this contingency, it can throw off the entire project financial plan. Not only is more capital required for completion, but the repayment plan will have been based on revenue being generated at a certain time in a certain amount that is not available.

Cost overruns. These are of most concern during construction and start-up, but can occur at any time.

Technical problems, such as the breakdown of a machine for which parts are not available.

Financial failure of the contractor. As noted, lenders look carefully at the contractor's experience and reputation. Contractors assume a large part of the risk of a project in the early stages: they may be required to provide certain guarantees as to completion, and they may be tied into a relatively fixed price construction contract. Given the size and complex nature of the activities supported by project financing, contractors need considerable cash reserves for their own operations, as well as contingency funds, and considerable experience in estimating and bidding these types of projects.

Government interference. It can take many forms, from those as obvious as nationalization to more subtle techniques such as holding vital imported supplies in customs.

Uninsured casualty losses.

Interruptions of vital inputs.

Changes in prices. Most feasibility studies of projects estimate their cash flows and expenses based on certain price assumptions. In turn, the entire project financing plan is linked in large measure to those same estimates. Changes in the prices of, say, key inputs or transport can throw off the entire financing plan. Nor can the project always raise its prices to adjust to the new costs, as it may be operating in a very competitive market.

Technological obsolescence. Today this is increasingly a potential problem, given the rapidity with which technology advances. The problem is compounded by the fact that many of the activities funded in project financing involve facilities and equipment with long lifetimes, such as a steel mill.

Loss of market.

Expropriation.

Poor management.

REFERENCES

Eiteman, David K., and Arthur I. Stonehill, *Multinational Business Finance*, 3rd ed., Menlo Park, Calif.: Addison-Wesley, 1982.
Rodriguez, Rita M., and E. Eugene Carter, *International Financial Management*, 3rd ed., Englewood Cliffs, N.J.: Prentice-Hall, 1984.

9

INTERNATIONAL SYNDICATED LOANS

Modeled after the U.S. multibank floating rate term loan, syndicated loans involve the lending of substantial sums, with the underwriting and management handled by more than one financial institution. Often the lenders come from different regions of the world, and rarely are they located in the home country of the borrower. This type of loan has been one of the most significant instruments in the world of international finance to emerge since World War II, although its popularity has been on the wane since 1982 except in industrial countries.

Eurocurrency syndicated loans had a particularly prominent role in the 1970s in providing financing for developing countries, as well as for centrally planned economies. From 85 percent to 95 percent of the medium- and long-term funds borrowed by the latter came from the Eurocurrency market, and even today, 50 percent of this type of borrowing is handled through syndicated loans.

Why has this vehicle been so popular? The reasons are several:

- The syndicated loan affords borrowers access to large amounts of money that single lenders could not or would not supply. Common uses of syndicated loans have been to cover balance of payments deficits and to finance the types of major development projects third world countries have been sponsoring. Because of the way syndicated loans are managed, there is also a convenience factor—the proposed credit, which may in the end involve anywhere from 4 to 5 to 20 or 102 lenders (the latter being the largest number ever)—is marketed and handled by a lead manager on behalf of the borrower.
- The syndicated loan allows a borrower new to the market with little credit standing to gain access to large institutions and other forms of borrowing.

- The syndicated loan permits a borrower to try to tailor the loan to meet specific needs and terms through the mechanism of requesting competitive offers that specify conditions the respondents must meet. A borrower's leverage, however, depends on whether the market is a borrower's or lender's and on other factors such as creditworthiness of the borrower and the size, purpose, and timing of the loan. Examples of conditions a borrower may specify are the length of the rollover period, the desired currency for a certain period, and a stipulation that no penalties be imposed in case of needed changes in the agreement.

- The syndicated loan may afford lenders very good profits, particularly if they are the lead manager or part of the loan management group. Further, they can participate in lending that they could not afford individually, and still have funds left for other lending. Their risk is less because it is diversified among all members of the syndicate. Further, a lender can participate with relatively little expertise, as a lead manager handles the technical aspects of the loan. Finally, syndicated loans are well-publicized by the lead manager, and that advertising is very helpful to future business.

THE EVOLUTION OF THE SYNDICATED LOAN MARKET

It is hard to say exactly when the syndicated loan market emerged. In a broad sense, syndications were already being carried out by British merchant banks in 1968. However, somewhere in that period Manufacturers Hanover Ltd. began to transform the syndicated loan from an occasional event into an ongoing business. It is clear, however, that the formative years were 1968 to 1972: the volume of lending went from about $2 billion in 1968 to around $11 billion in 1972.

Certain patterns emerged in this period. U.S. borrowers resorted to syndicated loans a great deal in the early part of the period, the reasons being high domestic interest rates and a tight monetary policy at home. Then in 1971, a reversal occurred, as conditions in the internal U.S. market changed for the better. That shift opened the way to other borrowers, of whom European corporations, the governments of developing countries, and centrally planned economies were prominent participants. Another trend was that the volume of sovereign (government) and sovereign-related loans rose. For lenders, this trend was a source of anxiety, because of the impossibility of performing precise country risk analysis.

Lenders in this period were dominated by investment/merchant bank subsidiaries of large U.S. and British commercial banks.

Boom and Bust Cycles

The popularity of syndicated lending and the volume of business attracted more and more lenders to the market. Each loan was highly publicized in an effort to attract more borrowers. In 1973 there was a major surge in syndications, with total volume almost doubling, at $19.5 billion. Ironically for the lenders, their very success also spelled trouble, for as the competition grew more intense, spreads and other charges came down, and with them earnings. Moreover, as the loans got larger, the management team also expanded, and the management fee, a lucrative source of income, had to be split more ways. Another effect of the rivalry was less prudent lending; the main concern seemed to be only more and bigger transactions.

The boom of 1973 was followed by a temporary bust in most of 1974. In that year the U.S. dollar was devalued twice, while the Yom Kippur war caused a decrease in confidence in the financial markets and in the economic growth of the industrialized West. The quadrupling of OPEC oil prices sent panic through rich and poor nations alike and threw the balance of payments in many countries into disarray. Paradoxically, though, the end result of the turmoil was very favorable to the syndicated loan market—the oil-producing nations flooded the money markets of Europe with their surplus revenues, just at a time when many governmental and corporate borrowers had need of funds to cover their balance of payment deficits and for other purposes.

Following the hard times of 1974 came another boom in syndicated lending, from 1975 to 1976. The terms for loans were once again commercial, as it was a lender's market: spreads were more satisfying (1.62 and 1.59 percentage points), maturity periods more advantageous (from 6.38 to 5.5 years). For their part, lenders seemed willing to pay the price. The basis for lending at this time centered on personal relationships, commitment, and reputation.

From 1977 to 1979, success again brought fierce competition that turned the market in favor of borrowers. Spreads again declined, averaging 1.29 between 1976 and 1977, 1.06 in 1978, and 0.81 in 1979, while maturities moved from the 6.0–6.5 range in 1977 to 7.5–8.0 in 1979. Borrowers realized they could get better than commercial terms by shopping around for the best offer, and they did so. Borrowers also started looking for larger loans—deal size went from $74.4 million in 1977 to $100 million in 1979. In part, this shift reflected a new class of borrower—not the private company, but public and governmental customers. On the other side of the fence, confidence in the Euromarkets was increasing, and senior management in banks continued to value the syndicated loan, which could, because of the high volume of business involved, be used for balance sheet growth purposes. The industrialized world believed it had found a considerable and stable source of long-term, fixed rate financing.

Given the availability of more favorable terms for borrowers, in 1978 there was a wave of refinancings, as borrowers sought to take advantage of declining spreads. In some cases, however, the reason was an inability to meet debt maturity schedules, a harbinger of trouble that was not paid much heed. This latter group of borrowers, lacking much leverage, was often unable to benefit from the more favorable terms.

By 1982, syndicated loans had become one of the most important instruments in the financial markets. The currency used most often was the U.S. dollar, which was used in almost 90 percent of the total financing, with deutschemarks, Swiss francs, and yen making up most of the balance. The main center for syndicated lending was London, but Hong Kong, Singapore, Bahrain, New York, Luxembourg, and the Caribbean were important secondary markets that challenged London more and more aggressively. They served areas too distant from London for easy transactions and marketing. As to the pattern of borrowers, they showed a heavy concentration on newly industrialized countries, especially in Latin America. By 1981, non-OPEC developing countries accounted for about one-third of total syndicated loans.

The Plunge of 1982

That degree of concentration brought about a severe contraction in the syndicated lending business. Lenders simply could not ignore the events of 1980–82; the debt crisis was no longer an abstract worry but a dismal reality. First there was the political tumult in Iran that culminated in a total and violent change in government, then the labor unrest in Poland, then other upheavals and tension elsewhere in the world. In 1982, Poland, followed in quick succession by Mexico and other Latin American countries, announced it could not meet the terms of its loans, which were very substantial. The immediate cause was a deteriorating world economy in which markets for exports contracted at the same time their prices went down and interest rates went up. As most loans by this time had floating interest rates, borrowers were caught in a squeeze—revenue from exports dropped as debt service obligations climbed.

Many lender banks in turn found themselves in serious trouble, particularly U.S. ones that had overconcentrated their lending in Latin America. In the heyday of syndicated lending, banks had vied hard to achieve top ranking among lenders. Now all that honor meant was a strong likelihood of a larger number of problem loans.

In the end, lending terms again tightened, as syndicators felt a need to reestablish, for the first time since 1975–76, a pricing differential that reflected the risk factor that now loomed large. In addition, there was less money available for new business, as the banks found themselves in the position of having to undertake massive refinancings and reschedulings of problem loans and of having to get their portfolios in order. Interestingly, it was at this time that U.S. borrowers turned to the Eurosyndicated loan market in a big way, realizing that only there could they find in a short time the large amounts of capital they wanted.

Thus, despite the problems, there was quite a large volume of business being engaged in, albeit much of it involuntary. One estimate was that only

25 percent of the deals transacted were new ones that banks wanted to enter into. By the end of 1982, the volume of syndicated loans for that year totaled $144.2 billion, as compared to $11.2 billion in 1972.

A New Era of Syndicated Lending

The nature of the market changed in the 1980s. Syndication lending returned to the pattern of the 1960s. Lenders wanted to deal in short-term financing at better terms; the medium-term Euroloan was in strong disfavor. Moreover, banks were looking for negotiable participation so that they would have more flexibility in the management of their portfolios; subparticipations increased in popularity and drew back into the market many of the smaller banks that had left it. Many lenders began to look to the lead management fee as the main and most secure source of earnings. It was a time in which banks in general were looking more to fees as a source of income and to the removal of marginal loans from their portfolios to keep their earnings up.

The degree of caution that entered the market is evidenced by the response rate to invitations to participate in syndicated loans at the end of 1982— less than 50 percent on average, with the range as low as 0 to 25 percent, as compared to 80 or 90 percent in the golden age.

Thus, for borrowers, the market was tighter and more expensive. East European, African, and Latin American borrowers had the worst of it and were often asked to provide guarantees for their loans. The most favorable terms in 1983 were 0.375 and 0.5 percent over the LIBOR, and that was awarded only in the case of the very unusual $4 billion loan entered into by France. More often, the spread averaged around 2 percent. One reason is that banks no longer wanted to rely on three- to six-month deposits to finance five- to ten-year year loans, given the volatility of the market. The Euromarket, then, had made a complete circle back to the transfer of overnight or short-term funds to centers where they were needed.

Another factor in the contraction of the syndicated loan market was the emergence of the Eurobond market, a cheaper alternative that has become increasingly popular with borrowers. In addition, many borrowers have been resorting to the Euronote market, where they can raise funds by the continuous sale of short-term paper at money market rates, and to the floating rate note. It should be noted, however, that the Euronote market has its own risks, and banks have been accumulating huge underwriting commitments. Some regulators and critics feel, as a result, that these new ventures should be included in a bank's risk/asset ratio.

Because there is a smaller supply of loans, and large loans in particular, it has become a lenders' market, and banks are paying far more attention to the terms of credit, including management costs.

Finally, banks are aiming at new objectives at the moment—improving their capital gearing ratios. This objective is most relevant to non-U.S. merchant banks whose dollar business is artificially high because of the rise in the value of the dollar. Many banks now prefer trading activities and other forms of off–balance sheet business, as opposed to new lending. One group is likely to continue seeking syndicated loans, however—the borrower of intermediate credit risk.

THE SYNDICATION PROCESS

Certain borrowers in need of credit may decide to go the route of a syndicated loan because of the amount of financing they want—it would be beyond the capacity of one lender—or because the risk factor necessitates dispersion over a number of institutions. Within the syndicated loan framework are a range of alternatives, and a borrower starts by designing a borrowing strategy and loan structure best suited to its needs and objectives. While clearly the credit itself is the primary objective, a borrower may seek to meet any number of subsidiary objectives, such as access to a certain bank's services in the future, improved relations with existing banks with which it deals, or access to a geographic region it is contemplating entering.

The Lead Manager's Proposal

As noted, syndicated loans are underwritten, in whole or in part, by a group of banks. A first task for the borrower, after deciding on the nature of the syndicated loan best suited to its needs, is to issue an invitation to one or more lenders to bid on the lead management job. The lead manager is the vehicle for structuring, placing, and managing the loan, and a critical element, perhaps the most critical, in the syndicated loan process.

The borrower may issue a general invitation for offers, or may choose from a short list of three to five candidates, or else negotiate directly with one lender. If the competitive bid route is chosen, the borrower has several options:

Open bidding. The borrower solicits a high number of offers. In the past, this approach has generated chaos in the market.

Select bidding. Here the borrower looks for bids either from a short list of three to five lenders or from several that have a speciality knowledge in a particular field in which the borrower operates.

Queue. Not strictly an option, it involves the borrower offering the mandate on a rotating basis if the first lender refuses.

Banks vie for lead management for two primary reasons. One is a greater return from the management fee. The other is prestige and the likelihood of new and repeat business as lead manager. They also want to be seen as being at the leading edge of the syndication business, which is hard to accomplish except as lead manager.

The Decision to Participate

When banks hear of a bid offer, they undertake an internal process to determine whether to make an offer and what offer to make. The process involves an analysis of credit risk, country risk, loan price, lending capacity, and the marketability of the loan. The latter is a key point, because lenders do not want to state they can handle the business and then fail to do so, as they lose credibility. The information from the analysis and a proposal go to the department that approves or disapproves the offer; it may request additional information or changes. If it does not approve the credit, it should give immediate notification to the borrower in a way that will not affect potential future business. Sometimes only a conditional approval is given. Then the task is to develop a bidding strategy, of which there are many, that will balance a high underwriting risk and/or a low return. For example, the bank can aim for a greater yield through an unequal fee distribution (for this option, the bank must have an unrestricted mandate), aggressive retention targets, or a combination of the two. Another factor is the potential for getting an unconditional mandate. If that proves unlikely, then price/return is the key factor.

The Proposal

If a decision is made to offer a bid, the bank must send the borrower a specific proposal. The basic objectives underlying the proposal are to establish the terms and conditions of the loan, clarify as much as possible all the points involved, and stimulate the interest of the borrower (Exhibit 1 contains an outline of the usual content of a proposal). The proposal may be sent by telex, to be followed up by letter, or by both methods. The bank may also follow up by telephone, personal visit, or further correspondence.

Before making its decision, the borrower may ask one or more bidders for further information or details and may seek to negotiate some of the terms and conditions. It may also ask for a market sounding, that is, a test of the market, to be carried out by the offeror.

Awarding the Mandate

As to the basis on which a decision is made to award a mandate, obviously a foremost criterion is the price of the credit facility. However, that factor can be modified by other determinants. A key one is the reputation of the proposer for professionalism and successful syndications, as defined by the

Exhibit 1
The Proposal

As noted, every lender interested in the lead manager role must submit a formal proposal to the borrower. Normally they are structured as follows:

1. Name of the lead manager and parent bank, and its contribution to the final take.
2. Terms—amount to be borrowed, and denomination(s) of the credit and who chooses it.
3. Purpose of the loan—what it can be used for.
4. Drawdown conditions such as final maturity, drawdown times and terms, and disposal of the balance at the end of the drawdown period.
5. Cancellation terms
6. Repayment terms, including grace periods and prepayment terms, interest rate, period of repayment of interest and principal, selection of banks on the basis of which the LIBOR will be determined.
7. Commitment fee—amount and payment terms.
8. Documentation and its negotiation, including the Credit Agreement.
9. Jurisdiction—laws, courts, and guarantee of the right to sue.
10. Management fee.
11. Out-of-pocket expenses—guarantee of payment regardless of whether the loan is placed.
12. Agent bank and agency fee.
13. Syndication strategy—the lead management group and how the money is to be raised from it, the general market syndication and how participation is to be solicited, and a determination of whether the borrower has an option on oversubscriptions.
14. Expiration date of the offer.
15. Miscellaneous conditions, for example, a contingency clause relating to changes in fundamental conditions in the international money and capital markets on which the offer was based, a request that the borrower undertake no interim borrowing that would affect the current offer, that the borrower make requisite information available to the lender, that the proper degree of participation is based on the lead management role and might change if that role is not awarded, and that the offer be kept confidential, as well as where and to whom to send the response to the offer.

---

ability to: place the loan within the timetable specified; negotiate an acceptable contract; manage the loan; work with and maintain cooperation and good relations among members of the syndicate, particularly those that competed for the lead; achieve a balance among the interests of lenders, borrower, and agent that leaves each party satisfied; and earn the stipulated return for the lead bank. A measure of success in terms of cooperation among syndicate members is the number of times the borrower is called on to resolve disputes among participants; it should never happen in a well-managed syndication. In addition, lead managers are expected to commit themselves to underwrite a considerable portion of the loan, although they have the option later of selling down portions of their participation to other lenders. A third determinant may be the borrower's prior successful experience with the manager. A fourth may be the borrower's desire to rotate the job among several banks with which it has close working relationships. Depending on the market, the availability of credit may also be a determinant.

In some instances, the borrower may decide to give the mandate to more than one lead manager. It will do so, for example, if it believes the loan will be difficult to place by virtue of its size, price, or status. Multiple lead managers offer more underwriting potential and more access to other lenders through their network of contacts. In addition, multiple lead management allows the power to be dispersed, so that responsibility does not rest with one institution, and it can result in more expertise being brought to bear. If more than a certain number of banks have a joint mandate, generally they appoint a coordinator or coordinating group.

A borrower may give the lead manager either an unrestricted mandate or a conditional mandate. Under the former, the mandated manager has full authority as to the formation of the management group, the fee distribution, and the placement in the marketplace. Conditional mandates impose limitations on the lender in terms of structuring and carrying out the loan. For example, a borrower contemplating later business in a certain geographic region may require that the lenders include a bank or banks from that area, as a means of entree down the road. Conversely, a borrower may exclude banks from certain regions. The borrower may have liked certain aspects of another bank's proposal relative to a certain function and ask that that bank be included and assigned that function. (There is no guarantee, however, that a proposer will accept a role other than lead manager, given that the management fee is for many the attractive element in syndicated lending.) Other typical restrictions include limitations on the terms of the loan. The conditions may be negotiable on the basis of the degree of difficulty of placing the loan, as perceived by the lead manager. For example, it may perceive the borrower to be a risky creditor, or the size or purpose of the loan may not be attractive, or the terms specified may be difficult to achieve given the nature of the borrower.

Lenders prefer unconditional mandates. They afford more control and a greater opportunity for profit and prestige. Whether an unconditional mandate is possible depends in part on the status of the borrower. Marginal ones generally will not give unconditional mandates.

The borrower may find that no lender is willing to undertake the syndication. At that point, there are only a few options. One is a private placement, a restricted syndication aimed at achieving limited selldowns or at placing the loan directly with a certain number of lenders that are not syndicate members. Having up to twenty banks as managers minimizes the risk, and the borrower may come up with close to the desired final take.

Sometimes a borrower will be advised that neither a private placement nor a syndication is feasible, as the community of lenders is price-insensitive to the deal. Two bases for this conclusion are the creditworthiness of the borrower and conditions in the market. The latter may include a tight, or lender's, market, or the borrower may have entered into a prior loan too recently.

Preparing for Placement

Having received the mandate, the lead bank then proceeds to place the loan. Generally the loan agreement specifies a time limit. How the task of placement is handled internally varies. Morgan Guaranty carries out its syndication business at a London branch and keeps syndicated loans distinct from other business, such as the Eurobond market, for better evaluation and tracking. Chase and Bank of America have more traditional approaches: their investment banking departments handle the syndications. In turn, those departments are split into buying and execution units. Sometimes merchant banks develop a syndication support group of specialists in this area of lending. In between are many other alternatives, geared in part to the market or divisional or geographic units in each bank. In-house politics can also play a role. No particular structure is better than any other; the key is to choose a system that best suits the bank and its personnel.

The lead manager spends the first days after the mandate is awarded largely on internal tasks: deciding on the structure of the syndication management group, preparing lists of potential managers and of general participants, setting the fee structure, and retaining outside legal counsel for the contract. Legal counsel is a vitally important element in the syndication team, and it is best to find the most competent lawyer possible. The team also devises a placement strategy. For example, the lead manager may suggest going for a lesser amount of the loan to make it look more feasible, with the expectation that there will be an oversubscription that will make up the balance. A very critical task is to decide on the formation of the management team. Much of this work will already have been done at the proposal stage, and some of the elements in the plan may be dictated by conditions established by the borrower. As for the structure of the management team, nowadays there are generally several managers and sometimes co-managers, some of whom the borrower may have specified for that role.

The Management Team

A number of factors go into decisions about the management team. One is the influence of the borrower and its objectives—does it want a certain bank included in order to enhance its relations with that institution? The lead manager may also be influenced by such considerations as the best way to get the loan placed—the bank may believe that participation by a specific bank will afford greater access to certain desirable participants. To encourage that bank to join, the lead manager may offer it a manager's role. A third variable is the ability of another bank to underwrite part of the loan. Underwriting is somewhat less popular now, with lenders unwilling to handle that task, and frequently they seek to sell down their participation when the loan target has been met. Where underwriting takes place, it is important to choose lenders that are capable of meeting their commitments, especially if the loan involves a long drawdown period. Generally, however, if a lender defaults on its commitment, the lead manager will cover the amount rather than run the risk of ruining its reputation as manager.

Another point to be considered in choosing the lenders is their access to certain currencies, and perhaps a certain geographic representation, both to broaden the base of participants and to spread the risk, yet another factor. Reciprocity is a final issue; if this type of arrangement is used, the lead manager must be very clear as to the terms.

Having decided on a desirable management group, the next step is to contact the prospective members again by telex or letter, with follow-up contacts. It is important for liability reasons not to seem to be selling the loan. Instead, the lead manager or whoever contacts potential participants should limit the invitation to specific factual information and allow the invited bank to decide whether to refuse, provide a conditional acceptance, or accept.

Once the group is formed, the managers meet to discuss syndication strategy, deal timing, and documentation. After their meeting, telexes are sent to all prospective participating banks. There is in this case intensive follow-up to encourage participation. The syndication may also be advertised, generally using "tombstones," public announcements that contain the details of the loan. The typical tombstone shows the borrower, the amount of the loan and the currency of denomination, the guarantor, the management group, the participants, and the agent. The lead manager must obtain the permission of all parties whose names are to appear. Tombstones are run in two to four magazines or journals, such as *Euromoney, Financial Times*, the *Wall Street Journal*, and *Institutional Investor*, on the basis of cost, geographic distribution, and type of audience to be reached. Borrowers like tombstones, as they are in effect a statement that large financial institutions are willing to extend credit to them. Similarly, lenders like them because they show to potential clients their economic strength or specialization in particular businesses. The lead manager may seek to advertise the syndication in other ways as well.

A central task in the placement period, often the responsibility of the lead manager but sometimes assigned to another manager, is to keep book, that is, to record all the contacts made and the responses.

There are two principal methods for selling syndicated loans:

Firm-commitment syndicate. The mandated bank commits itself to find the funds at specific conditions and terms. Should the bank fail to place the loan, its commitment ensures that it will underwrite the entire amount.

Club syndicate. A new placement technique, it involves a small group of banks arranging the syndication, with each committed to holding its share of the loan. This form is used for small loans in particular and ensures the borrower of immediate placement.

Documentation

There is extensive documentation involved in syndication lending, beyond the proposal. The most important documents are:

Offering telex. It contains the basic information on the loan, sufficient for the recipient to accept or decline, although clarification can be requested and is readily forthcoming.

The information memorandum. A 25- to 100-page report, it describes the loan, borrower, and guarantors; reviews thoroughly the terms and conditions, and the history, background, and financial situation, of the borrower; and analyzes the country risk. The memorandum has several main headings:

- Country background, if the borrower is a country, including its economy, monetary system, foreign trade and balance of payments, public finance, public debt, and political status.
- Corporate background, if the borrower is a corporation, including some of the above points, with the emphasis on the market environment for the company's products and other financial considerations such as leverage, cash flow projections, and credit.

The loan agreement. This document is the contract between the lender and the borrower (Exhibit 2). By signing it, both parties commit themselves to the terms and conditions specified in the agreement. In many ways, the headings are similar to those of the proposal, with the addition of information on the roles and responsibilities of all managers and participants, and certain other topics related to the actual borrowing. Important headings thus include: the parties to the loan; the borrowing provision (the procedure to be followed before a drawdown or borrowing); selection and amount of optimal currencies and option to change them; terms for repayment of the principal and interest and other costs; substitution basis (in case of difficulties in funding the loan, permissible changes in basic circumstances, with examples of difficulties, or in case of additional expenditures incurred by the lender or a key variable that might affect the borrower's ability to pay); representations and warranties (information about the borrower); events of default; agency;

Exhibit 2
The Loan Contract

A loan contract will include at least the following information:

1. The parties involved in the syndication, with clear mention of each one.
2. The information memorandum, containing a broad description of the country, the type and form of government, geographic location, population, extent of foreign trade, recent economic history, and total debt (local and foreign).
3. Purpose clause, which specifies what the loan proceeds will be used for.
4. Commitment clause, a provision that binds the banks to make the loan.
5. Borrowing/drawdown provisions, which encompass the notices and timing required for drawdowns, the minimum and maximum amount of each drawdown, and the obligations of the banks.
6. Choice-of-currency clause, which specifies what currencies may be used and the option of changing them, and the impact of the choice of currency on interest rate charges.
7. Repayment schedule, or the times at which the principal and interest are to be paid.
8. Prepayment terms and schedules and payment obligations, with specific reference to timing and to whom the payments go, the impact of prepayment on interest rates, and the distribution of funds to lenders by the agent.
9. Interest schedule, with the repayment dates and amounts, the LIBOR and how it is determined, along with the specific margins, and the interest levy in case of default.
10. Warranties and representation clauses, which cover such things as the identity of the borrower's agent, the borrower's obligation to provide periodic financial reports, and the borrower's obligation to make all repayments free of taxes and other liens.
11. Default clause, which covers how a default is determined, misrepresentations, failure to pay by the stated dates, cross-default provisions, and a bankruptcy clause.
12. Indemnification clause, which states who covers the losses if either party does not follow the agreement.
13. Agency clause, which describes the relationship of the banks among themselves and the agent's responsibilities, for example, as to the disclosure of information to members of the syndicate.
14. Fees and charges, which include the commitment fee, agency fee, management/arrangement fee, legal fees, stamp duties; and limits on out-of-pocket expenses.
15. Assignments clause, which deals with the assignment rights and obligations to another party.
16. Jurisdiction clause, which specifies which legal system will be used to interpret and enforce the contract, which courts will have jurisdiction in case of disputes, the currency in which a judgment will be made, and coverage against exchange losses.

Exhibit 2 (cont.)

---

17. Miscellaneous agreements and provisions, such as the Eurodollar unavailability clause, change-in-law contingency clause, increase-in-cost clause, how notices are to be sent, language of reports, and any other point not covered elsewhere.

---

jurisdiction in terms of country, body of law, and judiciary; fee distribution schedule; and arbitration of conflict.

Reports on the status of the loan and borrower. These reports are typically the responsibility of the agent (see below) and should go out periodically or when something of particular note should be passed on to all participants.

The Roles of Participants

It is useful at this point to review the roles of the key participants on the lenders' side of a syndicated loan. As loans have grown in size and complexity, so has management structure. Today, because of the large size of many loans, it is not uncommon to see a three-tiered level of management, consisting of the lead manager(s), managers, and co-managers. Which of the latter two roles a bank is assigned depends on its underwriting commitment. The management fee is distributed according to level and the deal status.

The Lead Manager

The mandated or lead manager performs four basic functions, called the Four S's, either alone or as part of a joint lead management group:

- *Sourcing* the loan, that is, making an offer to creditworthy borrowers, in response to an invitation to propose;
- *Structuring* the loan, that is, finding a form that meets the borrower's terms for the contract and that balances the interests of the various parties involved;
- *Selling* the loan, that is, looking for a group of lenders, taking into consideration the size of the loan, the likely response to the offer in the marketplace, and the preferences of borrowers; and
- *Servicing* the loan, that is, handling the operational aspects, such as fixing the interest rate on variable rate loans, collecting the interest and other payments, distributing the management fees, and updating lenders on any changes in the situation of the borrower.

Because of the importance of these tasks and their complexity, the lead manager(s) must have considerable expertise and preferably a broad geographic network that affords the greatest access to other lenders.

As to the managers and co-managers, they are named where the loan is particularly large. They are expected to make an underwriting commitment, and usually some are designated to carry out certain functions, for which they receive some additional portion of the management fee. Again, the inclusion of participants may be based on the requirements of the borrower or objectives of the lender. For example, the borrower may want a certain bank included as a way of gaining access to that bank's services at a later date.

Participating Banks

Participating banks are part of the syndication but have no underwriting risk. They join the syndicate for the potential earnings from their share of the loan, to diversify their portfolio with corporate, public sector, and sovereign loans, to benefit from the advertising through tombstones, and because of the flexibility in terms of deciding the degree of participation.

The Agent

Every syndicate designates one of the managers to serve as the agent. The agent's functions vary somewhat. For example, in the United States, the agent handles just mechanical and operational jobs, serving as an intermediary between the syndicate and borrower, whereas in Great Britain, the agent examines documents that are conditions to drawdowns, handles the bookkeeping, and sends out notices and reports on the loan. In some cases, the agent may decide if the borrower is in default and handle related tasks. Other functions may be ensuring compliance with the terms of the loan, rate fixing, and redrafting the provisions of the loan. The agent, who receives a fee for this work that is generally one-tenth of one percent of the total loan, must be very careful to carry out the functions properly and responsibly, as there are numerous areas of potential liability, such as failure to notify syndicate members of changes in the status of the borrower's creditworthiness.

The Credit Facility

There are three types of credit facilities:

Term loan. The most common form of syndicated loan, it allows the borrower to draw funds within a specified period after signing the agreement and to repay according to an amortization schedule.

Revolving credit facility. This option is generally favored for loans to cover balance of payments deficits and involves a commitment of banks to make funds available for a defined period during which the borrower, a sovereign government, can draw, repay, and redraw.

Mixed. A mixture of the previous two, this alternative allows the borrower, after the banks' commitment has expired, to convert into a term loan a portion of the funds drawn.

Obviously, the feature of a credit facility that draws the most attention is the cost. Six basic charges make up the cost of a loan:

Out-of-pocket expenses. The lead manager must be reimbursed for any out-of-pocket expenses, such as legal fees or photocopying, regardless of whether the loan is successfully placed.

Actual lending interest rate. The interest rate is usually based on a spread over the LIBOR (London Interbank Offered Rate) or SIBOR (Singapore Interbank Offered Rate), both of which are the rates at which leading banks offer to place deposits with other prime Euromarket institutions. Rather than taking the LIBOR of a single bank, usually the loan agreement specifies several banks, known as reference banks, whose average LIBOR will be used. Traditionally, reference banks have been the major lenders in the transaction, and as such, they are likely to benefit from the most favorable rates. The spread has ranged between 0.375 percent and 2.5 percent and has often been, and still is, the most important and competitive element in syndication lending. It is influenced by the borrower's rating and acceptability in the marketplace, the riskiness of the loan, the purpose of the loan (rescheduled loans are subject to higher spreads, a sort of penalty), availability of other loans (competition in the market), and general market conditions. Lenders look at the spread as a basic component of the total return and as a useful means of comparing competitive bids.

Management fee. This fee is paid to the management group, usually within 30 days of signature, although the timing may be negotiated. Of this fee, a part, called a praecipium, is paid to the mandated bank, with the amount based on the personnel and resources it assigns to managing the loan. The balance of the management fee is distributed to the managers and co-managers according to a negotiated arrangement. It should be noted that most borrowers accept the fee as a cost of business and leave the level to the lead manager to determine. Therefore a key task of the mandated bank is to determine what the market will bear, and its popularity and perceived success with the rest of the management group will depend on its obtaining the maximum fee.

Agency fee. This annual fee, one-tenth of one percent of the amount of the loan, or somewhat less if the loan is large, is paid to the agent.

Participation fee. This front-end fee is paid to the participating banks within 30 days of signing and is proportionate to the level of their participation.

Commitment fee. This fee is paid quarterly, every six months, or annually on the unused portion of the total funds committed, and usually ranges between 0.25 percent and 0.5 percent.

Other possible costs are a prepayment penalty, cancellation fees, and postdefault interest charges, a sort of penalty interest.

Repayment of the principal is usually done on a six-month basis, although there are variations, such as yearly percentage reductions of the credit, tailor-made cash flow project loans (the repayment is made out of earnings from the project once in operation, see Chapter 8), annual repayments, and bullet maturities.

Servicing the Loan

Once a loan is made, it must be serviced. To a large extent, this function involves monitoring the loan and borrower. The main purpose is to identify any problems or potential problems in time to take the most effective action. Servicing a syndicated loan is often the responsibility of the agent, who handles the operational aspects and compliance with the loan terms. The agent therefore needs to maintain close relations and communications with the borrower. As noted, a major responsibility of the agent is to determine defaults and handle any renegotiations that are necessary. To ensure responsible monitoring, the procedures should be spelled out clearly and be an integral part of the bank's operations.

What the monitoring looks at specifically is current financial conditions and projections, performance to date, outstanding loan balance overall, and any loan covenants. An analysis of future prospects should cover both what might go wrong and what might enhance the borrower's credit position.

Besides the monitoring of the syndicated loan by the agent, participating banks should have their own internal monitoring for this loan as for all other loans. Basically, this task means routine reviews, perhaps once a year, with more frequent analyses if conditions warrant. The review is designed to assess the borrower's compliance and to identify potential or actual problems and the position of the loan within the context of the overall portfolio and earnings of the bank.

FUTURE PROSPECTS

As noted, the Eurocurrency syndicated loan market has changed quite a lot since the beating of 1982. The market is still sluggish, the result of a combination of problem loans and the availability of other financing alternatives, as well as the restrictive monetary policies some major countries have instituted. Banks have also been paying more attention to domestic markets as the return from foreign lendings has worsened. And there are problems in the syndicated loan operation itself that have made lenders leery. Regional U.S. banks, Canadian banks with serious domestic loan difficulties, and Swiss banks, which have all along been less enthusiastic, have withdrawn from the market in large numbers.

Many believe that even in the best of times, syndicated loans did not reach their potential. The reason is said to be in part the system itself—that is, the dominant position of the lead manager, the difficulty of running a disparate group of competitive banks of different nationalities, the complexity of loans that encompass so many different countries and regulatory and legal systems, and the absence of some centralized unit to coordinate reschedulings.

The lead bank seems to be the pivot point for many of the problems. The most common criticism of the performance of lead banks relates to inadequate or erroneous information. It is unclear in what way a lead bank is responsible for the information it includes, for example, in the placement documentation, and to what extent it is liable for that information. In other cases, smaller banks have interpreted the lead bank's willingness to place the credit facility as an endorsement of the borrower, although that is not the case.

Two other general issues relate to the Eurocurrency market, where most syndicated loans are placed. One is that investments are being switched from the Euromarket to the stock markets of the United States and Europe, which have been growing substantially. Second, OPEC countries no longer have the large surpluses of cash that they had poured into the market in the 1970s. In fact, they are beginning slowly to withdraw their funds from the Euromarkets. Aside from the tighter supply of money, this shift in the market has produced mismatched maturities—at the same time that the OPEC countries are pulling out their funds, bank funds are tied up in medium- and long-term loans.

The syndicated loan market has gone through other rough times and is likely to survive this one. The belief is that the major banks will continue to syndicate loans, especially as the major reschedulings are finished. And they will lend to all classes of countries, the reasons being the interest they can earn on assets now locked into borrower countries and their desire to help stabilize countries in which they have loans. The future of many of their syndicated loans of the past depends on those countries' receiving further credit.

Thus the question is not survival, but what form and scale the market will take. As to form, banks are likely to shy away from long- and medium-term loans in favor of shorter-term ones. Moreover, they will want to minimize their participation and have it be transferable. A large portion of the syndication business in the future may involve intermediate-risk borrowers that have no other alternative, as individual institutions will want to steer clear of them, and they will need to offer guarantees.

The business will probably be carried on mainly by the larger banks; many smaller ones have already left the market, concerned about the risk and finding it hard to compete because of the low spreads. Among the larger lenders, the trend now is toward club deals. These transactions have the advantage of rapid consensus among the syndicate when something goes wrong, both because of the commonality of the members of the deal and because fewer of them make up the syndicate. And because there are fewer members, each receives a larger portion of the fees.

One prominent trend today is an outgrowth of the desire of the major lenders to minimize their participation. They are now selling what are called subparticipations of their share, usually available in relatively small amounts. Moreover, these subparticipations are readily transferable at any time a buyer can be found. As such, they have been attractive to smaller banks and may counter the trend of those institutions to pull out. Subparticipations provide an opportunity to participate in a relatively large and lucrative loan, while at the same time offering the flexibility of transferability. Dealing in subparticipations can be a good way for a small bank to maintain a diversified, balanced portfolio, and many are in fact using this technique. For the selling banks, the business is profitable and also leaves funds for other lending opportunities.

Subparticipation transactions tend to be short-term, with much of the business taking place in the rapidly expanding secondary market. U.S. banks have been particularly active in this operation. Generally, secondary market transactions are kept quiet so as not to damage the relationship between borrower and original lender, and because there is a perceived stigma to a bank's admitting that it is not holding all that it underwrote. Given the secrecy, estimates of the market volume are hard to come by; the annual turnover is said to range anywhere from $5 billion to $25 billion.

The disadvantage to subparticipations is that the purchaser has no voice should anything go wrong with the syndicated loan as a whole and lead to its being rescheduled. Their legal rights in such a situation and in general are uncertain. In fact, the reschedulings in Africa and Latin America have ended that secondary market there. Moreover, if the primary bank runs into hard times, the subparticipant may not receive its share of the interest.

As to the volume of syndicated lending in the future, the size of loans and their frequency is likely to fall. Another trend may be more competition with London as other financial centers take on syndicated lending as a major activity. Some offshore loans in Eurocurrency have already been arranged in the United States, Japan, and countries in Europe other than Great Britain. Banks will continue to expand this business as they acquire more expertise.

REFERENCES

Anderson, Jim, and Quck Peck Lim, "Syndicated Lending—Out for the Count," *Euromoney*, February 1983, pp. 36–40.

Citicorp, *The Global Financial System and LDC Debt: An Analysis by Four Senior Officers of Citibank/Citicorp*, New York: Citicorp, 1983.

Cline, William R., *International Debt and the Stability of the World Economy*, Washington, D.C.: Institute for International Economics, 1983.

DaCosta, Michael, *Finance and Development: The Role of International Commercial Banks in the Third World*, Boulder, Colo.: Westview Press, 1982.

Donaldson, J. A., and T. H. Donaldson, *The Medium-Term Loan Market*, New York: St. Martin's Press, 1982.

Donaldson, T. H., *International Lending by Commercial Banks*, New York: John Wiley & Sons, 1979.

Goodman, Laurie, "Bank Lending to Non-OPEC LDCs: Are Risks Diversifiable?" Federal Reserve Bank of New York *Quarterly Review*, Summer 1981.

Hertzberg, Daniel, "S&P Cuts Ratings of Certain Debt of Nine Bank Firms," *Wall Street Journal*, January 17, 1984.

Hilder, David B., and S. Karene Witcher, "Citicorp and Cigna Cancel Insurance Banking Firm Bought for Foreign Loans," *Wall Street Journal*, February 4, 1985.

Isaac, William, "The Implications of Bank Lending to Foreign Governments and Corporations," *Issues in Bank Regulation*, Summer 1983, pp. 11–15.

Kammert, James L., *International Commercial Banking Management*, New York: AMACOM, 1981.

Mendelsohn, M. S., "Commercial Banks and the Restructuring of Cross-Border Debt," Group of Thirty, New York, 1983.

———, *Money on the Move: The Modern International Capital Market*, Part 2, New York: McGraw-Hill, 1980.

Robert Morris Associates, "Reports on Domestic and International Loan Charge-Offs," Philadelphia, 1979–83.

Seiber, Marilyn J., *International Borrowing by Developing Countries*, New York: Pergamon Press, 1982.

Terrell, Henry S., "Bank Lending to Developing Countries: Recent Developments and Some Considerations for the Future," *Federal Reserve Bulletin*, October 1984.

U.S. Comptroller of the Currency, "Foreign Lending," *Quarterly Journal*, June 1983.

Weintraub, Robert E., *International Lending by U.S. Banks: Practices, Problems and Policies*, Fairfax, Va.: George Mason University, 1983.

Williams, Charles M., *Offshore Lending by U.S. Commercial Banks*, Washington, D.C.: Bankers Association for Foreign Trade; and Philadelphia, Robert Morris Associates, 1981.

10

INTERNATIONAL INSTITUTIONS IN MULTINATIONAL BANKING

The disparity between the income and developmental levels of nations and the realization that the poorer ones need assistance from richer ones has led over the last 40 years or so to the establishment of a number of specialized international, regional, and national institutions that promote development. Much of their effort has involved facilitating the transfer of funds to developing nations. The primary means are outright grants, direct and indirect loans, export credit facilities, and instruments such as guarantees, insurance, and cofinancing ventures that afford the borrower access to the private capital markets. The agencies also provide technical assistance in project implementation, institution-building, and other areas critical to national development.

This chapter reviews the key international institutions facilitating development in the third world through financing programs and technical assistance: Export-Import Bank of the United States; Private Export Funding Corporation, Federal Credit Insurance Agency, Overseas Private Investment Corporation, World Bank Group, Inter-American Development Bank, Asian Development Bank, African Development Bank, European Investment Bank, International Monetary Fund, and Bank for International Settlements.

EXPORT-IMPORT BANK OF THE UNITED STATES

The Export-Import Bank of the United States, or Eximbank, offers loans, guarantees, and insurance programs to assist the private sector in financing sales of U.S. exports. It was organized in 1934 as a banking corporation in the District of Columbia, and then in 1945 was made an independent U.S. government agency, located within the executive branch.

Programs

The Eximbank's operations are based on the following basic principles. (1) It offers financing for U.S. exporters in order for them to compete with exporters from other countries. (2) It does not provide financing unless private capital is unavailable in the amount required. Thus it supplements export financing without competing with private sources. (3) It requires that the transactions supported promise a reasonable assurance of repayment. (4) The host government must approve the project. (5) The Eximbank sets the levels of fees and premiums for guarantees and insurance in relation to the risks covered. (6) It authorizes loans for projects that have a favorable impact on the U.S. economy, especially on employment and real income, as well as on the development of productive resources. (7) It encourages new and small businesses to enter the agricultural export market, and to that end it offers educational programs to increase awareness of export opportunities among small agribusinesses and cooperatives.

It should be noted that most countries have comparable government agencies that assist exporters in their countries. Exhibit 3 lists the names of the most prominent in several major exporting countries.

Following is a brief discussion of the main Eximbank exporter credit and guarantee programs.

Direct Loans and Financial Guarantees

The Eximbank provides financing assistance for periods of between five and twelve years for U.S. exports of heavy capital equipment and large installations. The bank offers two forms of financing: (1) direct credits to a public or private overseas buyer; or (2) a financial guarantee assuring repayment of a private credit, which can be in U.S. dollars or any foreign currency acceptable to the Eximbank. Credits are available for up to 65 percent of the U.S. export value.

For a loan to a foreign buyer to occur, he must make a cash payment to the U.S. seller of at least 15 percent of the U.S. export value. The balance of the financing usually comes from private lenders. Moreover, according to the Eximbank's statutes, financial organizations in the buyer's country must assure repayment of the loans. Normally this guarantee is provided by governmental institutions or in some cases by large commercial banks.

Repayment of the principal and interest is scheduled in equal semiannual installments, normally beginning six months from the date of delivery or completion of the project. Repayment terms typically range between five and ten years; however, these terms vary and may be lengthened to enable U.S. exporters to compete with foreign exporters who have received credit

Exhibit 3
Foreign Competitors in Export Credits

France

Direction des Relations Economiques Exterieur (DREE)
Banque Francais du Commerce Exterieur (BFCE)

The Federal Republic of Germany

HERMES (a private company acting on behalf of the West German gov-
ernment that provides short-, medium-, and long-term insurance)
AKA (provides subsidized supplier credits)
KfW (provides buyer credits to developing countries)

Japan

Ministry for International Trade and Industry (MITI)
Japanese Export-Import Bank

United Kingdom

Export Credits Guarantee Department (ECGD)

---

with longer maturities. The Eximbank usually funds the later maturities so
that private lenders can be repaid within a shorter period.

Medium-Term Credit Program

The Eximbank introduced this program in 1983 in order to provide
medium-term loans at fixed interest rates for export sales by small businesses
facing competition from foreign exports supported by officially subsidized
credits. The program is directed toward transactions involving products
whose export value is $5 million or less, with the financing provided for
one to five years. The loan is actually made to the U.S. commercial bank
funding the purchase of exports for a foreign buyer, rather than going
directly to the exporter. In FY 1985, this program was budgeted for $500
million.

To be eligible for the program, the applicant bank must present evidence
of the subsidized credit with each credit request. Moreover, the foreign
buyer must make a cash payment of at least 15 percent of the contract
value.

There is a one-time advance commitment fee based on the amount of the
loan; it has to be paid within 30 days after the U.S. exporter wins the
contract.

Small Business Credit Program

This program, formerly called the Small Manufacturers Discount Loan Program, was set up in 1983 to help U.S. commercial banks meet the financing needs of small businesses for fixed rate export financing of products normally sold on terms of one to five years. The program is limited to the products of small businesses where the contract value generally is less than $2.5 million. The Eximbank's commitment covers up to 85 percent of the contract value of the export sale financed by a U.S. commercial bank. This program was budgeted for $100 million in FY 1985.

Working Capital Guarantee Loan Program

The Working Capital Guarantee Program enables exporters to meet critical pre-export financing needs, such as for inventory build-up or marketing, from commercial sources. It is aimed at supporting exports by small and medium-sized agricultural businesses. Under this program, the Eximbank will guarantee 90 percent of the principal amount of a loan issued for pre-export needs by any financial institution that demonstrates financial capability to the Eximbank's satisfaction. The loan must be for export-related activities. The guarantee runs only one to twelve months.

Interest Rates

The interest rates shown in Table 1, which come from the Office of Public Affairs of the Eximbank, were established on July 15, 1984, for the Direct Credit Loan Program, Medium-Term Credit Program, and Small Business Credit program. The actual rate charged, however, varies according to the classification of the country to which the exports will be shipped and the repayment period.

Future Trends

The Eximbank anticipates an increased demand for credits as countries work out their debt payment problems and come back into the world marketplace. As a result, the Eximbank requested for FY 1985: $3.83 billion for direct loans, of which $100 million was to go to the small business credit program; and $10 billion for the guarantee and insurance programs. The Eximbank will continue placing special emphasis on helping small businesses move into the export market. In addition, over the near term, it will help keep essential trade flows going between the United States and countries that are experiencing debt payment problems.

Table 1
Annual Eximbank Interest Rate (percent)

Country Classification*	2–5 Years	More than 5 Years
I Relatively Rich	13.35	13.6
II Intermediate	11.55	11.9
III Relatively Poor	10.70	10.7

Source: Office of Public Affairs of Eximbank, July 1984.

* The classifications, which are based on the OECD arrangement on officially supported export credits, include the following countries:

Category I: Per capita GNP of $4,000 or more as of 1979, International Bank for Reconstruction and Development (IBRD) figures—Andorra; Australia; Austria; Bahrain; Belgium; Bermuda; Brunei; Canada; Czechoslovakia; Denmark; Finland; France; Germany, Democratic Republic; Germany, Federal Republic; Greece; Iceland; Ireland; Israel; Italy; Japan; Kuwait; Libya; Liechtenstein; Luxembourg; Monaco; Netherlands; New Zealand; Norway; Qatar; San Marino; Saudi Arabia; Spain; Sweden; Switzerland; United Arab Emirates; United Kingdom; United States; USSR; Vatican City.

Category II: Per capita GNP of less than $4,000, not eligible for International Development Association (IDA) or a mixture of IDA and IBRD financing—Albania; Algeria; Antigua; Argentina; Bahamas; Barbados; Belize; Botswana; Brazil; Bulgaria; Chile; Colombia; Costa Rica; Cuba; Cyprus; Dominican Republic; Ecuador; Fiji; Gabon; Gibraltar; Guatemala; Hong Kong; Hungary; Iran; Iraq; Ivory Coast; Jamaica; Jordan; Kiribati; Korea, Democratic People's Republic; Korea, Republic of; Lebanon; Macao; Malaysia; Malta; Mauritius; Mexico; Monserrat; Morocco; Namibia; Nauru; Netherlands Antilles; Nigeria; Oman; Panama; Papua New Guinea; Paraguay; Peru; Poland; Portugal; Romania; St. Kitts–Nevis; St. Lucia; Seychelles; Singapore; South Africa; Suriname; Syria; Taiwan; Trinidad & Tobago; Tunisia; Turkey; Uruguay; Venezuela; Yugoslavia.

Category III: Eligible for IDA or a mixture of IBRD and IDA financing, or per capita GNP of less than $680—Angola; Bangladesh; Benin; Bolivia; Burma; Burundi; Cameroon; Central African Republic; Chad; China; Congo, People's Republic; Egypt; El Salvador; Ethiopia; Gambia; Ghana; Guinea; Guinea-Bissau; Haiti; Honduras; India; Indonesia; Kenya; Lesotho; Liberia; Madagascar; Malawi; Mali; Mauritania; Mozambique; Nepal; Nicaragua; Niger; Pakistan; Philippines; Rwanda; Senegal; Sierra Leone; Somalia; Sri Lanka; Sudan; Tanzania; Thailand; Togo; Uganda; Upper Volta; Yemen Arab Republic; Yemen, P.D.R.; Zaire; Zambia; Zimbabwe.

FOREIGN CREDIT INSURANCE ASSOCIATION

A private association of more than 50 marine, property, and casualty insurance companies, the Foreign Credit Insurance Association (FCIA) plays a significant role in the export credit system of the United States and in the overall operations of the Eximbank. It relies on the Eximbank to guarantee all its transactions, and in turn the Export-Import Bank has an influential role in its management.

The FCIA, in agreement with the Eximbank, provides insurance against certain commercial risks to exporters engaged in short- and medium-term export deals supported by the Eximbank. There is a limit, however, of a maximum coverage of $750,000 for up to five years. Anything over that limit is underwritten by the Eximbank itself, which also handles all insurance against political risk. The FCIA thus does not finance any export deals itself, although member companies may do so on their own.

Insurance rates for the FCIA are based on the type of buyer, amount of security risk, and repayment terms. The average rate for short-term insurance is 0.5 percent, and for a five-year policy, up to 3.5 percent.

PRIVATE EXPORT FUNDING CORPORATION

Like the FCIA, the Private Export Funding Corporation of New York (PEFCO), which was set up in 1970, is a private corporation that works closely with the Eximbank. It is composed of 54 commercial banks, 7 industrial firms, and 1 investment banking firm. In contrast to the FCIA, the PEFCO finances medium- and long-term export transactions, although it has emphasized primarily medium-term lending, with a few commitments of up to fifteen years. The role of the Eximbank is to help exporters in the United States by guaranteeing the repayment of the principal and interest of PEFCO export loans and of the interest on its collateralized debt. Before the Eximbank will provide any guarantees, however, it must approve the interest rate and repayment terms of PEFCO loans. Moreover, since the PEFCO is the recipient of the guarantee, it can deal only with those countries the Eximbank can deal with.

To obtain a PEFCO loan, an exporter applies for financing from a commercial bank, which then applies to the PEFCO for the loan. In turn, the PEFCO submits to the Eximbank the loan application, which states the amount to be repaid and the terms, for its guarantee. If the guarantee is given, the PEFCO makes the loan.

The PEFCO generally lends at fixed rates over the maturity of the loan, with the rate based on the cost of PEFCO's funds at the time of the loan, plus 0.5 percent for non-PEFCO members.

OVERSEAS PRIVATE INVESTMENT CORPORATION

The Overseas Private Investment Corporation (OPIC) was credited by the Foreign Assistance Act of 1969. Its purpose is to mobilize and facilitate the flow of private U.S. capital and skills to friendly countries of the developing world and thereby to complement the development assistance objectives of the United States. OPIC's programs also serve to support U.S. foreign policy and economic interests. OPIC's assistance is particularly important to poorer, less developed countries, as they have the least access to commercial funding and insurance and to sophisticated sources of information and analysis.

OPIC's fundamental role is to insure or finance projects by American investors that most banks or insurance companies are unwilling or unable to handle. It operates two main programs: insurance for U.S. private investments in more than 100 developing countries against certain political risks, and financing for eligible projects sponsored by U.S. investors in those countries.

OPIC's insurance program offers investors protection against currency inconvertibility, expropriation, and war, revolution, insurrection, and civil strife. The OPIC also offers special coverage for investors involved in contracting and exporting, energy exploration and development, and international leasing.

The insurance program has undergone remarkable growth recently: in each of the four fiscal years since 1981, the OPIC has carried out record volumes of insurance, with a four-year total of $12.8 billion, a level that exceeds by nearly 50 percent that of OPIC's first ten years of operations. In FY 1984 alone, the OPIC insured 124 projects (compared to 107 in FY 1983) and issued a total of $4.3 billion of insurance coverage, an increase of 10 percent over the record level of FY 1983 and almost three times the level in FY 1981.

The second OPIC program—financing—has become an increasingly important instrument in the mobilization and facilitation of U.S. private investment in the developing world. This source of credit is particularly important for small U.S. businesses, which are often unable to obtain financing for overseas projects on reasonable terms from private U.S. or developing country sources, particularly in the poorer developing countries, where foreign exchange is scarce. More than 70 percent of OPIC's annual finance commitments since 1981 have involved significant participation by small businesses; moreover, the majority of the projects for which funding has been provided have been in the least developed nations (defined as those with per capita incomes of $680 or less in 1979 U.S. dollars). These nations are located primarily in the Caribbean basin and sub-Saharan Africa.

THE WORLD BANK GROUP

The World Bank group includes the International Bank for Reconstruction and Development (IBRD, or the World Bank, as it is commonly called) and the International Development Association (IDA). Also linked to the group is the International Finance Corporation (IFC), which can be considered a private arm of the World Bank. These institutions, located in Washington, D.C., share the goal of promoting social and economic progress by channeling financial resources from richer to developing countries. The importance of the World Bank is indicated by the amount of funds lent from its inception in 1944 to 1984—$120 billion for about 3,500 projects in more than 100 countries.

IBRD

The oldest and biggest of the three institutions, the IBRD was created at the Bretton Woods conference in July 1944, along with the International Monetary Fund. It began operations in 1945. Any country can apply for membership, and acceptance is decided by a consultation between the applicant and the Bank. The next step is approval by the board of governors, which bases its decision on the financial and economic strength of the country and its financial participation in the International Monetary Fund. When a country becomes a member, it automatically gets 250 votes on the board of governors; additional ones depend on how many shares of stock the country acquires. Each share costs SDR 100,000 and brings with it one extra vote. The largest shareholder is the United States, with slightly over 20 percent of the subscribed capital and 20.6 percent of the votes.

Programs

The activities of the Bank have become far more diverse in its 40 years of operations. The emphasis has shifted from electric power and transportation projects, characteristic of its first 20 years, to lending for agricultural and rural development, with many intermediate steps along the way. The latter two areas have gotten the lion's share of expenditures, along with new sectors such as small-scale enterprises, urban development, health care, family planning and assistance, nutrition, education, and housing.

The Bank provides both financing and technical assistance for specific projects on the basis of the economic condition of the country and the characteristics of the project. Financing is provided only to those borrowers that are creditworthy and that promise a real rate of economic return to the country. Even then, a government guarantee is still mandatory. Recipients are governments, government agencies, and private enterprises whose loans are guaranteed by the government.

Typically, there are six stages to a project cycle:

Identification. Projects are identified by governments, assisted by an ad hoc Bank identification mission, and designed for submission to the Bank.

Preparation. The borrower, the Bank, and external consultants evaluate the project in terms of its technical, managerial, economic, and financial characteristics.

Appraisal. The Bank judges the economic need that the project is supposed to address and the project's effectiveness and features in terms of meeting that need. The appraisal constitutes one basis for the Bank's decision.

Negotiation and approval. The Bank negotiates with the borrower specific details such as revenue levels, rates of return, and organizational change, concurrent with the approval process of the executive directors.

Implementation and supervision. The borrower is responsible for implementing the project and has to submit periodic progress reports, while the Bank supervises the implementation, providing technical assistance as required.

Ex-post evaluation. The Bank, which conducts this auditing effort, has found it to be a very effective way to check on project implementation.

As noted, the Bank also provides technical assistance, for example, in areas such as engineering problems, technical and feasibility studies, project supervision, improvements in statistical services and other institution-building, and the like. This assistance may be provided directly by the Bank or may be arranged with another source.

Funding Sources

The Bank raises its funds through medium- and long-term borrowing in the world's capital markets and through the withdrawal of funds from paid-in capital, retained earnings, and repayments. The first source seems to be the most important, providing more than two-thirds of Bank revenues. These funds are raised in the private capital markets—individual and institutional—and directly from the governments of member countries. As to private lenders, investment, merchant, and commercial banks are used. With respect to governmental lenders, the Bank makes official placements of bonds and notes with them, their agencies, and their central banks. IBRD bonds have an AAA rating.

More recently, the Bank has also resorted to short-term borrowing. As a result, it will now change its interest rate every six months for loans made on or after July 1, 1982, in order to avoid undue interest rate risk. The Bank also avoids risk by maintaining a highly liquid balance; it does so by borrowing more money than it requires at the moment. In this way it is not compelled to borrow when market conditions are bad. Moreover, rather than relying on a few markets, it has diversified its borrowing to more than 100 countries. The most important sources, however, are the United States, the Federal Republic of Germany, Japan, Switzerland, and the Middle East. More recently, the Bank has also engaged in currency swaps (see Chapter 4).

In the last few years, the Bank has augmented the flow of funds to borrowers by cooperating in cofinancing, that is, by providing financial support in conjunction with other institutions. The key sources of funds here are official ones, such as governments and their agencies, and export credit institutions.

As noted, the interest rate changes every six months, based on the interest being paid by the Bank on money borrowed. Lately, the rate has ranged between 7.5 percent and 11.6 percent. Other changes include a front-end fee of 0.25 percent on the total amount of the loan and a commitment charge of 0.75 percent on undisbursed amounts. The maturity of its lending generally varies between fifteen and twenty years, with a grace period of three to five years.

Organizational Structure

The main organizational units of the IBRD are:

Board of governors. It holds all the powers of the Bank, such as policy-making, organizational issues, and election of the president. There is a governor for each country plus 21 full-time executive directors who represent the board at headquarters in Washington, D.C.

President. He is responsible for day-to-day operations. Since the United States has the largest number of votes, by informal understanding the president has always been an American.

IDA

The IDA was established in September 1960. The IDA's goal is to allow countries that cannot afford the terms of IBRD loans to obtain financing for their projects. IDA members are divided into two categories: developed, or high-income, countries, which pay their entire subscriptions at one time; and poor, or less developed, countries, which pay 10 percent of their subscription immediately and the rest when requested.

Programs

The kinds of projects funded are basically the same as those supported by the IBRD, although the emphasis is more on agricultural development. Recipients are governments, although in many cases they relend the money to private enterprises. Loans are made on the basis of a country's per capita income (usually less than $410 a year and no more than $715), their limited creditworthiness in the eyes of conventional lenders, and their economic performance in terms of efficient use of resources. Otherwise, the selection criteria and project cycle are the same as for IBRD loans.

Since its inception, the IDA has lent more than $30 billion for over 1,300 projects in 70-plus countries.

Because of its mandate, the terms of IDA loans are very different from those of the IBRD. No interest is charged, but there is a fee of 0.75 percent a year on the disbursed balance and a commitment fee of 0.5 percent on the undisbursed balance. That latter charge was established in 1982 to cover administrative expenses. The maturity period is fifty years, with a ten-year grace period.

IFC

The IFC, the third affiliate of the World Bank, was established in 1956 to complement the IBRD in terms of promoting the development of member countries by assisting the private sector in two ways. One, IFC lends only to private enterprises or to government organizations that assist the private sector in developing countries. Second, the IFC engages in cofinancing ventures with local investors and financial institutions.

Programs

Projects to be funded by the IFC must meet two requirements—they must be profitable and they must be economically advantageous to the country. The IFC, as noted, funds only a portion of the project cost itself, in addition to providing financial, legal, and technical assistance. However, the IFC helps the borrower obtain the balance from private resources, with IFC participation in itself serving as an incentive to private lenders. Recipients of loans may spend the funds however they choose, as long as the funds are used in a member country of the IBRD or in Switzerland. One main difference between the IBRD and the IFC is that the latter does not require government guarantees for its loans.

Another key difference between the IFC and the IBRD relates to the terms for lending. The IFC sets its interest rate on the basis of the market rate and charges an annual 1 percent commitment fee on the undisbursed amount of a loan. The average maturity is seven to twelve years, with a grace period of three years.

Funding Sources

The main source of IFC funds are internal capital and borrowing from the IBRD. Additional funds for joint ventures are obtained through syndicated loans, underwritings, and standby financing. To date, the IFC has experienced exceptional growth in its operations: it has gone from 31 members and $100 million of authorized capital in 1956 to 124 members and $650 million in 1983.

Organizational Structure

The IFC shares some of the bank's administrative staff but has separate legal and operational personnel.

INTER-AMERICAN DEVELOPMENT BANK

The Inter-American Development Bank (IADB), which commenced operations in 1960, promotes and directs financing to regional member countries, as well as providing technical assistance for development projects. It has 43 member countries, 27 of them in the region; those 27 are also members of the Organization for American States (including the United States and Canada). Sixteen others are from outside the region (including Japan, the Federal Republic of Germany, France, the United Kingdom, and Switzerland). The IADB is headquartered in Washington, D.C., and has field offices in London and Paris.

Programs

Since its inception, the IADB has supported balanced social and economic development in member countries. Loans are made for several different purposes:

- Specific projects.
- Multiple works projects of a similar nature.
- Integrated development programs involving interrelated projects.
- Projects contributing to the development of a specific sector.
- Complementary credit line financing, used to provide additional funds for productive projects that are also attractive to other financial institutions.

Usually the IADB does not finance more than 50 percent of the total cost of a project from its own resources.

To be approved, each loan proposed to the bank's board of executive directors is subject to a series of analyses that look at: institutional capacity (does the borrower have the necessary financial, administrative, and operational capability to implement the project?); technical feasibility; socioeconomic impact, for example, in terms of employment, production, income, and the environment; financial status (the profitability of the project and the likelihood of its being self-sustaining once implemented, as well as the creditworthiness of the borrower); legal issues; and the distribution of benefits, particularly with respect to low-income groups.

After the loan has been approved, it is monitored closely by the field offices of the IADB. In addition, the borrower has to submit periodic reports. At the end of the loan, the IADB performs an ex-post evaluation to check out its policies and implementation of the projects.

The bank fixes the interest rates it charges each year, with the rate actually applied to each loan dependent on the type of resources used and the level of poverty of the borrower. For loans from ordinary funds (see below), the interest rates declined in 1984 in relation to previous years. For loans disbursed in a foreign currency, the bank has charged 9.5 percent interest. The bank also imposes a supervision fee of 1 percent of the total loan for the entire period, and a credit commission of 1.25 percent of the undisbursed balance. If the loan is disbursed in a local currency, the interest rate is less— 4 percent—and there is no credit commission.

The length of the amortization period depends on the kind of project but runs between 15 and 25 years, as follows:

- For individual industry projects, 15 years.
- For productive sectors and economic infrastructure, 15 to 20 years.
- For productive sectors in low-income countries, up to 25 years.
- For social projects, 20 to 25 years.

The disbursement period is usually four years, with the grace period typically the same length. The largest debtors are Brazil (27 percent), Mexico (26 percent), Argentina (13 percent), and Colombia (7 percent).

The IADB operates with a gearing ratio (i.e., ratio of loans to capital) of approximately 2 to 1. Total lending in 1984 amounted to $3.5 billion.

The IADB also offers technical assistance in training and in the preparation, financing, and implementation of a project. This work is either granted or must be paid for, depending on the level of development of the borrower.

Funding Sources

As with most organizations of this kind, the principal source of funds is capital subscribed by member countries. The authorized level of the capital stock has been increased six times and stood at $15.7 billion in December 1983. Most of this capital has been callable, that is, it has involved no actual cash outlays by member countries; only 4.5 percent has been paid in. The United States is the biggest shareholder, with 51 percent of the capital; Venezuela is second, with 15 percent.

The IADB also borrows on the capital markets, with these funds guaranteed by the callable capital stock. Thus it can utilize private savings to implement high-priority projects. Much of the borrowing is handled through bond issues, which have an AAA rating, and through other arrangements, such as notes and direct loans. The financial markets used by the IADB are in the United States, Europe, Japan, Israel, and Latin America.

Additional funds are made available through cofinancing agreements, such as complementary credit line financing, in which the potential borrower asks the bank to obtain complementary financing from commercial banks and institutional investors. In this way, the IADB effectively grants two loans: the first from its own resources at its standard terms, the second at the commercial terms offered by banks and financial institutions.

The IADB's total resources in 1984 were $34 billion.

Organizational Structure

The main organizational units of the IADB are:

Board of governors. It reviews the operations of the bank and decides on most important policy matters. It has delegated certain of its powers to the board of executive directors, except for those it has expressly reserved, such as the admission of new members, changes in the capital structure, election of the president, and approval of the balance sheet. The board is composed of representatives of the member countries; it meets once a year or whenever necessary.

Board of executive directors. Elected by the governors (one by the largest shareholder, two by nonregional members, and at least eight by the others) for a three-year period, the executive directors are responsible for the ordinary operations of the bank. Their main tasks are to establish operational policies, approve loans and technical assistance proposals presented by the president, set interest rates, authorize borrowing, and approve the budget. They work full-time at headquarters. Each executive director designates an alternate who has full powers in case of the absence of the principal.

President. Appointed by the board of governors for a five-year term, the president proposes the general policy of the bank. He is also the chairman of the board of executive directors and the main executive officer of the bank, as well as its legal representative. With the assistance of the executive vice president (elected by the directors), the president is also in charge of day-to-day operations.

ASIAN DEVELOPMENT BANK

The Asian Development Bank (ADB) started operations in 1966, its purpose being to foster economic growth, cooperation, and advancement in the developing countries of Asia and the Far East. It has 45 member countries (31 in Asia and 14 in Europe and North America). The ADB is headquartered in Manila, the Philippines, and has an office in New York City.

Programs

General lending operations include concessions, participations, and guarantees of loans to the governments of ADB members, their agencies, public and private enterprises that operate in member countries, and other organizations involved in the economic development of the area. When examining investment proposals, the bank takes into consideration elements such as the economic, technical, and financial feasibility of projects, their effects on the general activities, savings, employment, and productivity of the country, and the ability of the country to borrow from other sources.

Another important activity of the ADB is technical assistance. It is provided on a grant or loan basis in conjunction with the implementation of development plans, evaluation of specific projects and programs, and creation of new institutions. Here the focus has been on the agricultural and energy sectors. Technical assistance consists of advisory services, missions of consultants or experts on a contract basis, and cooperation with other institutions.

The rate of interest the ADB charges, as well as the commitment and other fees, are set periodically by the bank, based on the particular features of each credit facility. The lending rate for ordinary projects is based on market conditions. The ADB requires a commission fee that is generally not lower than 1 percent a year, and a guarantee fee. Loans must be repaid in the same currency as the disbursement, or in gold or a convertible currency. The gearing ratio is 1 to 1.

Funding Sources

The ordinary resources of the ADB come from subscriptions and relative increases in the capital stock by member countries. These resources are either paid-in or callable. The bank also borrows in the international capital markets (Standard and Poor's and Moody's have given AAA ratings to ADB bonds).

The total share capital is $16 billion, with Japan providing 16 percent, the United States 16 percent, and Australia, Canada, the Federal Republic of Germany, and the United Kingdom as a group around 18 percent.

Depending on the resources used, lending operations are categorized as ordinary or special. The former are financed through the ordinary resources of the bank, while the latter, which include projects of high development priority requiring lower interest rates, longer maturities, and longer-deferred repayments, are financed through special funds.

Organizational Structure

The main organizational units of the ADB are:

Board of governors. Composed of a governor and an alternate elected by each member, it holds all the powers of the bank.

Board of directors. Its ten members, elected by the board of governors, are responsible for the general direction of the bank operations.

President. Elected by the board of governors, the president is in charge of the daily business of the bank and is the chief of staff.

AFRICAN DEVELOPMENT BANK

The African Development Bank (AFDB) was established in Abidjan, Ivory Coast, in 1963 "to contribute to the economic development and social progress of its members—individually and jointly." It has grown from 33 members to 51.

Programs

To reach its objectives, the AFDB pursues several avenues. It provides support using its own resources and others raised inside and outside Africa; it promotes private and public investment for development purposes; and it provides the technical assistance necessary to implement projects and programs, alone or in cooperation with national, regional, and subregional development institutions.

The bank can make or participate in direct loans with both ordinary and borrowed funds, can invest in the equity capital of institutions, and can guarantee, completely or partially, loans by others. Financing is provided for specific projects or groups of interrelated projects, with priorities in terms of particularly urgent needs relating to the social and economic development of the borrower taken into account. Recipients of AFDB assistance are regional governments and their political subdivisions, and institutions and international or regional agencies concerned with the development of Africa.

The terms of loans are specified in a contract with the borrower. Funds are to be repaid in the same currency in which they were disbursed, unless otherwise stated. The rate of interest on normal loans is approximately 7 percent a year, with maturities of twelve to twenty years, including a grace period of two to five years. The bank also charges a commission on each loan or guarantee of not less than 1 percent a year. Finally, there is a fee, determined by the board of directors and calculated as a percentage of the total amount of the loan outstanding, on each guarantee.

Funding Sources

Sources of ordinary funds are capital stock, borrowing (through sales of obligations on the financial markets of member countries), and repayments and income from loans.

Organizational Structure

The basic organizational units of the AFDB are:

Board of governors. The main function of the governors is to develop guidelines for the credit policy of the bank. The governors can delegate their authority to the directors, except in a few areas relating to the administration of special funds, changes in the capital stock, approval of the balance sheets and income statements, and decisions on possible cooperation with the governments of African countries that are not yet independent. Each member country elects a governor and an alternate for a five-year term. They meet once a year or when there is a need.

Board of directors. The directors are responsible for the general operations of the bank and exercise whatever powers are delegated by the governors, such as the election of the president of the bank, determination of interest rates for direct loans, and preparation of the work of the governors. There are nine directors, who are elected by the governors for staggered three-year terms; each director appoints an alternate who has full authority when the principal is absent. The directors meet whenever there is a need.

President. The president is the chairman of the board of directors (but with voting power only in the case of a tie), chief of staff of the bank, legal representative of the bank, and the person in charge of daily operations.

EUROPEAN INVESTMENT BANK

The European Investment Bank (EIB) was created, along with the European Economic Community (EEC), by the Treaty of Rome. It commenced operations in 1958. Its headquarters is in Luxembourg, and it has offices in Brussels, Rome, and London.

The goal of the EIB is defined by Article 130 of the treaty:

...to contribute, by having recourse to the capital market and utilizing its own resources, to the balanced and steady development of the common market in the interest of the Community. For this purpose the Bank shall, operating on a non-profit-making basis, grant loans and give guarantees which facilitate the financing of the following projects in all sectors of the economy: (a) projects for developing less developed regions; (b) projects for modernizing or converting undertakings or for developing fresh activities called for by the progressive establishment of the common market, when these projects are of such a size or nature that they cannot be entirely financed by the various means available in the individual Member States; (c) projects of common interest to several Member States which are of such a size or nature that they cannot be entirely financed by the various means available in the individual Member States.

The members of the EIB are the same as those of the EEC: Belgium, Denmark, the Federal Republic of Germany, Greece, France, Ireland, Italy, Luxembourg, the Netherlands, and the United Kingdom. Even though its membership is completely European and it has regional goals, since 1963 the EIB has gradually become involved in 77 countries outside the community.

Programs

The EIB grants or guarantees loans only for specific projects that meet the terms of Article 130; these projects fall mainly into the areas of industry, energy, and infrastructure. Regional development has been the most important objective of the bank, with 70 percent of the lending since 1958 channeled in this direction. Within this area, the emphasis has been on small and medium-sized investments through lending to entities that meet EIB criteria. Each project funded has to be approved by the country in which it is to be implemented, by the Commission of the European Community, and by the bank's board of directors.

EIB financing covers only a part of an investment and cannot exceed 50 percent of the cost of the fixed assets. There is no predetermined minimum amount for loans, but the figure has generally been 2 million ECUs. Recipients are public and private entities, states, and public authorities that are financially autonomous (councils, regions, etc.). The only condition on a loan is conformity with EIB lending criteria.

Small and medium-sized ventures can also take advantage of EIB financing. In this case, the lending is indirect. Another bank or financial institution acts as intermediary and actually enters into the contract with the EIB, after applying for and negotiating the loan on behalf of the borrower. If the loan is received, the intermediary then opens a line of credit for the borrower at its institution.

Loans made by the EIB can be disbursed in three main formats:

1. Several currencies in a standard mix, with the currencies generally being those in large supply at the bank, and with the terms fixed in advance;
2. A mix of several currencies according to the borrower's preferences and their availability at the bank; and
3. A single noncommunity currency (mostly U.S. dollars, Swiss francs, or Japanese yen).

The general length of a loan is seven to twelve years for industrial projects and ten to fifteen years for infrastructure, with a maximum of twenty years when market conditions permit it. There is usually a grace period of from two to five years; after that, the loans are repaid, in the currency received, in equal semiannual installments. In certain cases, a 3 percent interest rate subsidy can be provided from EEC budgetary funds. The bank maintains a gearing ratio (ratio of loans to capital) of 2.5 to 1.

Financing Sources

Subscriptions (or authorized capital) from member countries are the foundation of the financial resources of the EIB. It has 14.4 billion ECUs, about 10 percent of which is actual paid-in capital. Since 1958, the amount of capital has been increased six times.

The bulk of the EIB's funds come from borrowing, generally carried out through public and private bond issues on the international capital markets and those of member countries. The EIB has an AAA credit rating for its bonds. It is considered a sound borrower because it has a diversified loan portfolio, approves only projects that can generate sufficient operating profits, loans funds only for projects with a government guarantee, does not run any currency risks, and has the unpaid capital of its members as a safety reserve.

Organizational Structure

The main organizational units of the EIB are:

Board of governors. It establishes the broad framework of the bank's credit policy and approves the annual report and balance sheet. The board is composed of ten members who are ministers (usually of finance) of the member states.

Board of directors. Its powers include granting loans and raising funds, determining interest rates, and overseeing both bank operations and compliance with the enabling statute. The board has nineteen members and eleven alternates.

Management committee. Consisting of the bank's president and four vice presidents, it supervises current operations and submits its decisions to the directors for approval.

Audit committee. It monitors the bank to ensure that operations are being carried out responsibly and that the books are being kept properly.

INTERNATIONAL MONETARY FUND

The international Monetary Fund (IMF) was created, along with the World Bank, at the Bretton Woods conference in 1944. Its goals are:

1. To promote international monetary cooperation through a permanent institution which provides the machinery for consultation and collaboration on international monetary problems.
2. To facilitate the expansion and balanced growth of international trade, and to contribute thereby to the promotion and maintenance of a high level of employment and real income and to the development of the productive resources of all members as primary objectives of economic policy.
3. To promote exchange stability, to maintain orderly exchange arrangements among members, and to avoid competitive exchange depreciation.
4. To assist in the establishment of a multilateral system of payments in respect of currency transactions between members and in the elimination of foreign exchange restrictions which hamper the growth of world trade.
5. To give confidence to members by making the general resources of the Fund temporarily available to them under adequate safeguards, thus providing them with the opportunity to correct maladjustments in their balance of payments without resorting to measures destructive of national or international prosperity.
6. In accordance with the above, to shorten the duration and lessen the degree of disequilibrium in the international balance of payments of members.

More recently, the IMF has been an important participant in the re-scheduling of commercial loans made by international banks to sovereign borrowers. Any rescheduling or new financing is made contingent on ac-ceptance and implementation of an IMF conditionality program whose pur-pose is to get countries with debt-servicing problems to strengthen and stabilize their economies. Generally the program calls for specific measures designed to achieve necessary structural adjustments in the economies of borrowers. Agreement with the program involves the countries in often painful steps such as currency devaluations, elimination of subsidies, and reduction of inflation and government deficits.

All the industrial market economies except Switzerland, some socialist ones, and most of the developing ones are members of the IMF. That membership is a requirement for admission to the World Bank. The IMF is headquartered in Washington, D.C., and has offices in Paris and Geneva and at the United Nations in New York.

Programs

Since 1962, the IMF has used different arrangements and agreements to meet different needs:

General Arrangements to Borrow (GAB). This system, which became effective in 1962, allows the IMF to use lines of credit from the governments of Belgium, Canada, France, Italy, Japan, the Netherlands, the United Kingdom, and the United States, and the central banks of the Federal Republic of Germany and Sweden. In 1983 the lines of credit were extended from SDR 6.4 billion to SDR 17 billion. Successive amendments have permitted the Swiss National Bank to enter into the arrangements as a lender and for the Fund to borrow and lend to countries not participating in the GAB. The interest rate that lenders charge the IMF is relatively low.

Oil facilities agreements. These were set up in 1974 and 1975 to help countries affected by the oil price increase to stabilize their balance of payments. The interest being charged was 7 percent a year. These drawings were ended in 1976.

Supplementary financing facilities. Effective in 1979 and ending in 1984, these facilities were available at floating interest rates that changed every six months, based on the average yield of U.S. government securities.

Borrowing to finance enlarged access. This borrowing involves medium-term loans (maturities of up to six years beginning in 1981) from the Saudi Arabian Monetary Agency (SDR 8 billion) and short-term loans from the Bank for International Set-tlements (SDR 6.5 billion) and IMF members (6.5 billion). The funds are to be made available to expand the resources of countries with severe balance of payments problems. The interest rate is the weighted average of the five-year government securities of the currencies that compose the SDR.

Borrowing arrangement with Saudi Arabia in association with the GAB. This arrangement, concluded in 1983, provided for a maximum of SDR 1.5 billion for a five-year period, to be used to assist the financing of purchases that have the same modalities as are prescribed with the GAB.

Funding Sources

Each member of the IMF has to subscribe a quota in SDRs, calculated according to a formula that includes variables such as national income, imports, and diversity of exports; the quotas are revised at intervals of no more than five years. Each member has 250 votes plus an additional vote for each part of its quota equal to 100,000 SDRs. The United States has the greatest number of votes—126,325, or about 20 percent of the total.

Subscriptions are the main source of funds for the IMF. Since 1945, members' quotas have been increased eight times. The last raise, approved in 1983, brought the total subscriptions to about SDR 90 billion. The IMF can supplement these ordinary resources at any time by borrowing in any currency from any source, both official, such as national treasuries and central banks, and private, such as commercial banks and financial institutions. To date, only official sources have been tapped.

Organizational Structure

The main organizational units of the IMF are:

Board of governors. It has all the powers specifically given it by the enabling agreement, and any other powers not conferred on the executive board or managing directors. The board consists of governors and alternate governors elected by the members. It meets once a year.

Executive board. The board conducts the daily business of the IMF, such as examinations of financial requests, decisions on general policies, and recommendations to the board of governors. The executive board consists of a managing director and twenty executive directors. The five members with the most votes elect a director each, while the other fifteen are elected by groups of members. The board is in continuous session and meets whenever necessary.

Managing director. Elected by the executive board for a renewable five-year term, the managing director is responsible for the day-to-day business of the IMF and is the chief of staff. He is also chairman of the executive board and participates in the meetings of the board of governors and the Interim and Development Committees. By informal agreement, the managing director has always been a European.

Interim Committee. The official successor of the Committee of Twenty, it advises the board of governors on the management of the international monetary system and the adjustment process following any disturbances, and on amendments to the articles of agreement. The committee is composed of 22 members (members of the board of governors or ministers or officials of a comparable level) elected in the same way as the directors. The committee meets twice a year.

Development Committee. A second successor to the Committee of Twenty, it was established with the formal name of Joint Ministerial Committee of the Board of Governors of the Bank and the Fund on the Transfer of Real Resources to Developing Countries. Its role is to study the programs arising out of the transfer of real resources to developing countries and to propose effective measures for achieving the transfer.

Staff. The staff number about 1,500. They are recruited from about 100 countries by the managing director on the basis of competence and efficiency. They are organized into five regional departments, five functional ones, three special services, the IMF Institute (for training officials of developing countries), and other informational and support service units.

BANK FOR INTERNATIONAL SETTLEMENTS

The Bank for International Settlements (BIS) was established in 1930 under a charter granted by the Swiss Confederation in accordance with an international convention signed at The Hague earlier that year. It was originally established to facilitate implementation of the Young plan, which aimed at reducing the post–World War I German reparation debts. It distributed the reparation payments provided for by the Hague agreements.

The current objectives of the Bank are to promote cooperation among central banks, to provide additional facilities for international financial operations, and to act as trustee or agent with respect to those operations and international financial settlements entrusted to it under agreements with the parties concerned. The bank is owned by 29 member central banks.

Programs

The BIS can:

- Buy, sell, or exchange gold.
- Make advances or borrow from central banks.
- Purchase or sell, discount, and rediscount bills of exchange or other short-term obligations.
- Buy or sell securities other than shares.
- Discount bills from the portfolios of central banks and rediscount with central banks' bills from its own portfolio.
- Accept deposits from central banks on current and deposit accounts.
- Provide financial assistance to central banks. This is now the most visible, if not the most important, function of the BIS as a result of the recent debt crisis. Traditionally, the BIS has served as a low-key provider of short-term liquidities for central banks in times of emergency.
- Conduct economic and monetary research, particularly in terms of monitoring international banking flows, for which it is considered the leading source of information.

• Supervise international cooperation among central banks (particularly the Group of Ten and Switzerland) in terms of their exposure to sovereign loans. This function is based on the Basle Concordat, which was introduced in 1975 and strengthened in 1983.

Recently, the BIS has had a major role as short-term lender of last resort. It has launched many major financial rescue operations, such as a $3 billion credit to Great Britain in 1977 to shore up the pound, $1.85 billion to Mexico in August 1982, and similar loans to Brazil, Argentina, Hungary, and Yugoslavia, among others.

BIS loans are based on three guidelines. First, the loan must be used as a short-term bridge until another source of financing is secured. Second, the loan must be backed by some solid collateral, such as gold in the case of Portugal in 1983 or oil in the case of Mexico in 1982. Third, the loan must be linked to some form of automatic repayment, such as a pending IMF loan.

Organizational Structure

The main organizational structure of the BIS consists of:

Board of directors. It is composed of thirteen members, representing the central banks of the Netherlands, Great Britain, Belgium, Italy, France, Switzerland, the Federal Republic of Germany, and Sweden. The Banque de France, the Bank of England, the Bundesbank, the Banca d'Italia and the Bank of Belgium each have two votes. The U.S. Federal Reserve, the major shareholder, has never taken the two seats reserved for it. The board meets monthly in Basle. Although the board is all-European, outsiders such as the managing director of the IMF sometimes attend.

It should be noted that in order to keep the BIS the "central banks' bank," the rights of representation and of voting are completely independent of the ownership of shares. That is, the central banks have all the voting rights for the entire share capital.

REFERENCES

Asian Development Bank, *Annual Reports*, Manila, Philippines.
Export-Import Bank Act of 1945.
Inter-American Development Bank, *Annual Reports*, Washington, D.C.
International Finance Corporation, *Annual Report*, Washington, D.C., 1984.
Overseas Private Investment Corp., *Annual Report*, Washington, D.C., 1984.
World Bank, *Annual Report*, Washington, D.C., 1984.
————, *The World Bank*, Washington, D.C., 1981.

11

SOVEREIGN DEBT

World development relies on flows of capital from more developed to less developed countries. This capital transfer has taken different forms but altogether has been the basis for international business. Traditionally, the form it has taken is foreign direct investment. Since 1970, however, a more obvious type of capital transfer has become dominant: that of financial capital.

THE GROWTH OF INTERNATIONAL LENDING

An apparent increase in world trade in the 1970s stimulated a demand for capital beyond U.S. borders. However, much of it actually reflected the machinations of OPEC: by sharply boosting the cost of energy in 1973, it added to its own financial assets at the expense of the oil-importing nations. Unwilling to lend these surpluses to their customers, OPEC members instead channeled much of them into secure short-term deposits at large banks in the United States and elsewhere. In turn, the banks, flush with funds on which they were paying only moderate interest, recycled them by financing the fuel bills of oil importers. In the spirit of OPEC, consumers and producers of commodities then joined the inflationary bandwagon.

The Growth of Sovereign Debt

Among the borrowers at this time were many sovereign nations, some of whom had already embarked on massive foreign borrowing in the 1960s and were taking advantage of still more opportunities to meet new needs.

Thus there was a major increase in sovereign debt, defined as government borrowing in the international financial markets. Nations borrowed for such activities as building armies, waging wars, repairing devastation, constructing public works, financing trade, and covering their balance of payments deficits. In keeping with these ends, commercial bank lending to sovereign borrowers has gone primarily for three broad purposes: general or program-related activities or needs, project-related ones, and government guarantees for private loans.

The first category has consisted of credits for unspecified budgetary or balance-of-payments purposes. That is, these funds are not designated for an individual development project or state corporation, but instead may be used to finance the broad economic and social programs that are a key part of most national development plans.

Project-related loans are intended for a specific productive investment purpose and are generally self-liquidating. Examples are the construction, expansion, or modernization of railroads or ports. However, they may also be used for a socially and economically useful project, such as a secondary road network that will not yield any direct earnings, or at least sufficient revenue to retire the loan without government subsidies. In addition, the loan may go to autonomous state-owned entities for start-up or expansion of government-owned production.

As to the third category, it involves a government guarantee of a loan to a private lender such as a corporation, where the end result furthers the nation's general economic and social development.

A Ready Supply of Funds

Whatever the purpose of the loan, sovereign borrowers found a ready supply of funds. Several factors contributed to the willingness of bankers to accommodate both trade and development financing, beyond the very important availability of funds to loan. International sovereign lending seemed relatively safe, all the more so if the loans were spread across many countries and among apparently unrelated borrowing entities in the public and private sectors. Government guarantees appeared to provide additional protection for private lending, the common wisdom being that nations do not go bankrupt and would want to maintain the credibility of their private business community as well. Finally, it was felt that if short-term disturbances diminished export earnings and thus debt-servicing ability, the international organizations would intervene to rescue the borrowers.

International loans also seemed protected against another risk on everyone's mind in the 1970s—inflation. Much of the lending was priced with floating interest rates set at a fixed spread above the LIBOR.

The Crisis of the 1980s

In 1979, forces beyond the control of the banks undermined the basis for foreign lending. In October of that year, the U.S. Federal Reserve adopted a sharply restrictive monetary policy in reaction to OPEC-based inflation, fueled by the second round of price increases in 1978. Other central banks around the world followed suit. Unfortunately, a concerted disinflation initiated by the major financial powers in late 1979 to provide a basis for sustainable, uninflationary economic growth in the future had a more brutal combined effect than intended by any single government. The impact was especially harsh because the main burden of counterinflation was placed on monetary policy. The rise of nominal and real interest rates to exceptionally high levels and the accompanying stagflation of world output and trade over the three years through 1982 simultaneously increased the cost of debt and reduced the ability of debtors to service their obligations.[1]

Initially, however, despite the global contraction caused by the new restrictive policy, bankers continued their lending to foreign entities. After all, the prices of exports were still rising. Some of the new loans were used to pay off the principal and interest on old loans, as both borrowers and lenders had incentives to avoid formal declarations of defaults. This shift in loan usage should have been a warning, but it was not needed for the most part.

By the early 1980s, there was no way to ignore what was happening. The threat of large-scale default by foreign borrowers—major and minor businesses as well as sovereign nations—was hanging over many household-name U.S. banks that had acquired massive exposures in obviously troubled third world nations. Clearly, these countries were not facing temporary adjustment problems, as bankers had wanted to believe. As a result, the developing countries suddenly found themselves cut off from new credit facilities that had always been at their disposal and that had often allowed them to service their debts. The LIBOR reached an all-time high, while exports prices went into free-fall. First Poland, then Mexico, failed to meet their obligations in August 1982, with Brazil and Argentina following soon thereafter. Simultaneous default by Mexico and other Latin American nations could have brought some better known American banks to their knees. As it was, Continental Illinois National Bank and Trust Co., one of the largest U.S. foreign lenders, did collapse under the weight of its badly structured loan portfolio, although it was later bailed out by the Fed.

Some observers attribute the crisis to the prolonged worldwide recession, falling export prices, high U.S. interest rates that assaulted dollar-dominated loans everywhere, and other factors not related to the actions and prudence of borrowers and lenders. Others attribute it to the banks' having provided excessive loans to foreign entities for lucrative short-term earnings without adequate regard for the risks. One analysis of the recent crisis suggests five broad factors: the decline or, at best, stagnation in commodity prices; inappropriate borrowing strategies; financial problems within state entities; political unrest; and oil price increases. This analysis, however, leaves out one major additional factor—it is plain that the multinational banks bear much of the responsibility, driven as they were by competitive urges that led to shortsighted policies and poor lending policies.

POLICY RESPONSES AND SOLUTIONS TO THE DEBT CRISIS

It was believed that the heart of the crisis was a liquidity problem—the developing world was cut off from vital credit facilities. Had bankers not panicked at the prospect of delayed payments by Mexico and other countries, perhaps the crisis would not have emerged, it was argued.

Initial Responses

The crisis did emerge, and the banking world had to adjust. That process was in fact already underway when the crisis hit, and the efforts were simply intensified. One step was to renegotiate and restructure the debt of developing countries, a process that was facilitated by a group of creditors known as the Paris Club and by other international organizations, specifically, the Bank for International Settlements and the International Monetary Fund. Intercession by the U.S. government via the Treasury and the Federal Reserve also dampened the crisis, especially for Mexico, Argentina, and Brazil.

Another step in the United States was to implement new regulations for foreign lending. The Securities and Exchange Commission, acting under its authority to protect investors and its jurisdiction over bank holding companies, required that the latter, which owned all the large U.S. multinational banks, disclose problem foreign loans that exceeded 1 percent of their total lending. In 1983, in answer to charges of laxity, federal bank regulators issued a joint memorandum to the Congress that called for legislation with the following key provisions:

1. Strengthening of the existing program of country risk examination and evaluation;
2. Increased disclosure of banks' country exposures;
3. A system of special reserves;
4. Supervisory rules for accounting for fees; and
5. Strengthening international cooperation with foreign banking regulators and through the International Monetary Fund.

Finally, U.S. international bank lending was cut back, even in nominal dollars.

Perhaps most important, the banks tried to work with the borrowers to restore some stability. Restructuring agreements often resulted in net new financing, a pattern that tended to increase cross-border lending somewhat, and the repayment periods were sometimes lengthened. Nor did the stretch-outs of payment necessarily result in writedowns of asset values on the books of lenders. The terms involved in the reschedulings from 1981 to 1982 appear to have been less severe.

Further Measures

Banks must and will continue lending so that developing countries can meet their prior commitments. The issue, then, is to find more sophisticated methods of lending and to rely more heavily on better risk analysis.

Risk Analysis

A country's external debt and its ability to service it will remain the number one focus in risk analysis. However, overall debt should not always be the ultimate ratio in assessing a country's financial strength and weakness. For example, the Republic of Korea and Taiwan are both heavily indebted, but their economic performance is outstanding. They have been using their loans for projects that balance domestic and export needs, and at the same time are borrowing at a level they can handle. Thus it is necessary to look at quantitative factors in a relative framework and to take into account subjective factors that are not always easy to quantify. For example, does a country's political system provide a system of checks and balances on government spending and indebtedness, and how well does it work? Does a nation have a professional civil service and planning capacity, and what are their quality and depth? Is a country's previous payment record impeccable, and does it have the ability to maintain that record? What are its likely earnings from exports over the next five years? In other words, when financing developing country projects, banks need to pay more attention to the total economic, as well as industrial, political, and social, situation in a country. This task will be facilitated by better communications and rapport between central and commercial banks, an improvement being worked on by both.

Monitoring and Rescheduling Loans

Banks will have to watch the utilization of funds and new borrowings carefully. As far as loan rescheduling goes, it should be handled on an individual basis in relation to each borrower's repayment capacity. No standard pattern will work; each transaction will have to be tailored to the particular circumstances of that lender and borrower.

Governments and International Aid Institutions

Governments of industrialized nations and official agencies must become more involved than before. They may have to revise their criteria for aid and for government or IMF loans to better accommodate the needs and problems of developing countries.

There has been much discussion in the past few years about the roles of the World Bank and the International Monetary Fund in supervising or safeguarding current and future sovereign borrowing. As the financing needs of the third world increase, the World Bank should assist in both the provision of funds and the supervision of borrowing and repayment. Several suggestions have been made as to appropriate functions: (1) cofinancing, with the international institution participating along with private lenders in providing funds to borrowers; (2) the IMF's borrowing from the private sector to lend to major sovereign borrowers; and (3) Granting of guarantees for private bank loans.

The World Bank is already working more closely with commercial banks on cofinancing. The International Finance Corporation, a bank affiliate that deals exclusively with commercial investments, has also stepped up its development programs. Their efforts, and those of other international institutions, are designed to attract commercial funds to developing countries and to promote project lending and somewhat longer term credits by commercial investors, as well as their continued involvement with developing countries. They are not intended as bailouts.

Adjustment by Debtor Countries

Many debtor nations have taken impressive steps toward adjustment as they seek to mobilize and allocate their resources more efficiently. Prompt action on their part is, of course, critical, especially with respect to budgets and balance of payments deficits. It is important to maintain and build the confidence of creditors and to deal with structural and other problems before drastic steps with high political and social costs become necessary.

Addressing the Debt Problem

As to the debt problem specifically, the main solution being followed today is to reschedule problem credit facilities. The debtor country and the bank negotiate the interest and loans on new terms whereby payments are extended for a longer period. In addition, to qualify for new loans, often the debtor country must meet IMF requirements as to structural adjustment and the stabilization of its economy.

Several other proposals have been put forward. To some degree, they are fashioned on the basis of where the blame for the crisis is placed—on the banks or on debtor nations. Others, such as the one described below, see responsibility on both sides.

One proposal suggests that a new agency be established, under the sponsorship of the major industrial countries, to take over a portion of the debt of developing countries held by banks. In exchange for this debt, the agency would issue its own bonds to the banks. This exchange would be made at the face value of the debt. Under this approach, the banks would not have to accept losses through loan write-offs. Moreover, they could reduce their exposure to selected developing countries by acquiring the agency's bonds. The bonds would be issued at market rates, but with maturities adjusted to reflect the ability of debtor nations to repay. The interest and principal payments would be made to the new agency, which would use the funds to retire its bonds. The banks, their exposure reduced, would then be able to issue new loans to needy countries, for use both in meeting their interest obligations and in supporting new development projects that stimulate recovery. The banks would also keep trade-related credit and interbank lines open at precrisis levels. Finally, these measures would be complemented by a rise in the resources of international organizations such as the IMF.

By pursuing such a plan, the argument goes, debtor countries' chances of recovery would be improved. Similarly, the quality of bank balance sheets would be enhanced, and their shareholders would be better protected. Finally, confidence in the international financial system would be strengthened, and banks could therefore attract the funds needed for extending credit to developing nations.

While on the surface proposals such as this one seem excellent, they are in reality an unrealistic and superficial way to solve the debt problem. Such proposals address only the banks' problems, not the underlying structural weaknesses in developing country economies that permit debt crises to occur. Nor do these solutions guarantee that debtor nations will use loans properly, or that banks will extend them carefully and responsibly. Further, setting up a new world agency, even if it is possible, takes time.

The modus operandi for the foreseeable future will entail extending maturities, capping interest rates, and providing some new credits to the borrowers. These measures are applied on a country-by-country basis, with the IMF playing an integral part as a catalyst.

CONCLUSIONS

The global credit crisis of the early 1980s has resulted in a general reappraisal of the risks of international lending. Bankers, regulators, and many borrowers have adjusted to the lower economic value of many foreign loans. (The accounting adjustments, of course, are not likely to cause much loss of book value for lenders.) Bankers and their overseers are now monitoring international lending more carefully, as are investors, although with a slightly longer time lag. Increasing disclosure requirements, lenders' remembrance of past problems, and the distaste of the private market for third world lending all reinforce the measures installed by governments to preclude a repetition of the crisis of the early 1980s. Restraint in lending to non-U.S., less sound entities, under way for some years, is likely to continue.

Some analysts believe the "debt bomb" has sputtered out, although it will take a while for the smoke to clear. Other observers believe it could still explode. Over the long term, resolution of the fundamental difficulties will require favorable interest rates, exchange rates, and world trade. Multinational banks are still vulnerable to shocks beyond their borders. To a large extent, the quality of existing loans appears to depend on macroeconomic policies, within and outside national borders, that no amount of bank supervision can influence. Future "anti-inflationary" or other restrictive policies could, for example, once again depress trade and increase the riskiness of international loans.

Nevertheless, it does seem that the debt crisis, although still critical, is showing signs of a turnaround. The debt problems of developing countries seem to be manageable. What is most needed now is a sustained global economic recovery. Fortunately, the world economy has picked up in the last two years, although the recovery has been much stronger in the United States than elsewhere. And there are clouds on the horizon again. The sustained U.S. budget and trade deficits have many economists and businessmen extremely concerned about the long-term prospects for sustained recovery.

Two points are certain. Banks and borrowing nations will have to act responsibly from here on. World organizations such as the IMF and World Bank will have to adapt to the needs of the moment and help with problems of liquidity and urgent development tasks. Moreover, it is clear that no government or institution alone can tackle the problems; rather, they must join together in doing so. In part, they must strive to maintain world political stability. If the foreign exchange earnings of developing countries do not start to grow, their debt servicing burdens will become heavier and their living standards will continue to fall. For example, if the historical relationship between imports and income holds, there will be no growth in lending and exports, and average real income per capita in the middle-income countries will decline by one-tenth. In turn, it is likely that countries will cushion the impact by imposing import controls that hurt their economies' long-term growth.

Finally, the internal stability of nations continues to cause concern. The realistic possibilities and actual occurrences of economic hardship, rising levels of malnutrition and child mortality, and high unemployment are worrisome. They strain the ability of institutions to cope, aggravate social conflict, and threaten vital stability.

NOTES

1.   M. S. Mendelsohn, "Commercial Banks and the Restructuring of Cross-Border Debt," Group of Thirty, New York, 1983, p. 6.

REFERENCES

Aliber, Robert Z., *A Conceptual Approach to the Analysis of External Debt of the Developing Countries*, World Bank Staff Paper, no. 421, Washington, D.C., October 1980.

"The Banker's Guide to LDC Debt," *The Banker*, May 1984, pp. 92–93.

Baughn, William H., and Donald R. Mandich, *The International Banking Handbook*, Homewood, Ill.: Dow Jones–Irwin, 1983.

Bogdanowicz-Bindert, Christine, "A Long-Term Solution for LDC Debt," *Business Week*, July 11, 1983.

Boyer, Edward, "Why Lenders Should Still Be Scared," *Fortune*, December 12, 1983.

Clausen, A. W., "Let's Not Panic about Third World Debts," *Harvard Business Review*, November–December 1983, pp. 106–14.

Cline, William R., "International Debt: From Crisis to Recovery?" *American Economic Review*, May 1985, pp. 185–90.

"Country Credit Bounces Back," *Institutional Investor*, March 1985, pp. 60–80.

"A Debt Panorama: Who Owes and How Much," *American Banker*, July 27, 1983.

Doan, Michael, Kenneth Smith, and Patricia Schershel, "Front-Loading: A Quick Fix That Really Isn't," *U.S. News & World Report*, March 12, 1985, pp. 95–96.

"Drying Out the Debt Addicts," *The Economist*, April 20, 1985, p. 86.

Khoury, Sarkis J., *Dynamics of International Banking*, New York: Praeger, 1980.

———, *Sovereign Debt: A Critical Look at the Causes and the Nature of the Problem*, Columbia: Center for International Business Studies, College of Business Administration, University of South Carolina, 1985.

Lassila, Jaakko, "Banks Failed to Appraise Risk and Discern Trend Toward Recession and High Interest Rates," *American Banker*, July 27, 1983, pp. 38–39.

Ryan, Reade H., Jr., "Defaults and Remedies under International Bank Loan Agreements with Foreign Sovereign Borrowers, A New York Lawyer's Perspective," *University of Illinois Law Review*, 1982 (1), p. 132.

Stein, Marcel, "International Lending Problems Need Not Be Horror Story," *American Banker*, July 27, 1983, pp. 64–65.

"That's the Way the Money Goes," *The Economist*, May 4, 1985, p. 84.

"The Way Out of the Country Debt Crisis," *Euromoney*, October 1983, pp. 20–26.

12

A LOOK AT THE FUTURE

International banking worldwide has undergone an astonishing transformation since the end of World War II, but particularly since the early 1960s.
Just as it would have been virtually impossible to forecast then what international banking would look like in the early 1980s, so it is extremely
difficult to predict today what the industry will be in another ten years.
Thus this look at the future is by necessity limited, with the focus on likely
trends through the end of the decade in both external and internal bank
operations.

INTERNATIONAL BANKING IN THE MID-1980s

Following the end of World War II, international banking in general was
quite limited in scope. Just a small number of banks in only a few countries
had ventured beyond their borders, except perhaps through correspondent
institutions; transactions involved mainly trade financing and services for
incipient multinational corporations. The United States was no exception
to the rule, although the Marshall Plan did lead to some additional activity
by American banks.

By 1985, about 30 percent of the assets of U.S. banks were international.
Nor was this shift unusual—the top ten banks in the world in terms of
assets were from three countries, five of them Japanese, while the top fifty
were from ten countries. Whereas London was for a long time the only
financial center of significance, eventually to be successfully challenged by
New York, now there are major financial centers in every time zone of the
world. Virtually every country is involved in international banking in one

way or another, and the banking community is now as much a global entity as it is a collection of national ones. Many foreign banking enterprises have acquired U.S. institutions in whole or in part, and vice versa.

Similarly, the range of activities and services has grown with bewildering speed, turning international banking into a highly specialized field. Many banks have become "global financial supermarkets," as they have sought to find new ways to meet their own and their customers' needs for profits and to keep up with the competition.

At the same time, the popularity of certain transactions has ebbed and flowed. Initially banks dealt almost exclusively in trade-related lending, which generally involved straightforward fixed interest rate three-year loans. Soon lending came to encompass a wide range of end uses, from balance of payments support to development of steel mills overseas, with a comparable array of financing techniques, from syndicated loans to interest rate swaps. Now even international lending has fallen into disfavor, the victim of shrinking profit margins, excessive amounts of problem loans on the books, and the need to strengthen capital bases. What lending there is goes mainly to low-risk borrowers; although banks once rushed to join a syndicated loan, now they take a very close look at the reputation not just of the borrower but also of other participants. One final reason for the drop-off in lending is that traditional borrowers such as large corporations have become financially so savvy they now raise their own capital by issuing commercial paper themselves. According to the Boston Consulting Group, in 1972 corporate commercial paper came to $35.2 billion. By September 1985, the figure was $274 billion, equal to one-half of all the business loans on banks' books.

Banks are instead resorting to transactions that do not affect their balance sheets and that generate fee income and commissions, as well as to activities that offer a greater return on investment. These include more exotic transactions such as interest rate arbitrage and options, as well as the better known securities underwriting business. Eurobond issues are particularly popular. Whereas Eurobonds had amounted to only $10 billion in 1965, in 1985 the figure was about $200 billion.

Another feature of today's international banking world is the extraordinary volume of business—transactions are routinely running into tens of millions of dollars (the largest was $4 billion, raised by France for an energy project). The volume of business in the interbank market has reached trillions of dollars a day. Banks make scores of transactions every 24 hours, in different currencies and with different interest rates and maturities and other conditions; they hold thousands more on their books. And many of these transactions are carried out in a matter of minutes.

Along with all this change has come, for various reasons, a substantial increase in the riskiness of bank business. Despite the intentions behind the managed float for exchange rates, they have proved extremely volatile.

Economic conditions have boosted interest rates, which show the same degree of unsteadiness. No longer is there the certainty about the cost of business that once existed. As the debt problems of the 1980s have shown, country risk is also major concern. Much of the risk derives from the way banks do business—borrowing short-term funds to make longer-term, sometimes fixed rate loans in the face of a very narrow profit margin on lending—0.125 to 0.25 percent—that can easily be wiped out by the constant shifts in interest and exchange rates. Thus the banking environment today is far more unstable than banks and customers have been accustomed to.

A number of forces have led to this profound transformation in international banking. After World War II, the United States channeled massive amounts of dollars primarily into Europe, but also into Southeast Asia and the Far East. As Europe recovered, worldwide trade expanded rapidly, and capital began to flow back and forth again. At first it was the industrial nations that were most active, but in the 1960s third world countries became prominent customers. Many had recently gained their independence and were setting out optimistically to become the new wave of traders and industrialists, goals that required and got massive lending from industrial nations. At the same time, U.S. banks moved overseas in an effort to escape restrictive legislation at home. The 1970s saw two floods of petrodollars that banks were called on to recycle. The ebb and flow of regulation and deregulation, combined with the creativity of banks in using loopholes in the legal framework, were yet other forces driving the growth and diversification of international banking.

As the banking industry grew, so, too, did the participants. Now they include not just banks, but also a variety of nonbanking institutions, such as insurance companies, building associations, money market funds, major retail chains, and brokerage houses. This competition quickly narrowed the profit margins on traditional activities such as lending and is one reason for the rapid growth in the diversity of bank activities.

The global political and economic environment has likewise been very dynamic. The movement of the world economy through successive cycles of recession and growth has fueled international banking in both positive and negative ways. While it encouraged business, it also created tremendous uncertainty and is one of the sources of both the existence and continuation of the third world debt crisis. Whereas surplus funds were once in the hands of the United States and later of oil-exporting Middle Eastern countries, which preferred to place their assets in banks in the form of short-term deposits, now Japan has emerged as the major creditor nation. Its investors want securities, and that demand has contributed greatly to the current strength of the Eurobond market.

At present, there is a great concern over the growing U.S. deficit and the volatility of the U.S. dollar. Persistent trade imbalances in many countries, including the United States, are major worries, particularly as they lead to growing pressure for protectionist measures. Many experts feel that a resurgence of protectionism will not only slow economic growth worldwide, but will hurt the economies and balance of payments of developing debtor countries in particular. In turn, they will find themselves hard pressed to find the revenue with which to meet their debt terms, even as rescheduled, while they will face greater pressure at home to channel the reduced flow of revenue into domestic uses that enhance growth and development.

As to political conditions, clearly they affect the ability of countries and borrowers to pay off loans and the profitability of bank operations. And they are another element of uncertainty, particularly today, when international banking sometimes becomes a political pawn of competing countries. National policy toward foreign banks is often based on reciprocity; foreign assets can be seized or frozen by antagonistic nations; assets are threatened by social and political unrest. Banks are now intimately involved with the politics of the International Monetary Fund, which is making its assistance conditional on countries' getting their houses in order along lines it prescribes. On the one hand, banks are pressured by the IMF to work out rescheduling of loans for countries that comply with IMF conditions. On the other, those countries are saying that the IMF conditions are too stringent and that they need to channel more income into growth and development, not interest, both to quell social unrest and to guarantee their future. And at home U.S. regulatory agencies are calling on banks to tighten their banking practices and reduce their portfolio of risky loans.

ON BALANCE

Owing to the various crises within the banking industry over the last fifteen years, from the collapse of the Herstatt bank in West Germany to the near failure of Continental Illinois and the default of many third world debtors on their private debt, many experts have taken to predicting the demise of the international banking system. Reformers call for radical changes in the system, retrenchment by banks, greater regulation, more rigorous oversight, and so on. They point out that it is not coincidental that the problems have cropped up since banks moved into the unregulated Euromarkets.

Are the fears and calls for reform justified? This question is important, because the next few years promise further profound transformation in the banking system. Many key issues that have been extant for many years will probably be decided, and the nature of banking operations and organization are likely to undergo some major changes. Thus it is important to understand the evolution of the past few decades, and to put international banking in proper perspective.

It is true that there have been problems with international banking—the debt crisis is a daily reminder. Many banks have not managed their operations well: they have pursued the wrong goals, believing that market share, the overall size of assets, and absolute profits were the keys to success; they miscalculated or ignored risk; few paid enough attention to the cost of business; many just followed the herd. These tendencies were unfortunately compounded by sometimes lax supervision by regulatory authorities. Finally, the distortions produced by domestic regulatory systems were compounded as overseas business grew.

Despite these and other problems, it is legitimate to ask whether the international banking system is really in its final throes or even in serious shape. Too often publicity follows only the bad and ignores the good. In fact, as many experts point out, for the most part international banking has a better loss record than does domestic banking, and profits from international business have been rising steadily. Most of the banks that have failed have been smaller ones whose business has been mainly domestic. Many banks of their own accord, or spurred by the suggestions of regulatory agencies, have begun to institute sounder management practices, to build up their loan loss reserves, to improve their capital bases, and to ensure adequate liquidity. Moreover, there is always a lag time as institutions catch up to profound changes in systems. That principle certainly applies here to both banks and regulatory institutions. In fact, rather than looking at the diversity and riskiness of bank activities as negatives, some experts see them as evidence of the dynamism and health of an industry that still has the capacity to meet challenges, cope with distortive regulations and fierce competition, and adapt to major changes, all the while achieving respectable profits.

It is unquestioned that international banking has fostered worldwide economic growth by providing countries and businesses with the funds and flexibility they have needed for expansion and innovation. The international banking system has been integral to the rapid and efficient allocation of resources worldwide, as evidenced by the successful recycling of the vast petrodollar surpluses that followed the oil price increases.

THE PATH OF THE FUTURE

To a large degree, international banking in the latter half of the 1980s should be familiar. Conditions in the broad economic and political environment within which banks operate are unlikely to change suddenly; internal practices should follow the same trends that have been emerging recently; and the types of activities toward which banks have gravitated in the last few years should hold. Instead, the next five to ten years or so should see a consolidation and fine-tuning of current trends.

At the same time, there will be some new features, although their exact nature can hardly be identified at this point with any certainty. For example, the continuing advances in telecommunications are likely to affect the organization of banks and the nature of their operations, but what the final outcome will be is hard to say, if for no other reason than that the future of technology is hard to foresee. Competition is going to produce new services and types of transactions as banks vie for customers, but again, what those products will look like is hard to tell. For one, today's banking world is driven by customers and their demands, and both are very fluid. Moreover, much of what a bank can do will be determined by the course of deregulation. While some of the regulatory changes are clear, just how far deregulation will go is anyone's guess.

One area that is likely to see a fairly major transformation is bank management. Banks are going to have to operate more like businesses in their approach to operations, especially in the areas of strategic planning, marketing, cost consciousness, product life cycles, and management style.

The balance of this chapter looks at the external and internal forces and trends that will influence the nature of international banking in the short term and at the likely directions in which banks will move.

The External Environment

One of the dominant economic issues today is likely to remain so five years from now—the massive U.S. deficit. It is clear that it will not be eliminated in the immediate future; in fact, the foremost question is whether its growth can be curbed. Along the same lines, there are still serious concerns about the state of the U.S. dollar.

The continued imbalances in trade in many countries, including the United States, guarantee that the tug-of-war between protection and free trade will continue, and no one is predicting the outcome. The imposition of some protectionist measures is likely in some countries, notably the United States, at the same time that others such as Japan are beginning to open up their markets. Whether the raising of barriers will invoke retaliatory measures and set off another trade war is not clear.

Should wide-scale protectionism emerge, it will have a very negative effect on economic growth. The markets for the exports of both developing and industrial countries will shrink. The implications in the case of the latter are severe for international banks, for repayment of their loans hinges on steady growth of income-generating exports. But any contraction in the global economy is serious, given that economists are predicting only moderate growth as it is. Another factor with implications for global growth is the economy of the United States. Should it falter, perhaps because of the strength of the dollar, the trade gap, or the huge deficit, it will no longer be able to serve as the engine of expansion on which economic predictions hang. The question then becomes whether other industrial countries can pick up the slack. And there is the omnipresent question of oil prices.

It is obvious to all that just as the U.S. deficit is nowhere near resolution, neither is the debt crisis. Clearly, the principal of the debt will not be repaid in this century. However, it is now questionable whether even the rescheduled interest payments will be forthcoming. Mexico, the country with the best record of compliance with the IMF adjustment program and debt repayment, recently announced that it could not meet the terms it had agreed to. And that was before the devastating earthquake of September 1985. Peru has stated similarly that it will not comply with the IMF package and the terms of its repayments, although that pronouncement may have been the political rhetoric of a newly elected president. Many countries are, however, challenging the feasibility of continued implementation of the austerity programs of the IMF and the continued outflow of funds to commercial banks in the face of social pressures at home and the need to fuel development. Once again, the specter of a debtor cartel opting for default is on the horizon, although most analysts consider that prospect unlikely. Developing countries realize they might face a bankers' cartel, while banks themselves cannot afford to be unaccommodating. But the years ahead will test the ability of nations to cooperate.

The International Banking Environment

And what of the forces within the international banking environment? Several stand out: deregulation, competition, specialization, the cost of business, and technology. Although these forces are discussed here as discrete, it is important to note their close interconnectedness in real life. They both are driven by one another and drive one another. For example, deregulation will determine what activities banks can move into, but at the same time the ability of banks to contravene regulations legally and the disparities among national regulatory systems have contributed to the decision to deregulate.

Deregulation and Supervision

Deregulation is a worldwide trend and the result of several factors. One is the principle of reciprocity: the treatment of country A's banks in country B is based to some extent on the treatment country B's banks receive in country A. An additional factor is that most governments have recognized the distortions their regulations cause and the cost to their banking industries in a highly competitive environment. Yet another is the way banks in most nations have been able to exploit loopholes or ambiguous language in laws and regulations. Finally, the entrance of nonfinancial institutions into traditional banking business while banks are excluded from their domains has produced an unfair situation that calls for deregulation.

The Nature of Deregulation. Deregulation has had and will continue to have a great impact on the shape of international banking in many ways. For one, it has opened up new areas of business to banks at home and abroad. In the United States, the deregulation of the past decade or so has allowed banks to enter into insurance, real estate, and broking. Given the parallel trend of nonbanking institutions' entrance into banking areas such as deposit-taking and checking accounts, as well as money management, investment, and lending, the distinction between financial and banking services has broken down, as has the distinction between banking and certain other types of business. Banks have even found a limited way to handle securities underwriting: a company can register a future issue with a bank that then places it with institutional investors, a technique known as shelf registration. Nevertheless, the overall ban on banks underwriting securities issues and holding shares in industrial and other nonfinancial enterprises seems unlikely to fall.

U.S. deregulation has also led to the removal of most interest rate ceilings; the last cap, that on passbook savings and loan accounts, is set to expire in 1986. Banks have also been whittling away at the prohibition on interstate banking. Through holding companies, several banks have acquired ailing savings and loan companies in other states, and many have credit card operations, cash management services, and automatic teller machine (ATM) networks that cross state lines, while other computerized operations have broken down state boundaries in other ways. Though a restricted form of interstate banking, the use of international banking facilities and Edge Act and Agreement corporations has also allowed banks to cross borders. And many foreign banks have branches in two states, as well as other units, because of grandfather clauses in the legislation that closed the loopholes for outside banks. The betting is that interstate banking will be uniformly available in the late 1980s.

As noted, banks in other countries are experiencing parallel processes of deregulation. In Great Britain, for example, banks had been having to compete with building societies and other associations that were offering interest-bearing checking accounts and with the government itself, which marketed its debt directly to private savers. The government has now decided to designate certain banks as primary dealers in its stock, with relations between the two clearly spelled out, in return for which the banks have the right to make two-way markets. Other regulations were modified to allow banks to offer interest-bearing checking accounts. Banks are now also allowed in the securities business, and they have been acquiring securities brokerage and jobber firms in large numbers. To quell fears about a market running amok, the banks are to be self-regulated through two boards of practitioners and users, rather than regulated by a government agency such as the Securities and Exchange Commission.

In West Germany, the government has okayed such activities as floating rate notes (FRNs) and zero coupon bonds, as well as issues in which foreign banks are the lead manager. Australia has finally let foreign banks in. Perhaps the most anticipated deregulation has been that in Japan, long the most restricted of markets. The government has opened up the Euroyen bond market, lifted the prudential limits on overseas yen lending, and permitted foreign exchange speculation by Japanese residents. Very soon a limited number of foreign banks will be able to undertake trust activities.

The Controversy Surrounding Deregulation. Deregulation in the United States has been accompanied by a great deal of controversy. For one, critics claim that large banks will swallow up small and regional ones, creating an unhealthy concentration in the industry at home and abroad. Moreover, they will make bigger mistakes and take harder falls. Finally, the conglomerates are likely to channel savings away from the local scene and into more profitable activities and loans elsewhere.

To these arguments adherents respond that many banks will not want to handle local business, as it involves greater numbers of smaller transactions and services for a smaller customer base, and that type of operation is too costly these days. They also point out that the segmentation of the market is what forced some banks, such as those in the Midwest, to concentrate their lending in unprofitable areas such as agricultural loans, a situation that is in large measure responsible for the problems they are having today. Interstate banking would allow these banks to diversify their portfolios and to add to their resources, thereby gaining strength. Customers in turn will benefit, because financing is likely to become less costly and services more diverse. Finally, research indicates that customers are very loyal to their banks, and it may prove hard for outside banks to wean them away. For this reason, as well as cost, it is likely that interstate banking will take the form of acquisitions and mergers, with the local bank retaining its name and identity.

Just as deregulation has created controversy in the United States, so it has in other countries. Basically the issues are the same—the effect of open banking on smaller banks and nonbank institutions, the safety of banks, and the need for supervision. And there are some international issues. One is a concern that the opening of national borders will permit the growth of a few superbanks that will dominate the market, especially U.S. and Japanese ones. Some believe that only restricted access to overseas markets has prevented that from happening. To this issue banks respond that, again, it is difficult to wean away loyal customers, particularly to a foreign bank. Moreover, it is hard for foreign banks to get started in certain operations, such as consumer business, as they have neither the contacts nor an existing network. More likely, they will enter other markets by acquiring interests in local banks, which will be left with substantial autonomy.

Two other concerns address some broader issues. One is the fear of central banks that deregulation will make it more difficult for them to control monetary policy, as they will lose substantial control over reserves. The second involves the threat of protectionism. Some people worry that if there is not uniform deregulation, the remaining restrictions on trade in financial services will invite retaliation against countries with more restrictive measures. Many expect to see international banking become a topic at the GATT (General Agreement on Tariffs and Trade) meetings.

Supervision

A final refutation of the arguments against deregulation involves what some see as confusion over what exactly that process means. Certain critics of deregulation seem to imply that it will leave banks with a totally free hand, as they have in the Euromarkets, with the same disastrous consequences as in the 1980s.

Proponents of deregulation respond that the issues of the 1980s are not a consequence of deregulation but of bad management and inadequate supervision. It is the latter that is actually more critical to the soundness of bank operations. Deregulation does not imply "desupervision." To the contrary, most countries that are undertaking extensive deregulation have at the same time stepped up their supervision of banks and have raised operational standards (although the two are not necessarily causally related). It is likely that as banks enter new fields and the rules of the game change, regulatory agencies will exercise closer supervision, if for no other reason than not to get caught out again.

In one respect, deregulation may enhance supervision. As banking becomes even more interlinked globally, nations are seeing a need to institute more uniform supervisory and accounting practices and techniques for measuring bank performance. The authorities realize that there is a great disparity in the scope of supervision now applied across countries. The fear is that customers may gravitate to banks that offer cheaper services because of less regulation but that are therefore riskier. Further, banks in some countries are required to disclose more information to the public than others, a requirement that should be made uniform. The OECD and other international associations are now working to achieve greater uniformity and more careful supervision.

The Intensity of Competition

Fueled in part by deregulation, but also by the growing sophistication of more and more banks, as well as the entrance of nonbanks into traditional banking areas, competitiveness can be expected to intensify. It is likely that the new entrants will come from smaller or developing countries, as the major banks from the industrial world are all already in the market. It will also come from nonbanking institutions that are now getting into the banking field.

Whereas at one time banks faced competition in relatively few areas of operations, primarily deposit-taking and lending, now they will be facing challenges in virtually every type of endeavor. As they introduce new products and services, they can expect to find other institutions copying them rapidly and offering the same items, perhaps at better rates. Banks will also continue to face competition from the traditional corporate client. These institutions are now raising their own capital by issuing commercial paper directly, instead of going through banks or borrowing from them. Not only has this shift cut down on the bank's market, but the corporations are competing for the same investors banks are looking to.

Specialization

As competition grows worse, the cost of business rises and profit margins shrink. One solution is for banks to specialize. Most realize that they can no longer be all things to all people: the costs are too great and the required skills too diffuse. Only a few major banks will survive as global financial supermarkets, offering a full range of services to a full range of customers. And they will be able to do so because the volume of their business will make up for the narrowness of the profits per transaction.

Specialization is probably a keynote trend in the coming years. Experts point out that whereas before deregulation banks were regulation-driven, that is, their areas of operation were defined by laws and rules, now they are customer-driven. Given the competitiveness in the marketplace, it is a customers' market, and banks must address their special needs in order to attract their business.

The Cost of Business

Banks will have to continue to do battle with rapidly increasing costs of business. The necessity to do so is driven by two factors: (1) as profit margins shrink, cutting costs becomes a key means of raising the return on assets and boosting profits; and (2) the intense competition will necessitate banks' keeping costs down. The three prominent areas of cost are: funds for financing, operations, and technology.

The Cost of Funds. Banks will need to continue finding cheaper sources of funds, as they have been doing through currency and interest rate swaps, and through fee income such as note issuance facilities.

The Cost of Operations. As to the cost of operations, it has several facets. A big expense for many banks is their network of branches and other offices, primarily because of the pattern of offering full services at each one, a very labor-intensive approach. Overseas offices are particularly expensive because of the added administrative costs and distance. One way banks have sought to cut back on this expense is through automation, particularly automated teller machines. However, automation has not necessarily been cost-effective. The equipment is initially very expensive, and a certain number of transactions must take place before the break-even point is reached. These considerations are ones that some banks have overlooked in their haste to keep up with their competitors.

In a similar vein, banks traditionally have provided a number of services to individual, corporate, and bank customers gratis as a means of capturing larger market shares and in the interest of reciprocity. They have paid for, or cross-subsidized, these services by the fees charged for other activities.

It has become clear that this approach is not cost-effective. Take the case of correspondent banking. For the major banks, their correspondents, especially in more remote locations, will never run an even balance in terms of exchange of services. Similarly, with individual customers, the cost of maintaining their demand checking accounts in comparison with the yield from their business does not justify such services as free checking. Banks are also moving from a concern about market share to one about pure profits and are looking closely at the advantages and cost of free services in relation to the secondary gains, such as capturing a market share or selling other services.

The Technology of Banking

Perhaps the greatest changes in international banking will involve new technology, although its application is already underway and some desired directions are already charted. The impact of modern telecommunications has already been seen. Banks can deal easily and quickly with clients and associates anywhere in the world in minutes, if not seconds. Transactions can be completed in minutes instead of days. That capability has not only allowed banks to transact more business, but it has opened up activities, such as arbitrage, that would otherwise have been impossible. For those who choose to do so, banking can be conducted 24 hours a day.

Technology has also changed the internal operations of banks. Their treasury departments, where such vital tasks as assets and liabilities management are carried out, are now often computerized. The analyst can tell instantly what the bank's global position is by type of transaction, currencies held, interest rates, maturities and due dates, country exposure, risk exposure, end-use of loans, borrower, and the like. This capability has the potential for vastly improving management.

An offshoot is that it may vastly enhance supervision as well. Most likely, the wire clearing services will be tied into this data pool, and the regulatory agencies may choose to do so as well.

The one big concern here is security. As banks become more computerized, how will the integrity of their data bases and files be ensured? It is likely that a major service industry will grow up around this need. Already there is a big business in the development of plastic cards that can provide the user with both greater security and instant updates on his account, including the transaction being undertaken.

Another aspect of technology that bears considering is cost. One of the rationales banks put forward for investing in automation and advanced equipment is that it reduces operational costs. Often overlooked is the start-up cost in terms of equipment, software, and training, and the volume of business that must be carried out for the expenditure to pay for itself and cover maintenance expenses. A second point that is often overlooked is the rapidity with which technology changes today. A multimillion-dollar system may become obsolete well before its cost is covered.

Banks will need to be aware of the danger of being led by technology, as many now are, rather than making deliberate, farsighted decisions regarding its use. While the appearance of modernity is important, so, too, is that of sound management and cost-effective operations. Moreover, as is discussed further below, there are alternative ways to acquire a technological capability.

THE IMPLICATIONS FOR INTERNATIONAL BANKING

What do these forces and trends mean for international banking in the next few years? The implications are discussed here in two categories—international banking activity and bank management.

International Banking Activity

Perhaps the dominant forces influencing the types of international activities banks will engage in over the next few years are competition and standards of performance and of bank soundness. Competition has two primary effects. One, it means that profit margins will face constant downward pressure. Second, there will always be more suppliers than there will be demand. As to performance standards, regulatory agencies are going to monitor banks very closely, both because of the problems of the 1980s and because deregulation is going to change the rules of the game substantially. And banks themselves are concerned about maintaining the public's confidence, which is based on perceived capital adequacy and profitability. As such, banks will continue to focus on building their capital and on maintaining liquidity, as well as on minimizing their risk in terms of imbalanced exposures.

The Decline in Lending

These forces will sustain the trend away from lending. In fact, some banks are even selling off loans, a move that is controversial, as discussed later. The reasons for the unpopularity of lending are several: the profits are too small; the risks, as embodied in volatile interest rates and currencies alongside a small spread, are often too great relative to the return; and loans show up on the balance sheet at a time when banks are trying to rebuild their capital. Finally, the demand is not there to the degree it once was; investors in capital-surplus countries want securities, while corporations are issuing their own commercial paper.

At the same time, lending will not disappear. There is, for example, one source of demand that will remain constant and that banks cannot ignore—

debtor developing countries. Their demand is likely to be reinforced by the governments of industrial countries, the World Bank, and the IMF, as most schemes that these three are proposing today envision a collaborative effort with the private banking sector. Recently the World Bank has been engineering cofinancing, or "B," loans, in which it joins with a private lender to extend funds, as well as offering its own lending. Some governments have followed suit, putting together mixed public and private credits. Not all banks like these options, but there is little they can do. There have also been complaints from some quarters that this approach is tantamount to subsidizing interest rates. Where the ultimate aim is to support exports, the debate falls into the realm of protectionism versus free trade.

Banks will also continue to lend voluntarily, with the loans going mainly to low-risk borrowers for low-risk purposes. For example, preference will be given to self-liquidating lending, such as that involved in project loans, rather than to blanket balance-of-payment loans or recourse or precompletion loans. Moreover, banks will want floating interest rates and maximum liquidity. They may even ask creditworthy borrowers to provide insurance or guarantees.

Banks will also look for lending opportunities that involve more than just lending, such as expertise, management, and advisory services for which they can charge fees. For many, syndicated loans will only be of interest if their bank can be lead manager, because of the fee. Similarly, project financing is attractive because it entails putting together a financing plan and package for which the bank can levy a charge. Finally, banks will try to design and package loans that they can then sell off in the secondary markets, as some have already been doing with their participations in syndicated loans. As to the participants, it is likely that only the larger banks will engage in heavy lending, as only they can carry the volume to compensate for the low profits.

By the same token, investors and depositors will also be looking for more profits and security. They will demand a higher return for their funds, and they may begin to require trigger clauses that will force banks to repay the principal should the investor have reason to question the bank's soundness.

Two contradictory forces relating to lending should be noted that have some observers concerned. These forces are apparent in the decision of banks to sell off some of their loans in order to shrink their assets, as regulators are calling on them to do. The tendency has been to sell off the safer loans, because they yield less, and to retain higher-risk ones, as their spreads are greater. Thus, when it comes to lending, the desire of banks to boost their profit performance may come into conflict with sound banking practice.

Preferred Banking Activities

As banks move out of the lending arena, where will they head? Some trends have already become clear. Banks will want to continue engaging in transactions that are off–balance sheet, liquid, and of high quality, that do not tie up assets, and that do not involve the assumption of risk. Activities with these characteristics are foreign exchange trading, leasing services, floating rate notes and floating rates in general, swaps, currency futures and options, and fee income. With respect to the latter, beyond that offered by certain lending operations, as discussed above, other alternatives are arranging long-term swaps, cash management services, advice on how to raise capital, designing and carrying out tailored financial packages, serving as broker or agent in putting parties or deals together, and acting as lead manager. There will probably be an increase in charges for services carried out for correspondent banks, although less so in the Euromarkets.

A new area of fee income relates to trade financing. Given the problems governments are having with their budgets and the need to trim spending, many have been cutting back on the availability of export credits. As a result, exporters are having to resort more frequently to banks. Rather than offering direct loans, however, banks are using some innovative approaches, such as putting together forfaiting and counter and trade bartering deals. In turn, they are paid a fee by the participants.

One area that is likely to grow, particularly if furthered by deregulation, is the securities business. As noted, investors prefer the capital market now for raising money, with the Eurobond a particular favorite. Banks are collecting lucrative fees for handling issues. As this market grows, so, too, will the alternatives. Already banks are offering perpetual notes—only the interest is payable, and there is no set maturity. At the same time, these types of transactions are leading to more use of floating interest rates for banks.

A new area of business for some of the larger banks will be the provision of technological services and products to other banks. Because of the start-up costs of automated systems and the rapidity of obsolesence, many smaller banks may choose to acquire or rent technological packages or franchises from other banks. They may also choose to tie into the main banks' system, as is done with data banks.

While clearly there are many opportunities for both new and old business, it should be remembered that the competition is commensurately fierce. Banks seem to have two options—either they can go for high volume and low profits, or they will have to specialize to bring down the unit cost and to offer the best services in a given area. Because only the largest banks can afford the first approach, the next few years are likely to see increasing specialization. The implications of that shift in terms of bank management and practices are discussed further below.

Managing the International Bank

New aspects of management are likely to come to the fore, to complement measures that banks have already taken. As a whole, they will derive from the practices of the business world, to which banks increasingly will have to look for guidance, given the nature of the banking environment today. The key areas at issue here are strategic planning, costing and rationalization of operations, marketing, product life cycles, performance standards, and management style. In addition, banks will need to address organizational issues related to the incorporation of widely differing areas of business, such as bank and stock brokerage.

Strategic Planning

Traditionally, successful businesses have engaged in strategic planning of their operations, setting both short-term and long-term goals. To date, banks have not paid much attention to this area of management. However, today's competitiveness, the complexity of international business, limited resources, the risks, and the likely necessity of specialization require that international banks undertake global strategic planning.

The exact nature of this effort will vary from bank to bank, but most likely it will involve certain fundamental tasks. These include the development of clearly defined goals and objectives in terms of markets, geography, activities, and management standards. As part of that process, banks will need to assess their strengths and weaknesses, what resources they have and what is required for certain activities, what the competition is doing, and what the external environment is likely to bring. Planning may also have to address specific sectors, as the strategy may vary for different regions or areas of business. In considering such options as acquisitions, banks must look seriously at the purpose of the undertaking, what it will accomplish, and whether there are better options. In general, planning will involve a comparative framework, looking at alternatives both in isolation and relative to one another.

Costing

Typically, banks have not paid much heed to the cost of services; they have simply provided them in order to gain a greater market share (without looking at the actual gain relative to the cost) or to keep up with other banks. Today banks will need to follow the lead of businesses and focus more on profits and less on market share, unless the latter can be justified economically. Costing will have to cover specific operational functions, such as branches and acquisitions, as well as services and products. Prices will in turn be based on the cost of services.

To the extent that banks adopt this approach—and many of them already have—customers of all types are likely to see more and higher charges for the services they get. Branches and other offices overseas will be scrutinized to see if they are truly necessary and if so, whether they are providing the optimal range of services. Much attention has been paid to the cost of offering a full range of services at the same outlet, as some services may not be in sufficient demand to generate revenue in excess of cost. Here the biggest item is personnel.

Research has shown that customers are willing to travel further for certain specialized services they use sporadically. Based on this type of information, it is likely that banks will reduce the services at some locations to those in greatest demand—that is, those that generate enough business to be profitable. Other services will be offered only at certain sites, whose locations will be determined on the basis of a profitable volume of business or regional demand. Even these sites might be scaled down somewhat, with back-up support from headquarters or a larger regional center.

Countering to some degree the concept of restricting the services offered at any bank outlet is the principle of cross-selling. That is, banks will try to sell as many services as they can through the same unit in order to reduce that unit's cost. Thus they may offer insurance or accept payment of utility bills. Again, however, only those services will be available that generate enough demand to yield a positive return.

Cost will also be a factor in determining what type of presence to maintain in the new overseas markets opening up as a result of deregulation. Other factors will be the nature of the business to be conducted and whether it can be handled by telecommunications or requires a permanent presence. If the latter is necessary, then the question is whether to set up a proprietary presence or link up with a domestic bank. Again, a critical determinant will be cost, along with the nature of the transactions, how the competition, both foreign and local, will respond, and the constraints on entering the local marketplace. Where the country's own banks are still relatively unsophisticated and have a narrow consumer base, a foreign bank may be able to enter the retail market and gain a large enough share to justify a local presence. Where there is a strong local banking industry, acquisition of minority (off–balance sheet) interests and telecommunications may be more cost-effective and viable.

Costing is likely to be a big ingredient in future acquisitions and mergers. Some banks have found out the hard way that they have paid dearly for institutions which have proven to be liabilities, at least in the short term. The Midland-Crocker venture is a case in point. Now banks are likely to be far more hard-nosed about the true value of acquisitions and at the future balance sheet.

Marketing

As has been said repeatedly, a foremost trend in banking is likely to be specialization. Here, too, banks have much to learn from business, particularly the retail chains against which they are competing. Banks will have to spend more time and effort identifying, or segmenting, their markets and choosing target groups or areas on which to focus. Sears, for example, undertook a study that indicated it should target the middle-income consumer that its sales operations are directed at, and has pursued that market effectively. Experts see as potential viable targets the next tier of corporations below the Fortune 500, as well as individuals who have high net worth that is relatively recently acquired and who are less savvy and price sensitive than older market clusters. Included in this category would be the first or second generation businessman. Another target might be foreigners who want hard currency out of their government's reach. Banks may choose to segment even those markets, for example, by geographic region.

Once a market has been decided on, banks will need to identify what services that market wants and then to design products that meet the need. This whole area of marketing is a new one to banks, but will be critical to their success.

Product Life Cycles

Given the competition in the industry and from nonfinancial institutions, banks will need to think in terms of another reality of the business world—limited product life cycles. No matter what service a bank introduces, almost immediately the competition will pick up on it, in many cases successfully in terms of both cost and quality. Thus banks must be prepared to get in and out of the market quickly, or to aim for high volume and low profit margins. Fortunately, here banks have an advantage. Most services need little start-up time and investment, and as a rule, most bank assets turn over every five years anyway.

The above point raises another issue with which banks are not familiar—the need to read the competition. Typically banks have not paid much attention to what other banks or institutions are doing and how they are likely to respond. Now that will have to be a prime variable in the development of any marketing strategy and program.

Performance Standards

The trend toward strengthening banking practices will be ongoing, with some of the reform measures instituted after the crises of the early 1980s becoming permanent features. Banks will have to continue building and then maintaining adequate capital; and they will have to ensure appropriate liquidity, loan loss reserves, and diversification in their portfolios in terms of funding sources, profit-making transactions, borrowers, country exposure, risk, currencies, interest rates, maturities, end-use of loans, and clearing exposures. The emphasis on assets and liabilities management will be as strong as ever, as will comprehensive risk analysis. Wherever possible, banks will support those efforts with computerized treasury departments that allow up-to-the-minute determination of a bank's global position, broken out any way managers and bankers want.

Regulators are likely to insist on more transparent balance sheets. That is, they will want to know more about the off–balance sheet business, or the "invisible bank." In some cases, they are likely to insist that banks include some of those transactions on the balance sheet when determining the level of capital adequacy. In fact, that is already such a requirement in some countries, while banks in the United States, anticipating that move, are doing so voluntarily. Finally, banks will have to provide consolidated reporting. That shift would probably have occurred anyway, as banks are moving of their own accord in the direction of global management.

Perhaps the most controversial aspect of the new standards involves capital adequacy. Even though most banks accept the need to boost capital, they question the way the requirement is being handled. The main issues are twofold. One is the definition of capital. To get an idea of the importance of this question, Salomon Brothers has estimated that U.S. banks will need to raise over $6.6 billion in capital by 1990 just to maintain their current capital ratios. Thus what is considered to be capital has major implications. For example, should preferred stock, subordinated debt, or loan loss reserves be included? This question has international dimensions in terms of the cost of business and competitiveness. For example, West Germany does not allow the inclusion of subordinated debt or of loan loss reserves, whereas the United States allows both to some degree.

The second issue is the blanket application of capital requirements to banks with widely differing portfolios and operating standards. Many banks complain that they are being penalized for the faulty operations of a few.

The answer to both these issues may affect the nature and profitability of bank operations in the next few years. In the meantime, banks are working to build up capital, a process that in itself is affecting operations. U.S. banks are finding that they cannot raise money in the stock markets at present, as their shares are selling at below par. Thus they are resorting to new debt/equity ratios, improved profits (through cost-cutting measures and the removal of low-yield, high-risk transactions from the books), greater retention of earnings, less interbank dealings, fewer loan activities, and on occasion, the sale of physical assets.

Banks are going to have to fine-tune the measures they now use for soundness and performance. The focus on absolute size of assets, absolute profits, and return on equity will have to give way to new measures. They include return on assets, quality of assets (risky assets to total assets), diversity, and ratios that emphasize different qualitative aspects of operations.

Management Style

It is clear that, more than ever, personnel will be important, and here, too, banks must look to the business world for guidance. Traditionally, banks have viewed change as anathema and have emphasized a paternalistic management style. In light of today's banking world, a new approach is needed that places a premium on creativity, risk-taking, teamwork, and strong management. Banks will have to accept the occasional loss as a cost of innovativeness. At the same time, they must reward the gains.

Another issue with which banks will have to grapple as banking becomes more diversified is how to structure operations that run the gamut from stock brokering to deposit-taking. It appears that the most successful approach is to establish a company-wide mentality and policy, but to allow the individual units their own identity and operating styles.

The Keys to Success

As the international banking industry shakes down, it is hard to say who the winners and losers will be. It is, however, possible to point to some of the factors that can lead to success. In some cases size will be one, in that it will permit banks to continue offering a range of low-cost services because of high volume. In other cases, banks may choose to specialize and either offer limited services at high volume to a small market, or focus intensively on certain areas and offer exceptional expertise and service. In any case, segmenting and understanding the market will be a critical ingredient to profitable operations.

In general, banks that are characterized by strong management as discussed above and that apply business approaches to their operations will probably fare the best. In particular, they must pay close attention to assets and liability management. But perhaps the key factor will be the quality and innovativeness of their professional staff, who must find new and cost-effective ways to beat the competition. In turn, what they are able to accomplish will depend on the support they get from senior management and bank directors.

As noted, the profit goals of the last decade that focused on high-growth and high-margin foreign markets have lost their appeal. Instead, there was a shift toward specialized services such as leasing, cash management, advisory services, foreign exchange trading, and corporate finance, and these activities should become still more important. These will depend, to a large degree, on the exploitation of technology, particularly in the area of telecommunications.

Undeniably, international banking in the next decade will hinge on the close cooperation between banks and their regulators. If the system is to continue to serve its paramount function of providing capital where it is needed most, the world's governments must recognize the benefits of free trade and free capital movement.

REFERENCES

Bailey, Norman A., "A Safety Net for Foreign Lending," *Business Week*, January 10, 1983.

Bergsten, C. Fred, William R. Cline, and John Williamson, "Bank Lending to Developing Countries: The Policy Alternatives," in *Policy Analyses in International Economics*, 10, Washington, D.C.: Institute for International Economics, 1985.

Cho, Kong Rae, *Multinational Banks: Their Identities and Determinants*, Ann Arbor: University of Michigan Research Press, 1985.

Fishlow, Albert, "The Debt Crisis: Round Two Ahead?" in Richard E. Feinberg and Valeriana Kallab, eds., *Adjustment Crisis in the Third World*, New Brunswick, N.J.: Overseas Development Council and Transaction Books, 1984.

House of Commons, Select Committee on the Treasury and Civil Service, *International Monetary Arrangements: International Lending by Banks*, London: Her Majesty's Stationery Office, 1983.

Lessard, Donald R., "North-South Finance: Implications for Multinational Banking," *Journal of Banking and Finance*, December 1983.

Marris, Stephen, *Deficits and the Dollar: The World Economy at Risk*, Washington, D.C.: Institute for International Economics, 1985.

Mendelsohn, M. S., ed., *The Outlook for International Bank Lending*, New York: Group of Thirty, 1981.

Oman, Charles, *New Forms of International Investment in Developing Countries*, Paris: Organisation for Economic Co-operation and Development, 1984.

Van Agtmael, Antoine, *Emerging Securities Markets*, London: Euromoney Publications, 1984.

Williams, Charles M., "International Lending in the Decade Ahead: An Overview," in F. John Mathis, ed., *Offshore Lending by U.S. Commercial Banks*, 2nd ed., Philadelphia: Robert Morris Associates, 1981, pp. 263–86.

Williamson, John, "The Why and How of Funding LDC Debt," in S. Al-Shaikhly, ed., *Development Financing: A Framework for International Financial Cooperation*, Boulder, Colo.: Westview Press, 1982.

INDEX

About the Author

DARA M. KHAMBATA is Associate Director of the International Business Center and Professor of International Business at the American University in Washington, D.C. He is the author of *International Lending: Structure and Policy Response*, *The Multinational Enterprise in Transition*, and *Current Issues in Managerial Finance*, and of numerous articles in international business and finance. He has served as a consultant to government and international agencies, as well as private businesses.